The Moral Fables of Aesop

The Moral Fables of Aesop
by ROBERT HENRYSON

An Edition of the Middle Scots Text,
with a Facing Prose Translation,
Introduction, and Notes by
George D. Gopen

University of Notre Dame Press
Scottish Academic Press Limited

Publication of this volume
was assisted by a grant from
Loyola University of Chicago

Library of Congress Cataloging-in-Publication Data

Henryson, Robert, 1430?–1506?
   The moral fables of Aesop.

   Text in English and Middle Scots.
   Bibliography: p.
   1. Fables, Scottish. 2. Animals—Poetry.
I. Gopen, George D. II. Title.
PR1990.H4M613   1986   821'.2   86-11298
ISBN 0-268-01361-6 cloth
ISBN 0-268-01362-4 paper

ISBN 0-7073-0505-5 Scottish Academic Press Limited

Manufactured in the United States of America

To my mother

CONTENTS

ACKNOWLEDGMENTS

This work benefitted in its early stages from the guidance of Professors William Alfred and B. J. Whiting and in its later stages from the comments of Professor Denton Fox and the thoughtful critical attention given it by Professors William Kretzschmar and Mary Carruthers.

My thanks are due Professor Anna Chave, who as a student of mine many years ago produced the mousy riot of appetite that adorns the cover.

Some of the introductory material appeared originally in *Studies in Philology*, vol. 82.

I wish to thank Richard Allen of the University of Notre Dame Press for his steadfast interest in this project, for being its guide through the many vicissitudes of its publication, and for his general good sense. Henryson is fortunate to have found him.

Bernadette Bosky and Deborah Whitman were of great help in the preparation of the manuscript. Loyola University of Chicago provided subvention aid for the publication.

My deepest dept is to my wife, Gillian Einstein, for her support, for her keen perception, for her caring criticism, and for her putting up with all that Haydn.

INTRODUCTION:
ROBERT HENRYSON'S
MORALL FABILLIS OF ESOPE

Anyone familiar with the fables of Aesop will be puzzled at first by the contents of Robert Henryson's *Morall Fabillis of Esope the Phrygian*, for its size, shape, and structure, its content and intent, differ greatly from any of the fable collections that precede it. Most fables take but a few lines to tell their symbolic story through the actions of animals, with but a single proverbial statement to articulate the moral application of the action; Henryson averages 230 lines per fable and 43 lines per *Moralitas*. All previous fable collections are merely collections; Henryson's not only develops certain themes throughout (e.g. the proper use of reason, the dangers of an unchecked appetite, the pitfalls of moral blindness), but also integrates all the fables into a subtle and complex structure which by itself establishes a critical moral perspective in the work. Previous fables tended toward the monolithic, one character trait dominating each character, one action or series of actions dominating the plot, and one moral interpretation dominating the moral application; Henryson develops his characters somewhat and builds the action into miniature dramas, then confusing and challenging the reader with multiple or unexpected morals. While we can enjoy Henryson's *Moral Fables* on first reading because of the sheer delight produced by his wit, his humor, his love of language, his sensitive ear, and his keen perception of human nature, a fuller understanding of the literary aspects of the work—the structure, the use of fable form, the possibilities of allegory, the richness of intratextual and intertextual reference—can lead us to the additional appreciation of his fundamental seriousness, his frustration over human weaknesses, his deep sense of pity, and, ultimately, his rather bleak view of life in Fifteenth-Century Scotland. Neither the bright view nor the bleak one necessarily dominates our attention; they are both continually present in the work, and the friction between the two may be the very agent that keeps our interest alive on rereading.

I. ROBERT HENRYSON

We know little about the life of Robert Henryson. We are convinced that he died before 1508 because in that year William Dunbar's poem 'Lament: Quhen he was sek' appeared in the Chepman and Myllar print, lamenting the deaths of twenty-four Scottish and English poets, including Henryson's:[1]

> In Dunfermeleyne he hes done roune
> With Maister Robert Henrysoun.

We cannot date his death precisely; scholarly guesses range from 1490[2] to 1508.[3] Sir Francis Kinaston wrote a 'gossipy note' about Henryson around 1640 (printed in 1796)[4] in which he states that Henryson was 'very old' when he died. Despite the clear difficulties Sir Francis has with dates elsewhere (he states with confidence that Henryson wrote the 'Testament of Crisseyde' around 1532), many have been willing to believe him on the subject of Henryson's longevity and have agreed that Henryson was born between 1420 and 1435, living into his seventies.

The same quote from Dunbar's poem mentions Dunfermline as Henryson's home. That assertion is corroborated by the title-pages of the manuscripts and early printed editions of Henryson's works, and again by Sir Francis Kinaston, who refers to the poet as 'sometimes chiefe schoolmaster in Dunfermling.' The manuscripts and prints concur in the title of schoolmaster.

The term 'Maister,' used of Henryson by Dunbar, Kinaston, and the poet Gavin Douglas, might simply reflect his contemporaries' respect for him; but more likely it indicates that Henryson had taken a Master of Arts degree, which would have qualified him for the rather prestigious position of schoolmaster of such a well known school. The records of the University of Glasgow show that in September 1462 a *venerabilis vir Magister Robertus Henrisone*, master of arts and bachelor in canon law, was admitted a member of the University. However since no other mention of a man by that name appears in the fastidiously kept records of Glasgow or of the other Scottish University, St. Andrews, it is probable that Henryson never attended a Scottish University. He may well have studied at a University on the Continent, as so many Scots did at that time. (The unstable relations between Scotland and England would make it unlikely that he attended an English University.)

We must also be wary of assuming that the 1462 record at Glasgow, or the later records of a notary public named Robert Henryson witnessing three deeds in Dunfermline, refer to the poet. David Laing, the first scholarly editor of Henryson's works (1865), made a thorough search for all Henrysons and Hendersons (the names were later interchangeable) in the Dunfermline area; he found thirty, six of them with the Christian name Robert. He cautions, moreover, that the list may be substantially incomplete; modern biographers suggest that the number could be tripled or quadrupled.[5] We simply are not in possession of the facts. On the other hand, both the quality of the poems and the nature of the subject matter lead us to want to believe that Henryson was trained at a University, schooled in the Law, and capable of being the schoolmaster, Bachelor in Canon Law, Master of Arts, and Notary Public that we suspect him to have been.

The prestige of the position of Schoolmaster at Dunfermline should not be underestimated. The program at a Grammar School was the entirety of formal education for the majority of educated people at the time. In it one would learn Latin (the language of education) in order to study grammar, logic, and rhetoric. Geometry, arithmetic, music, astronomy, and philosophy were reserved for study at Universities; the task of the medieval university was specifically to prepare people for service to the Church. The post of Schoolmaster, then, at the famous Abbey school of one of Scotland's leading cities, carried with it substantial distinction and dignity.

The most colorful comment we have about Henryson's life comes from the manuscript of the unreliable Sir Francis Kinaston. Although it reads suspiciously like local legend, no biographical note on the poet can do without it:

> For this Mr Robert Henderson he was questionles a learned &
> a witty man, & it is pity we haue no more of his works being
> very old he dyed of a diarrhea or fluxe, of whome there goes
> this merry, though somewhat unsauory tale, that all his
> phisitians hauing giuen him ouer & he lying drawing his last
> breath there came an old woman vnto him. who was held a
> witch & asked him whether he would be cured, to whome he
> sayed very willingly. then quod she there is a whikey tree in
> the lower end of your orchard & if you will goe and walke
> but thrice about it. & thrice repeate theis wordes whikey tree
> whikey tree take away this fluxe from me you shall be presently
> cured, he told her that beside he was extreme faint & weake
> it was extreme frost & snow & that it was impossible for him
> to go: She told him that vnles he did so it was impossible he
> should recouer. Mr Henderson then lifting upp himselfe, &
> pointing to an Oken table that was in the roome, asked her
> & seied gude dame I pray ye tell me, if it would not do as
> well if I repeated thrice theis words oken burd oken burd garre
> me shit a hard turde. the woman seeing herselfe derided &
> scorned ran out of the house in a great passion & Mr Hender-
> son within halfe a quarter of an houre departed this life . . .[6]

II. FIFTEENTH-CENTURY SCOTLAND

Henryson lived during the chaotic reigns of James III and James IV, when political factionalism and lawlessness at all levels were commonplace.

James III (r. 1460-1488) was a particularly inadequate leader, disaffecting
both the nobility and the populace by seizing for the crown inheritances
large and small, by administering the laws with open personal prejudice,
and by attempting to strengthen his own position by arranging marriages
with the English. He is pictured as a wretched character by many writers
of the time,[7] and his mismanagement and the hard times it created may
possibly be reflected in the violent and passionate nature of much of
their poetry. (See for example Dunbar's 'Flyting of Dunbar and Kennedy,'
or Blind Harry's *Wallace*, or Henryson's 'Three Powis.')

At the same time a new economic prosperity was appearing, accompanied both by an acceptance of corruption and a forced extreme show
of piety amongst both merchants and landowners. One critic suggests
that the collision of promise and disillusionment had a great deal to do
with producing two poets (Henryson and Dunbar) who excelled in both
tragic and comic verse, and whose special skill lay in the tragicomic.[8]
He contrasts Scotland's gloomy outlook with Sir Thomas More's *Utopia*
(1513-15), suggesting that the Scottish were more aware than the English
that the arrival of the Renaissance would bring with it an erosion of
firmly grounded traditions:

> In Scotland the Christian and national traditions were at least
> alive enough to make the best minds aware of what they were
> in danger of losing, and serious enough about the loss to make
> a profound response. It may be argued that Scotland was
> merely more backward, less progressive, but the fact remains
> that in the last quarter of the century its poetical response
> was the most considerable that Europe had to offer, particu-
> larly from one man of genius [Henryson] who was moved by
> the time's dilemma to look beyond the present scene to the
> human scene as it would always be.[9]

So the age was one of contrast: culture was flourishing as it had never
before; the economic strength of the middle classes and the upper classes
was increasing; and yet the political storms were dangerous and debili-
tating. Political life was constantly shifting and uncertain: The barons
were never completely at peace with one another or with the king; the
country was continually at odds with England over territorial boundaries
and feudal relationships; and both France and Burgundy were constantly
seeking Scottish alliances in order to weaken the position of the English.

James I (d.1437) had done a great deal to make the country more secure
from international pressures, but his heavy-handed policies at home eventually resulted in his being put to death by a group of conspirators who
objected to the centralization of power in the national government. James
II succeeded to the throne at the age of six, at once becoming the pawn

in a political struggle for baronial control during his minority. He asserted himself vigorously when he became of age, but died at thirty (of a wound from a cannon incurred at a formal ceremony), too soon to have left a lasting impression of stability.

His successor, James III, was only eight at the time, and the old baronial struggles for control were revived. James III proved less capable and more capricious than his predecessors, and eventually died during a rebellion led by his own son and several of the most influential barons (1488). James IV was able to form a court party that brought a substantially greater sense of stability to the country, giving him the chance to improve Scotland's international relations and ushering in a remarkable period of excellence in Scottish culture.

To add to the political instability, the Church was struggling with internal corruption on the one hand and with the government's attempt to take over the conferring of benefices on the other. At the same time the country was changing rather rapidly from a wholly agrarian economy to a significantly mercantile economy. A period of centuries of comparative stability and changelessness had ended.

It is not difficult to see why several critics have mined Henryson's works for political allegory and social commentary;[10] but to view them only as such, or even primarily as such, would be to obscure their relationship to the fable tradition, to ignore their original, innovative use of the fable form, and to limit the possibilities of interpretation and response. I therefore turn now to the nature of the fable tradition and to Henryson's imaginative transformation of the genre.

III. AESOP AND THE FABLE

The term "fable" generally signifies a short, fictitious narrative which reflects common ideas about the proper conduct of daily life. Often a moral statement is appended to direct the attention of the reader to a specific didactic interpretation. The characters are usually animals who act according to their bestial instincts but at the same time converse and reason like humans. The reader is both entertained by the incongruity of animals acting like humans and disturbed by the ease with which human actions can be imputed to brute beasts. This ancient combination of humor, morality, and character drawing, which approaches drama on the one hand and myth on the other, dates back at least to the Eighth Century B.C.[11]

By the Fifth Century B.C. the name of Aesop had become so closely associated with the fable form that he was presumed to have invented it and to have composed all the existing works in it single-handedly.

There is no proof that such a man ever existed, but it does seem certain that more has been attributed to him then he could possibly have accomplished. For example, the fable of the eagle and the vixen which Aristophanes attributes to Aesop[12] appears in the Fragments of Archilochus at least 150 years before Aesop is supposed to have lived.

If we can believe Herodotus,[13] Aesop was a storytelling slave who lived on Samos in the middle of the Sixth Century B.C and was killed by the citizens of Delphos. Writers later than Herodotus identify Aesop as either Phrygian or Thracian by birth. Aristophanes and Plutarch both contend that he was hurled to his death from a cliff when the Delphians discovered in his baggage a golden cup stolen from a temple.[14] (The story, however, is a common one: compare Joseph and Benjamin in Genesis, chapter 44.) By the Middle Ages these stories had gained acceptance as the truth and had bred a host of other episodes and details. Most accounts picture Aesop as a deformed hunchback, grotesquely ugly, partially crippled, and defective in his speech, whose lively wit and imagination in storytelling allowed him to escape disaster in the direst of circumstances. (This too, however, has been a commonplace in literature: compare the story of Scheherezade.) Some sources even resurrect him after death and send him off to fight in the battle of Thermopylae, handicap and all.

The Aesopic fable may well have made its way to England with St. Augustine, since fables always appear as teaching devices in primary education; but our first actual traces of them date from the Norman invasion in the Eleventh Century. The great Bayeux tapestry, a pictorial chronicle of the invasion, furnishes the earliest examples, portraying the tales of the Wolf and the Lamb and of the Swallow and the Other Birds, both of which Henryson used in the *Moral Fables*. The earliest written fables, all of them Latin, were brought to England by John of Salisbury in the 1150's as a message of warning from Pope Hadrian IV to the English prelates. Fifty years later Richard the Lion-hearted used the fable of the Man, the Lion, and the Snake to reprove his restless nobles.[15]

The earliest known collection made in England was that of Gualterus Anglicus ("English Walter"), who was Archbishop of Palermo and chaplain to Henry II of England. We know of as least 84 manuscripts of his work, and between its first printing in 1473 and 1500 it went through more than twenty editions. Its frequent use as a school text makes schoolmaster Henryson's knowledge of it almost a certainty.[16]

The Aesopic fables were long considered on a literary and educational par with Ovid's *Metamorphoses* and were known to all who had received schooling. They appear to have been used as the basis for rhetorical exercises, for training in reading, ethics, and argumentation. Given a fable, a student might be asked to deduce a moral; given a moral, he might have to create a fable to fit it; given both fable and moral, he might have to write another fable to dispute the moral of the first or write an argument showing how the first moral was improperly applied.[17] The pedagogical use of fables described by Quintilian during the Empire remained virtually unchanged throughout the Middle Ages.

> Pupils should learn to paraphrase Aesop's fables, the natural successors of the fairy stories of the nursery, in simple and restrained language and subsequently to set down this paraphrase in writing with the same simplicity of style: they should begin by analyzing each verse, then give its meaning in a different language, and finally proceed to a freer paraphrase in which they will be permitted now to abridge and now to embellish the original, so far as this may be done without losing the poet's meaning. This is no easy task even for the expert instructor, and the pupil who handles it successfully will be capable of learning everything.[18]

Much of the critical attention devoted to Henryson's *Fables* has concentrated on tracing his sources. (A concise summary of those efforts can be found in Denton Fox's introduction to his edition of Henryson's complete works.) But whatever sources Henryson may or may not have used, this much seems clear: He developed the fable form in a way far different from any of his predecessors, arriving at a final product of striking originality. He faithfully reproduced the cast of characters, the moral dilemmas, and the human/bestial balancing found in all fables before his; but his extension of their length, his development of the stock characters, his deepening of the complexity of the moral issues, his subtle use of purely literary techniques, and his stunning use of the structure of the collection distinguish his fables from all previous collections. Indeed, the *Moral Fables* is not a "collection" at all, but rather a unified literary work that uses fables as its substance.

Generically, fable form allowed its user to ignore any possibility of literal interpretation: foxes, wolves, mice, and lambs were not actually supposed to have talked and interacted with each other the way they are portrayed. The means of signification for fable form were straightforwardly (1) representative, (2) figural, and (3) symbolic.

(1) In representing human motivations through the conversations and actions of animals, fable form could use the humor of incongruous recognition (bestial traits appearing in humans, human traits unrealistically displayed in animals) to engage the attention and make its points.

(2) In making the animals and their actions figures of humans and specific human actions, fables could make moral statements, articulated in epigrammatic form at the tale's end, that drew direct connections between "their" doings and "our" doings. One could "signify" the other.

(3) By generalizing behavior symbolically in "types," fables could also comment not only on human actions but also on the human "condition," on the moral propensities that complicate human action and interaction.

Henryson's animals behave in part like the animals of all fables before his. In responding to the problems at hand, they could call upon "reason" (the logical faculty), or "science" (knowledge or cognizance of something specific or implied), or "prudence" (the ability to discern the most suitable, politic, or effective course of action). In doing so, they would be swayed by their natural tendencies (signified by the word "kynd") and be called upon to do battle with the negative among those tendencies (such as "sensuality," "carnal lust," "appetite," and the whole list of sins, deadly and otherwise).

Henryson's animals differ from their predecessors in that they inhabit a greater expanse of text in which to interact with each other and make these decisions. As the characters are allowed to develop, they have many opportunities to express themselves, allowing the burden of moral interpretation to be made more complex, resulting in functional ambiguities for the reader. The figural (one thing standing for another) gives way more often to the symbolic (a series of things, actions, ways of being, expressing itself through the emphasis provided by repetition). Henryson then adds to that the functional signification of the structure of the whole work, the nature of which is suggested below. If we look, even briefly, at the delight produced by his representational and figural modes, and the seriousness produced by his symbolic mode and the work's structure, the complexity and surprising originality of the *Moral Fables* may begin to appear.

IV. THE HUMOR OF THE MORAL FABLES

Henryson has long been credited as a master of the light touch, the charming detail, the humorous insight. He seems to have captured some of the whimsical nature of his animal characters and translated that in poetic style. Perhaps it was his experience as a schoolmaster that convinced him of the value of entertainment as a pedagogical aid. He made the point early in the *Prologue*:

> Moreover, scholars think it most profitable to in-
> clude a merry sport in their earnest teachings, to
> lighten the spirit and make the time seem short.
>
> For as we see, a bow that is always bent even-
> tually warps, and its string will lose its snap; so
> it is with the mind that is constantly diligent,
> even in earnest thoughts and ever studying. It
> makes good sense to mix some merriness with
> matters that are sober; that is surely why Aesop
> said, *Dulcius arrident seria picta Iocis*.
>
> (Stanzas 3-4)

Since he fears that 'holy preaching has no good effect' (Stanza 198),
he gives us merry though moral tales in its place. They are populated
with animals who sometimes walk and talk like people, and at other
times scurry about and behave like animals, blurring the distinction between the two in an entertaining and instructive way. He restricts the
humor, however, almost entirely to the narrative, the tale itself, balancing it with sober reflection and interpretation in the *Moralitas*. As long
as we think of the Mouse in tale #13 as mouse, we can be amused by
her frantic behavior as she despairs of getting across the river to the attractive delights on the other side:

> She could not wade across, her legs were so
> short; she could not swim; she had no horse to
> ride. By sheer necessity she was compelled to re-
> main there; and back and forth beside that deep
> river she ran, crying with many a piteous peep.
>
> (Stanza 397)

The Disney-like entertainment stems from the clever combination of
bestial details (the Mouse's inability to swim, the scurrying motions, the
peeping sounds) with human details (the inability to wade, the lack of
a horse), but the picture remains one of a human-like mouse. When the
Mouse decides to disregard her own observations of the significance of
the Paddock's physiognomy and to take a chance on the crossing, the
emphasis shifts, and we find ourselves contemplating a mouse-like human.
Then when the *Moralitas* informs us that the Mouse represents the Soul,
we are persuaded to view both mouse and human in allegorical terms.
The humor resides in the incongruity; the moral lesson resides in the
figural representation; and the simultaneity of the two produces the
literary tension that is so intriguing.

Henryson varies the way he mixes the human with the bestial. At times he combines them by mixing the details of a single description, as with the Mouse just mentioned. At other times he allows a single description to stand equally well for either: Friar Wolf Waitskaith (Stanza 97) has bare feet, a lean cheek, a pale face, and a grey-russet cowl, a description that applies equally well for both a holy Friar and a hungry wolf.

At still other times he combines the two through irony: When the City Mouse tells her sister that 'the crumbs I leave behind on my plate are equal to your whole expense,' (Stanza 36) she is unaware that for a real mouse crumbs might well suffice for an entire meal. One Fox complains that he is unfit for ambassadorial duty because he has a crooked leg (Stanza 142), but foxes are natually formed with crooked legs. Another Fox tells Chanticlere of the aid he supplied Chanticlere's father, the details ironically sounding human and noble to the Cock, but sounding bestial and murderous to the reader.

> 'I would be much to blame if I did not serve you
> as I have served your progenitors; your father full
> oft has filled my stomach and sent me food from
> his dungpile to the moors. And at his death I
> carefully did my duty, holding his head and giv-
> ing him warm drinks, until in the end the dear
> one died in my arms.'
>
>   (Stanza 63)

Sometimes he alternates letting the human and the bestial dominate, occasionally commenting on the differences: When the Country Mouse brings forth 'nuts and peas, instead of spice' (Stanza 30), or when she and her sister drink 'clear water instead of wine, but even so they made good cheer' (Stanza 39), they are behaving entirely as mice; but when the City Mouse is pictured 'with pikestaff in her hand,' leaving town 'as a poor pilgrim' (Stanza 26), the bestial has disappeared in favor of the human. In like manner, the Fox demonstrates his knowledge of Astrology (Stanza 91-93); the two Mice discuss their ownership of real estate (Stanzas 31 and 36); and the Wolf vows to give up all of his clothes if he can but get a glimpse of the Nekhering (Stanza 303), even though wolves have no clothes.

In addition to his manipulation of the human/bestial balance, Henryson also manipulates the tone and style of the dialogue throughout the *Moral Fables*, creating a psychological realism in the drama of the interaction. (Such realism had heretofore appeared in fables mainly through the allegorical application of the action, rarely through the working out of relationships between characters.) See for example the seminar of the hens in 'Sir Chanticlere and the Fox' (Stanzas 71-77), in which the style of each response to the abduction of Chanticlere varies with its content: Pertock's lament (Stanzas 71-72) is in the high style, complete with anaphora, heightened diction, and inverted syntax; Sprutock's deflating rejoinder (Stanzas 73-74) is in the middle style, featuring unpoetic diction and straightforward syntax; Pertock's reply (Stanza 75), in which she agrees with Sprutock, begins in that same middle style but ends with a low sexual colloquialism; and Toppock's peroration (Stanzas 76-77) has all the marks of a fire and brimstone sermon. The whole debate is made even more humorous by its being conducted over the unconscious body of the Widow.

Sometimes the style works against realism, to equally humorous effect. The Cock in the first tale is allowed a lengthy disquisition in the high style on the virtues of the discovered jasp and its inappropriateness for his needs. Learning in the *Moralitas* that the Cock is a fool and the jasp representative of wisdom, we discover that the real inappropriateness in the tale was the condescending style and content of a speech by a rooster contemplating wisdom.

In addition to varying the style, Henryson also varies his use of the narratorial voice throughout the *Moral Fables*, sometimes with a distinctly humorous effect. The work is delivered to us through the voice of an omniscient first-person narrator, who often gives up his own voice to present dialogue between the beasts themselves. This first-person narrator usually describes (in the tales) or preaches (in the *Moralitates*); but on occasion he steps into the tales as an analyst of the action, an active participant, or a sharer of our experience.

He seems highly conscious at times of his responsibility to report the truth first-hand:

> I have heard it was a humble abode, poorly made
> of moss and fern, a simple cot under a heavy
> stone, the entrance of which was neither high
> nor broad.
>   (Stanza 29)

He sometimes takes this to an extreme, with the result being comic understatement. When the two Mice are surprised at their feast by the appearance of the Steward, the narrator is particularly cautious to distinguish between fact, inference, and analysis:

> They did not pause to wash up, I believe, but ran
> off, each on her own. The City Mouse had a hole,
> and in she went; but her sister had no hole
> in which to hide; it was a great shame to see that
> poor Mouse, so desolate and not knowing what to
> do; for very fear she fell into a swoon, near dead.
>   (Stanza 43)

At one point he takes this fastidiousness to an extreme:

> 'Well' (said the Wolf), 'kneel down upon your
> knee.' And he, bare-headed, knelt down very
> humbly and then began with *Benedicite*. When I
> saw this, I stood a little further off, for it is im-
> proper to hear, see, or reveal anything said in
> such a privileged communication. In the follow-
> ing manner the Wolf spoke to the Fox:
>
> (Stanza 99)

Note that the narrator's sensitive withdrawal does not hinder him from giving a word-for-word account of the ensuing confessional dialogue.

The narrator is at his most prominent in the three central tales, #6–#8. In the sixth (unique in the *Moral Fables* in this respect), an animal is allowed to wander into the *Moralitas* and have a moment to speak (Stanza 185). The narrator's response (Stanzas 185-188)[19] intensifies his involvement in the work, as it moves from description to deploration. The seventh fable is unique in having its own prologue, a scene between the narrator and Aesop, in which the sense of omniscience is transfered from the narrator to his mentor. For several stanzas, the narrator becomes a central character in the work. This presence is repeated at the begin-ning of the eighth fable, as the narrator comments on nature and then remains as a significant presence, observing the dialogue between the Swallow and the other birds. Having been an eyewitness to the Fowler's butchery at the end of that tale, the narrator loses his air of humorous detachment. It never fully returns.

The humor of the *Moral Fables* stems from Henryson's control over his art, his decision to teach through keeping his audience awake and engaged, and his ability to portray the weakness of humans through the part-human part-bestial interactions of his beasts. In the first and brighter half of the work, these moments appear as incongruities; in the latter, darker half of the work, they appear more often as ironies, more witty than comic. Throughout the work they are interlaced with a solemn con-centration on the seriousness of moral failings.

V. THE SERIOUSNESS OF THE MORAL FABLES

A. Clues to the Serious Character of the Work

Henryson tells us straightforwardly in the 'Prologue' that these humorous incongruities serve a most serious purpose, to show 'how many men in their actions behave as if they were beasts' (Stanza 7); but since we are unaccustomed to such unvarnished moral preaching in modern literature, we are in danger of not taking him at his word.

> Do not marvel that a man can come to resemble
> a beast, which ever loves carnal and foul delights;
> for in despite of shame, which can neither restrain
> nor arrest him, he grasps at every pleasure and in-
> dulges his appetite; and thus through habituation
> and daily rite, sin roots itself so firmly in his mind
> that he becomes transformed into a brute beast.
>
> (Stanza 8)

There is every indication in the *Moral Fables* that he took himself most seriously and expected his audience to do the same.

Henryson gives us three clues at the outset that the *Moral Fables* will be a work of high seriousness. The first is his choice of stanza form, Rhyme Royal, which was intended only for elevated poetry dealing with the most solemn of subjects and occasions, perhaps originally limited to public ceremonies at which the monarch was present. It was the first consciously shaped stanza of high style in English Literature. After Chaucer used it with such great flexibility in the *Troilus*, it set the mode for serious, elevated long poems in the English language until the sixteenth century.[20] While Henryson's use of the form by no means guarantees the seriousness of his content, it should at least prepare his readers for the possibility of a solemn literary experience, despite his displays of humor and homeliness.

Henryson gives us the second clue in his 'Prologue' when he raises the question of how to justify the use of frivolous verse and, simultaneously, warns us that we will have to work hard to extract his deeper meanings. In his opening stanza he defends 'the fabulous tales of old poetry,' which, although not 'all grounded in truth,' still have an important function, 'to reprove man's evil-living by representing it in terms of another thing.' He implies that most writing of this sort tends towards the dour and the dull, and informs us that he will lighten the task by using his sometimes humorous animals.

> Moreover, scholars think it most profitable to in-
> clude a merry sport in their earnest teachings, to
> lighten the spirit and make the time seem short.
>
> (Stanza 3)

He repeats the thought in the next stanza: 'It makes good sense to mix some merriness with matters that are sober.' Note, however, his emphasis: lightness must be *added* to the general solemnity; he writes in earnest and mixes in the merriness. We misunderstand his purpose, then, if we allow his delightful touches to dominate our attention.

We are also warned that these fables are tough nuts to crack (stanza 3) and that we must expect to strain our minds somewhat if we are to make complete sense of the work. This, then, is our second clue: we should not be fooled by the presence of 'merriness' into disregarding the essential seriousness of the work. Since fifteenth-century readers considered fables to be literary works of the highest seriousness, we should not hesitate to apply Denton Fox's statement about the tragic poem, 'The Testament of Cresseid,' to the *Moral Fables* as well: 'Henryson took for granted an audience who would see, because they were looking for it, the evidence that this poem was serious, moral, and Christian.'[21]

Henryson gives us our third clue by his particular use of the traditional content of the first fable, the 'Tale of the Cock and the Jasper.' Because of its direct applicability to the reader and to the experience of reading fables, this tale has often appeared first in Aesopic collections. While looking for food one morning, a Cock finds a rare gem on a dunghill but passes it by in favor of finding something more digestible. In the usual moral application, the Cock represents the foolish man, and the Jasper, wisdom, an allegorical formula that warns the readers against the folly of disregarding wisdom (i.e., the fables that follow) when it lies before them. Henryson follows this tradition, and in his *Moralitas* he laments the disappearance of moral wisdom in his world ('But now, alas, this Gem is lost and hidden'), urging us to seek it out in his book: 'Go, seek the Jasper, you who will, for there it lies.'

Simultaneously, however, Henryson differs from all previous recounters of this fable by expanding the tale with a great many details which make the Cock's rejection of the Jasper look rather praiseworthy. This bird rises early and sets about his major task with diligence, in contrast to the young girls 'wanton and insolent' who have so little regard for their work that they sweep out precious jewels with the trash. The Cock recognizes the nobility of the Jasper immediately, knows its true worth and rightful place (11.78-84), considers the irony of a lowly animal having found it (11.85-91), considers his own needs and limitations in life (11.92-105), rhetorically wishes the Jasper better fortune (11.106-12), and departs. Henryson is handing us a particularly hard nut to crack by complicating the story with these compelling details.[22]

> If the Cock does not reject the jewel out of arrogance or ex-
> clusive preoccupation with bestial appetite but because a real
> barnyard cock cannot pocket or possess a gemstone, the
> simplistic moral proposition that the free agent, man, willfully
> disregards the wisdom that could secure him all the possible

benefits of this and the next world gives place to a powerful impression that man, the prisoner of his inescapable limitations, has no plain and easy choice of wisdom and folly.[23]

The third clue, then, is our uneasiness when we discover the Cock was meant to represent the fool who disregards wisdom, instead of the wise man who knows his own limitations and has a sense of relativity.

The seriousness of the *Moral Fables* is transmitted to the reader in three ways: (1) through the reappearance of moral themes expressed in consistent imagery; (2) through the complex and meaningful structure of the work as a whole; and (3) through the use of the *Moralitates*.

B. The Imagery of Morality

When an action or a state of mind reappears often in the same work of imagination, it tends to call for a weight of response different from that which might be given it in any one of its appearances. Henryson, aware of this, has his animals act and react in certain consistent ways that eventually appear behavioral, from which he derives grist for his mill of morality. The two most prominent of these in the *Moral Fables* are the recurrences of appetite and momentary blindness.

Henryson develops his sermon against appetite in a relatively inobtrusive manner. It is so natural for animals to spend much of their time and effort in finding food that the reader may not ascribe to the action any special significance, even though it appears in the first stanza of the first fable:

> One day, early in the morning, a Cock with bright
> and colorful feathers, high spirited and cocky, despite
> his being poor, flew out and landed on a dunghill;
> his only care was to find his dinner. While scratch-
> ing about among the rubbish, he happened upon a
> gorgeous Jasper, a most precious gem, which had
> been swept from the house in the daily cleaning.
>
> (Stanza 10)

In showing us that we were wrong if we considered this action natural instead of foolish, the *Moralitas* establishes the symbolic significance of appetite in the work. We should be well warned then when the same concern becomes so important to the two Mice in the following fable (see Stanzas 30-36, 39, and 41). They suffer for their overindulgence, as does every "good" character in the work. Some of the villains are allowed to fill their stomachs without suffering divine retribution (e.g. the Foxes in #9 and #10, the Wolves in #11 and #12, and the Kite, representing death, in #13); but all these instances are accompanied by a profound sense of moral injustice.

Some of the characters get into trouble from making strenuous efforts to find or reach food (e.g. the Cock in #1, the Country Mouse in #2, all the birds except the Swallow in #8, the Mouse in #13); others suffer the consequences of too much food having made them unaware of present danger (e.g. the Fox in #4, the mice in #7). The effect of the message increases as the number of instances of the image increases. Eventually the moral flaw emerges not merely as the sin of desiring food (gluttony), but as the pervasively sinful desire for wordly things that are beyond our immediate reach (covetousness). The action so natural and forgivable in a beast turns out to be just as natural but not at all forgivable in humans.

Henryson works the same kind of pattern with the imagery of blindness. But its presence is perhaps more subtle, and it appears in different forms. The Cock in #1 is figuratively "blind" for not "seeing" the true worth of the jasp; but the Cock in #3 is literally blinded, momentarily, because he makes the mistake of responding to the challenge of the Fox:

> 'Well done, so might I prosper; you are your
> father's son and proper heir. But yet you lack
> one special skill of his.' 'What?' asked the Cock.
> 'Have no doubt about it, he would close his eyes
> and crow and three times turn about.'
>
> The Cock, then, inflated by conceit and vanity,
> which throw so many into confusion, trusting
> thereby to win great admiration, shutting his eyes
> unwarily and walking up and down, braced him-
> self to sing and crow. But suddenly, before he had
> crowed a single note, the Fox was ready and
> grabbed him by the throat.
>
> (Stanzas 67-68)

The Wolf in #9 makes this same mistake. When the Fox tricks the Cadger, the Fox keeps his eyes wide open (Stanza 293); but when he gives instruction to the Wolf in preparation for the repetition of the ruse, he carefully includes the admonition 'let your tongue hang out, and tightly close your eyes' (Stanza 305). This is the same Fox who has just argued 'you might as well call a beast blind that is not able to escape from me by a mile' (Stanza 284).

Blindness—moral blindness—appears in nearly every fable, though in varying ways. The Fox in #4 sees his fate figured in the stars but refuses to repent; the Swallow is unable to convince the other birds (whom she calls in Stanza 256 'blind birds') of the significance of the planting process they are watching; the Fox in #10 is able to deceive the Wolf into thinking that the reflection of the moon is actually a great cheese; the Mouse in #13 refuses to let what she sees (the Paddock's moral ugliness as expressed by the Paddock's physical ugliness) deter her from what she craves by appetite (the food on the far side of the river). There are many more examples; the theme is pervasive.

These repeated thematic images and references lend a sense of unity to the thirteen fables, a sense that a single moral force is informing them all. As we turn our attention to the structure of the work, that unity becomes more clearly perceptible and highly significant.

C. The Significance of the Structure

A careful look at the way the Moral Fables is put together reveals three different, simultaneously functional symmetries, all of which taken together demonstrate the unity of the work and its fundamentally serious moral intent.

Although Henryson entitled his work The Moral Fables of Aesop the Phrygian, he took only seven of his thirteen fables from Aesopic sources. The other six come from French tales of the Reynardian tradition and from other sources. In the order that they appear in all but one of the major manuscripts and early prints, they form a neat symmetry according to source.[24]

The Synthetic Symmetry[25]

Aesopic —	1) The Cock and the Jasper
	2) The Two Mice
	3) The Cock and the Fox
Reynardian —	4) The Confession of the Fox
	5) The Trial of the Fox
	6) The Sheep and the Dog
Aesopic —	7) The Lion and the Mouse
	8) The Preaching of the Swallow
	9) The Fox, the Wolf, and the Cadger
Reynardian —	10) The Fox, the Wolf, and the Farmer
	11) The Wolf and the Wether
Aesopic —	12) The Wolf and the Lamb
	13) The Paddock and the Mouse

This symmetry is "synthetic" because it cannot be perceived by the reader during the process of reading. By itself it seems relatively unimportant— order for the sake of order; but considered in conjunction with the other symmetries of the poem, this ordering takes on additional significance. For the moment we should note in particular that it leads us to considering the fables in five groupings according to source and that in this regard tales #6 through #8 form the center of the work.

Medieval poets generally considered themselves craftsmen, builders of literary works, and we should therefore never feel safe in imagining that any of their perceptible structural devices are meaningless. The very word "poet" means "one who makes something" (from the Greek *poien*), and the Scots in particular refer to their poets as "makars." Such a hidden structural device might be created in imitation of God's creation of the world, using a divine plan that is imperceptible to the mortals who are living through the experience. The structure of many Medieval and Renaissance works of art reflects this concept of creative order (cf. Dante's *Divine Comedy* or Spenser's *Epithalamion*).

There is a second symmetry which could be called the "climactic" symmetry. It also focuses on tales #6–#8 as the center of the work, but unlike its synthetic counterpart it can be and must be sensed in order for the reader to experience the moral impact of the work as a whole. This symmetry consists of a linear development which continues throughout the work, creating a crescendo from the first tale to a climax at the mid-point, tale #7, and then a decrescendo until the fictional world disintegrates in the final tale.

This development depends upon the special nature of the middle fable, 'The Tale of the Lion and the Mouse.' That tale is the work's numerical midpoint not only because it is the seventh in a group of thirteen, but also because it is preceded by precisely 200 stanzas and followed by precisely 200 stanzas.[26] Moreover, the seventh fable stands out from the others in several striking details: only this fable has its own prologue; only this fable is presented in the form of a Medieval dream-vision; only in this fable do characters actually listen to and follow wholesome advice from others; and only this fable ends in unmitigated triumph for all of the central characters. This central fable seems to bear a unique significance.

Looking closely at the progression of the fables before and after the seventh fable, we can see the denouements of Henryson's tale increase in harshness as the work proceeds. In the first six tales (those preceding the central fable), none of the "good" characters suffers any permanent damage. The Cock in #1, the City Mouse in #2, and the Mare in #5 suffer no harm whatever; the Country Mouse in #2 and Chanticlere in

#3 undergo ordeals but escape intact; and the Sheep in #6 must suffer through a bitter Winter but may survive to grow another coat of wool. Only the Fox in #5, the Wolf in #5, and the Fox in #6 suffer severe physical injury or death, and they, being predators and rogues, have earned only their just rewards. For the most part, everyone receives the fate deserved.

In the six tales that follow the central fable, however, the relatively sympathetic characters suffer increasingly harsher consequences: the Swallow (#8) is saddened and deprived of companionship; the Cadger (#9) is robbed; the Farmer (#10) is badly frightened and must pay a ransom; the Wether (#11) is shaken to death due to his pride; the Lamb (#12) is eaten despite his innocence and humility; and the Mouse (#13) is flayed alive. The evil characters, on the other hand, fare increasingly well: the Wolves progress from being beaten (#9) to being cheated (#10) to being scared but victorious (#11) to being well fed (#12); the Foxes (#9 and #10) succeed in cheating everyone; and the Kite (#13) encounters no resistance whatever in his murderous attack. Thus Henryson gives us a substantially and increasingly grimmer view of life in the second half of the work than in the first, demonstrating that in a deceitful and sinful world good often falls prey to evil.

All this fits into a symmetrical design that emphasizes the progression away from a world wherein frail men are forgiven or punished by a just God, and toward a world which is dominated by evil and powerful men and from which God has withdrawn.

Along with this climactic development we can perceive yet a third kind of symmetry, which can be called the "concentric" symmetry. Again, fable #7 is the focal point, but this time we can consider the tales in parallel groups receding from the center like ripples around a stone dropped in the water. The chart below demonstrates this organization.

The first and last tales are isolated as introduction and conclusion. In each the central characters misuse their power of self-determination; the former escapes harm, but the latter does not. Tales #2 and #12 both concern innocent non-predators (the comparatively innocent Country Mouse and the spotless Lamb, both referred to by Henryson as *sillie*), whose sound reasoning is ignored; the former escapes harm, but the latter does not. Moving still towards the center, #3 and #11 both concern proud non-predators who lack the restraint of reason; the former escapes harm, but the latter does not. The obverse situation occurs in #4 and #10, and in #5 and #9. In the earlier tales the Fox, despite his trickery, suffers death; in the later tales the Fox, despite the immorality of his trickery, succeeds.

The Concentric Symmetry

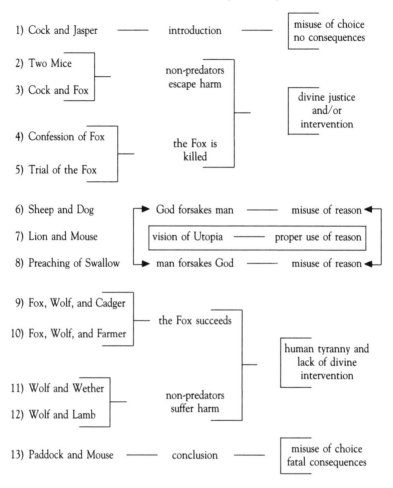

1) Cock and Jasper ——— introduction ——— misuse of choice / no consequences

2) Two Mice
3) Cock and Fox — non-predators escape harm

4) Confession of Fox
5) Trial of the Fox — the Fox is killed

divine justice and/or intervention

6) Sheep and Dog → God forsakes man ——— misuse of reason ◄
7) Lion and Mouse   vision of Utopia ——— proper use of reason
8) Preaching of Swallow → man forsakes God ——— misuse of reason ◄

9) Fox, Wolf, and Cadger
10) Fox, Wolf, and Farmer — the Fox succeeds

11) Wolf and Wether
12) Wolf and Lamb — non-predators suffer harm

human tyranny and lack of divine intervention

13) Paddock and Mouse ——— conclusion ——— misuse of choice / fatal consequences

We therefore have three different conscious arrangements—synthetic, climactic, and concentric—all of which point to tales #6–#8 as forming the core of the work and marking its turning point. The central vision of human justice (#7) is surrounded by the tale of the innocent Sheep who can find no justice (#6) and the tale of the proud flock of birds who ignore wisdom and suffer an unhappy end in which justice is no longer a question (#8).

In tale #6 the Sheep laments the lack of divine intervention in his world:

> Shivering from the cold, lamenting sorely all the
> while, he cast his eyes up to the heights of heaven
> and said: 'Lord God, why sleep You so long?
> Awake, and pass judgment on my cause, which is
> founded on truth; see how I by fraud, corruption,
> and deception, am stripped full bare'; and so is
> many a one in this world now, plagued in the extreme.
>
> (Stanza 185)

The world literally has been God-forsaken. In the central tale, #7,
Henryson demonstrates that we could still survive, even without divine
intervention, if we only would listen to reason. The Lion, Lord of beasts,
literally "awakes and passes judgment" on the Mouse's cause, temper-
ing his personal sense of outrage with reason and open-handed justice:

> When this was said, the Lion reconsidered his
> words and tempered his thoughts with reason,
> and let mercy assuage his cruel anger; and he
> granted the Mouse remission. He opened his paw,
> and she fell down on her knees and raised both
> her hands to heaven, crying 'May almighty God
> requite you!'
>
> (Stanza 215)

Henryson follows this fable with 'The Preaching of the Swallow,' which
demonstrates by contrast what happens in a God-forsaken world when
we do not listen to reason, when we abandon righteous teachings.

> Alas! It made the heart lament to see that bloody
> Butcher beating down those birds and to hear
> their woeful song and lamentation when they
> could tell they were about to die. Some he
> clubbed unconscious to the earth; he beat the
> head of some, he broke the neck of others, and
> some he stuffed into his bag half-dead.
>
> (Stanza 268)

Henryson uses the symbol of the net to represent human disaster. The
Lion is able to escape the hunters' net because his previous use of reason
had gained him allies who could bite the cords; but the birds of the following fable are caught fast in the fowler's net because of their having ignored reason beforehand.

   The solidity of complex structures in the *Moral Fables* depends to a
great extent upon the ability of the central fable to support the weight

of its central position and function. In its unique prologue, the narrator walks out into the beautiful fields (representing perhaps the natural goodness of the God-given world), falls asleep, and has a dream-vision. Aesop appears, and after complaining that holy preaching no longer has any effect, consents to tell the following tale. A Mouse, having been captured by a Lion whom he had awakened from a deep sleep, forcefully and intelligently pleads to be released. The Lion is convinced by the Mouse's reasoning and therefore sets him at liberty. Later, when the Lion has been entrapped by villagers' nets, the Mouse summons other mice, frees the Lion, and all happily go on their ways. The narrator then awakens and returns home.

The importance of this tale (and only this tale) being a dream-vision cannot be underestimated. 'The Lion and the Mouse' is Henryson's Utopian vision, presentable only as a dream: a world wherein men listen to each other, allow themselves to be swayed by reason, justice, and mercy, and remember their debts to each other with gratitude. It is a glorious world, in which the Lion can lie down with the Mouse; but unfortunately, it is only a dream, and at its end we must awake and return to the real world.

To underscore this, Henryson repeats the process with significant alterations in the following tale, 'The Preaching of the Swallow.' There the narrator also walks out into the beautiful fields, but this time he remains awake. Again he sees characters reasoning with each other, but in this non-dream world the Swallow's logic is ridiculed and ignored. As a result, the other birds must suffer a bloody death, described in the harshest detail of the work to that point (see Stanza 268, quoted above).

Aesop's complaint seems to have been justified: the Swallow's holy preaching had no effect. Henryson never allows the shock of this return from Utopia to die away, and he constantly increases the harshness of the tales' outcomes, saving the most hideous for last. Blindness, appetite, and the ignoring of reason have so completely taken over then that Henryson dares put the good advice into the mouth of the very character who ignores it. The Mouse recognizes that the frightening physiognomy of the Paddock bodes ill for any alliance between them (Stanzas 403-404), and even listens to the Paddock decry silken tongues that disguise deceit (Stanza 407); yet still she allows her appetite to overwhelm her good sense, which results in a most grisly death for her. When the Kite comes to destroy them both, we view an image in little of this world's day of destruction: the Kite (who represents death, as we are told in the *Moralitas*) pulls the skin of his victims (who represent the body and the soul) over their heads in one deft motion that suggests the ultimate in thoroughness and cold-bloodedness.

The *Moral Fables* began with a warning that hard nuts are tough to

crack but worth the effort. It ends with a tale of a Mouse who admits
to being unwilling to crack hard nuts and who prefers more elegant and
less challenging fare (Stanza 399). In that last tale, Henryson includes
verbal, narrative, or thematic echoes from almost all of the other twelve
fables. For a few examples, compare the following pairs of stanzas: 399
with 3; 405-407 with 210-214 or 377-384; 411 with 28; 413 with 48;
410 with 17; 415 with 213; 418 with 54. The work gives us many clues
why it should be considered a unified whole, and that unity offers us
more in the way of meaning than does the sum of the meanings of the
individual fables.

The tension between despair over the future and amusement in the
details of the present gives Henryson's work its intriguing quality of
restlessness. With the exception of the central dream vision, the world
of the *Moral Fables* is not a happy one, despite the elegance of the art
and the persistence of the humor. As the work progresses, the world of
deadly sins, with sadness overcoming joy and depravity overcoming innocence, increasingly dominates. It is filled with persecution, suffering,
irresponsible trickery, studied injustice, and sheer gratuitous malevolence.
Some moral indictment is levelled at all the characters except the Sheep,
the Swallow, and the Lamb, who instead are subjected to some of the
harshest fates in the *Moral Fables*. In each tale but the central one, an
animal either is called to obey reason but ignores it, or tries to follow
reason but is prevented. The work as a whole charts a progression of
increasing frustration that finally reposes in despair. We move from the
admonition to seek out wisdom (in 'The Cock and the Jasper') through
the discovery of Utopia (in 'The Lion and the Mouse') to the finality
of universal destruction (in 'The Paddock and the Mouse'), and we find
that Henryson has suggested *through his structure* the common Medieval
resolution to the human predicament, the same resolution that he makes
explicit in the complaint of the Sheep in tale #6.

> Lord, do you not see this world is thrown into chaos,
> just as if someone were to change pure gold into lead
> or tin; the poor man is stripped bare, but the great
> man can do no wrong; and Simony is considered no
> sin. Now he considers himself happy who can win the
> greatest profit by extortion; kindness is slain, and pity
> is a thing of the past. Alas (good Lord), why do you
> suffer it so to be?
>
> You suffer this even for our great offense; you
> send us troubles and sore plagues, as hunger,
> dearth, great war, and pestilence; and yet this

causes few to mend their way of living. We poor
people, as of now, may do no more than pray to
Thee. Since on this earth we are so oppressed, in
heaven may God grant us rest.

(Stanza 187-188)

C. The Function of the Moralitates

Despite etymology, many *moralitates* of fables before Henryson's did not
concern themselves with morality as much as with propriety and
practicality.

> Since the fable is essentially a popular *genre* of literature, it
> naturally reflects the ideas of ordinary people about the con-
> duct of life. It has little to do with the ideals of virtue and
> the pursuit of perfection inculcated by the great ethical
> philosophers of antiquity. The virtues recommended by the
> fabulists are chiefly the social virtues which make life com-
> fortable and redound to the credit and interest of those who
> practice them—loyalty, gratitude, moderation, resignation,
> industry, and so on. Sometimes the lessons they teach are not
> really moral lessons at all, but merely counsels of prudence
> and worldly wisdom based on observation of people's behavior
> and degenerating at times into frank *im*morality—how to get
> the better of an enemy (or even a friend), how to keep a
> whole skin by subservience to the possessors of power, how to
> profit by other men's misfortunes and mistakes, and in general
> how to turn everything to good account for oneself.[27]

Henryson, in contrast, goes out of his way to emphasize the moral
retribution visited upon his rogues (in the first half of the work) or to
dramatize the viciousness of their behavior (in the second half of the
work). The Fox in tale #4 entertains us with his ingenuity, transforming
a kid into a salmon by a false baptism ('Go down, Sir Kid; come up again
Sir Salmon'); but his death comes quickly thereafter and the last joke
is on him, as he invites fate to consider his swollen belly a perfect target
for an arrow. The ironic touch of the Fox's comment and the almost
domestic charm of the final scene up to the fatal shot appear nowhere
in the story's sources and analogues; they bring to the tale a new emphasis on retributive morality.

He also develops the *Moralitas* far more extensively than any fabulist
before him, even as he expanded the length and depth of the tale itself.
In fact, these extensions depend upon each other: by giving us a longer
tale, he gave himself greater opportunities for interpretation of the tale,

and vice versa. His development of the final fable, 'The Paddock and the Mouse,' is a good example of this.

It is generally agreed that Henryson used as his source the following fable of Gualterus Anglicus:

The Mouse and the Frog

The mouse's journey being interrupted by a lake, a
    talkative frog
Met the mouse, and after he agreed to help, he wished
    to harm him.
For in all creatures a discordant mind prevails over
    words of ruin;
Flowery speech embellishes guilty souls.
The frog allied the mouse to himself with words, ventured
To bind his feet with a rope, to break his faith with deceit.
Foot therefore joined foot, but heart retreated from heart.
Lo, they swam, the one was drawn, and the other drew.
The frog was immersed so that he submerged the mouse
    with him; making
A shipwreck with his friend, that faith sank.
The frog pursued the diver, but the mouse emerged and
    resisted
The shipwreck: the same fear moves men.
A kite was near, and he seized the wretched little pair
    with his fierce claw:
One lies dead, both lay dead, burst organs flow.

Thus those who claim that they are useful, and are in
    the way, perish.
One may learn that suffering returns to its author.[28]

Comparing this to Henryson's treatment of the tale, one is immediately struck by the difference in length: 14 lines of narrative and 2 of moral in the Gualterus version; 132 lines of narrative and 66 of moral in the Henryson. Henryson adds description, character development, dialogue, scientific theory, and philosophical musings, all of which enhance the literary appeal of the narrative and give greater opportunity for interpretation in the *Moralitas*. For example, he spends more than 20 lines (see Stanzas 397-400) on a moment covered by Gualterus with the phrase 'The mouse's journey being interrupted by a lake.' Henryson takes this opportunity to reintroduce the continuing theme of unreasonable appetite, to echo the 'hard nuts' of the 'Prologue' and the 'Tale of the Two Mice' (Stanzas 3 and 32), to represent again the role of fortune through the verbal echoes of 'to and fro' and the formulaic 'sometimes up, sometimes down' (see Stanza 48) as well as the piteous 'peep' of distress (see Stanza 44), and to begin preparation for the allegory by having the Paddock, who stands for the body, respond to the Mouse's call for 'some *body*' to help her (Stanza 398). He goes out of his way to establish a psychological justification for the Mouse's binding herself to such a threatening character as the Paddock, especially in light of the Mouse's keen awareness of the danger (developed at length in Stanzas 403-409).

Since Gualterus simply presents the mouse being deceived by the frog, he could limit his attention in his brief moral to the problem of deceit; we are warned quite simply that we should not cause trouble for others because it will return to our own harm. In contrast, Henryson's enlarged and more complex narrative allows him the opportunity to suggest a number of practical conclusions:

1) A wicked tongue and a fair countenance are more dangerous by far than any pestilence (Stanza 416);
2) Be careful what company you keep (Stanza 416);
3) Do not soon believe fair-sounding words (Stanza 417);
4) Cherish freedom, even in poverty, more than wealth accompanied by slavery (Stanza 418);
5) Fortune is fickle, and nothing in this life is secure (Stanza 420);
6) Death comes quickly and without warning (Stanza 423, supported by the brevity of the Kite's appearance in both the tale and the *Moralitas*).

He then adds to this practical advice some moral interpretation, detailing for us the allegorical significances of the tale: The Mouse is the soul, the Paddock the body, the river the world, the far bank heaven, the string that binds them life, and the Kite death. Further moral significance arises from the placement of this tale as last in the *Moral Fables* and the resulting denouement it provides for the work as a whole.

As pat as the allegorical solution may sound, the *Moralitas* manages to avoid offering a single, "correct" interpretation for the tale. For example, it makes good sense to regard the far bank as heaven, since it is that which is beyond the world, the goal of the journey of life when body and soul are joined. However, at the beginning of the tale the far bank was the object of the Mouse's interest solely because it would satisfy her needs of appetite. The conflict between these two interpretations need not be considered an internal weakness in Henryson's plan; it reflects the problems of interpretation encountered in biblical exegesis and legal argumentation, both of which may well have occupied a good deal of Henryson's time during his training. Also, it leaves to the reader the hard nutcracking that had been promised in the 'Prologue.'

Henryson often hints that he has not told us all that can be told in his *Moralitates*:

> Of the significance and nature of this false Fox,
> of whom I have spoken before, and of this Kite, at
> the present time I will say no more.
>
> > (Stanza 183)

> Adieu my friend; and if any should ask you about
> this Fable (and shortly now I will conclude), you
> can say I left the remainder to the Friars, to use
> in their examples and interpretations.
>
> > (Stanza 424)

We find that if we return to a particular tale with the details mentioned in its *Moralitas*, they spawn a good deal more interpretation than we might have expected. This is especially so in the case of significant verbal echoes. He does this to a far greater extent than the fabulists who preceded him.

Compare the moral application of several of Henryson's possible sources with his own for the tale of the two Mice. Phaedrus states the main point clearly enough:

> It is better to live by oneself in one's own little poverty than to be gnawed by the anxiety of wealth.[29]

Caxton's *Aesop* states it equally simply and straightforwardly:

> And therefore hit is good to lyue pourely & surely
> For the poure lyueth more surely than the ryche.[30]

Gualterus Anglicus adds a food metaphor but keeps the emphasis is on the advantages of security:

> A pleasing, small mouthful of bread is better for me
> Than to take with sadness a banquet from a plate;
> I do not wish to fear the surfeit of a fatted calf;
> I do not wish to fear the plenty of honey-sweet food.[31]

Odo of Cheriton shifts the emphasis to the sin of gluttony, using it as a metaphor to preach against simony and usury. He is also concerned with security, but that of the immortal soul, not of the mortal body:

> Thus if very many rectors of churches, who are unworthy and simoniacal and usurous, would understand with how much danger they eat, seeing that upon morsels unjustly acquired sits the Devil, sits the Cat who devours souls, they would

prefer to eat barley bread with good conscience than all delights with such company.[32]

The *Isopet of Lyon* introduces the element of the folly of social climbing:

> For him who fears the shame of falling from too high
> It is wise if he does not climb too high.
> Happiness and sufficiency make
> Wealth, not abundance.
> It is poverty, not wealth,
> If one spends goods in sadness.[33]

Henryson, again using the greater length of his fable to advantage, complicates the moral focus of his *Moralitas*. Like his predecessors he praises security; but he also praises poverty, previously presented as something of a necessary evil—'Of earthly joy, the highest degree is to have happiness in heart with few possessions' (Stanza 56). He adds to the susceptibility of fallen humanity to its own worldly appetites, the falsity of the concept of unbounded freedom, the insistence that all earthly joy must be mixed with adversity, the foolishness of attempting to climb above one's station in life, and a demonstration of how retribution will be visited upon those who neglect basic Christian ceremonies and procedures. He accomplishes all this by rather subtle echoes in the *Moralitas* of details in the tale proper.

'No estate is free, without trouble and some vexation' (Stanza 53). If we look back to the tale, we can see Henryson preparing for this particular application by giving the word 'free' special emphasis:

> The other Mouse, that lived in the town, was a
> member of the Guild and made a *free* Burgess,
> also *free* from tolls, exempt from both the Great
> and Little Customs, and with *freedom* to go wher-
> ever she wished, among the cheese in the cup-
> board and the meal in the chest.
>
> (Stanza 25, emphasis supplied)

The three-fold reference to her freedom stresses the luxurious quality of her city life and builds a mock-heroic crescendo to the mousiest freedom of all—the free run of the larder. The *Moralitas*, in echoing these freedoms, explains that while poor mice may not be free to indulge their appetites at will, rich mice also lack total freedom because 'the Cat comes and has his eye on the Mouse' (Stanza 55). Thus 'no estate is free, without trouble and some vexation.'

Another echo in the *Moralitas*:

> As vetches are mixed in with wholesome seed,
> so intermingled is adversity with earthly joy, . . .

The word 'intermingled' recalls the farewell speech of the Country Mouse: 'Your meal is mingled all with care' (Stanza 50); looking further backward we can find several examples in this tale of joy being mingled with care. Early moments of happiness are balanced by later moments of pain. Their joy at meeting (Stanza 28) is balanced by the bitterness that marks their parting—'Farewell, sister, your feast I here renounce' (Stanza 49). The hope expressed in the charming 'Come forth to me, my own sweet sister dear! Cry "peep" once!' (Stanza 27) is transformed later into the distress following the Steward's visit—'How fare you sister? Cry "peep" wherever you are' (Stanza 44). A single stanza brackets the very height of their enjoyment at the fulfillment of their appetite ('and "Hail, Yule, Hail" they cried on high') with the threatening arrival of the Steward, at which we are told 'Yet after joy oftentimes comes care, and trouble after great prosperity' (Stanza 42). The delight and the distress are mingled.

When the *Moralitas* warns of trouble and vexation 'especially for those who climb most high' (Stanza 53), it echoes the description of the Country Mouse's escape from the Cat: 'Then up in haste behind the partition wall she climbed high enough that Gilbert might not get at her' (Stanza 49). From this echo we discover that the Country Mouse is not to be considered blameless for her own precarious position. By agreeing to turn her back on her humble home she was succumbing to the temptation of appetite that had already corrupted her sister. However, the Country Mouse remains aware that all is not well—'Yes, Dame, . . . but how long will this last?' (Stanza 40))—and she redeems herself by returning in haste to the country.

Other kinds of references, perhaps more subtle, also refer to parts of the narrative. 'Blessed be the humble feast in quiet' (Stanza 54) recalls the noise with which they cheered 'Hail, Yule, Hail' during their feast (Stanza 42). The 'sweetness' of 'the sweetest life therefore . . . is security with few possessions' (Stanza 54) harkens back to the description of the City Mouse comforting her dazed sister: 'And when her sister found her in such straits, for the sake of pity first she grieved a bit, then comforted her with words *as sweet as honey*' (Stanza 45, emphasis supplied). (Henryson's source, Gualterus Anglicus, uses the words 'sweet' and 'honey' three times each within ten lines at this moment in his tale, echoing them in his *Moralitas*—'I do not wish to fear the plenty of honey-sweet food.') 'The Cat comes and has his eye on the Mouse' (Stanza 55) suggests that the Cat in the tale, or some force motivating the Cat, had visited retribution on the mice intentionally, a conclusion supported by another echo, this time within the tale itself: On his entrance, the Cat bids them 'Godspeed' (Stanza 47), a reminder to the reader of the unceremonious, grace-less beginning of their gluttonous feast: 'Without Godspeed they took their shelter in a larder filled with great plenty of food; . . . later, when they were disposed to dine, without saying grace they washed and went to their food' (Stanzas 38, 39).

Compared to the fabulists that preceded him, Henryson could richly diversify the messages of his *Moralitates*, mainly because he had so enriched his narrative with detail; but rather than spell out everything for the reader in the *Moralitas*, he chose to urge the reader to discover that richness through rereadings of the fable with the *Moralitas* in mind. By taking this approach, Henryson created the first thoroughly literary fables, a feat for which he has not yet been adequately recognized. It turns out that the solemn advice he advice he gives in the 'Prologue' is by no means merely *pro forma*:

> In the same way that up through the rough
> earth (so long as it be worked with great dili-
> gence) spring the flowers and the first shoots of
> grain, wholesome and good for the sustenance
> of man, so springs a Moral of pleasant meaning
> out of the ingenious language of poetry, to good
> purpose for those who can apply it wisely.

(Stanza 2)

NOTES

1. J. W. Baxter argues for 1505 as the date of composition for Dunbar's poem. See *William Dunbar: A Biographical Study* (Edinburgh: Oliver & Boyd, 1952), 133-34.

2. See John MacQueen's 'The Literature of Fifteenth Century Scotland,' p. 204.

3. See the Introduction to the 2nd edition of H. Harvey Wood's *Poems and Fables of Robert Henryson*, p. xi.

4. See the Introduction to G. Gregory Smith's edition of the Poems, p.xx.

5. See Robert L. Kindrick, *Robert Henryson*, p. 17.

6. *The Kinaston Manuscript* (Bodl. Ms. Add. C. 287), reprinted in G. Gregory Smith's edition of the Poems, pp. ciii-civ.

7. See Matthew P. MacDiarmid, 'The Kingship of the Scots in their Writers,' *Scottish Literary Journal* 6 (1979).

8. See Matthew P. MacDiarmid's *Robert Henryson*, pp. 35-41.

9. MacDiarmid, *Robert Henryson*, 35-6.

10. See especially the books on Henryson by Marshall Stearns, John Mac-Queen, Robert L. Kindrick, and Matthew MacDiarmid, and the articles by Mary E. Rowlands, and Nicolai von Kreisler.

11. See Hesiod's *Works and Days*, 202-212, and Archilochus's Fragments 81ff. and 89ff.

12. Aristophanes, *The Birds*, 651-653.

13. Herodotus, *Histories*, II, 134ff.

14. See Aristophanes, *The Wasps*, and Plutarch's *De Sera Numinis Vindicata*, 12.

15. Max Plessow, *Geschichte der Fabeldichtung in England bis zu John Gay (1726)*, *Palaestra*, LXII, Berlin, 1906.

16. Denton Fox, 'The Scottish Chaucerians,' *Chaucer and Chaucerians*, ed. D. S. Brewer (University of Alabama Press, 1967), pp. 164-200. For an excellent summary of Henryson's probable sources, see Denton Fox, *The Poems of Robert Henryson* (Oxford: The Clarendon Press, 1981), pp. xliv-l.

17. Herbert Thompson Archibald, *The Fable as a Stylistic Text in Classical Greek Literature* (Baltimore: J. H. Furst, 1912), p. 16. See also Denton Fox, *The Poems of Robert Henryson*, pp. xliv-l.

18. Quintilian, *Institutes of Oratory*, I, 9, trans. H. E. Butler (Cambridge: Harvard University Press, 1936). See I. Carruthers, 'Henryson's Use of Aristotle and Priscian in the *Moral Fables*,' p. 284.

19. There is some editorial disagreement concerning the closing of the sheep's quotation. I follow G.G. Smith, Wood, and Elliott in ending it at l. 1298, allowing the rest of the *Moralitas* to be spoken by the narrator. Denton Fox, following Laing, Murray, and the advice of Jamieson, extends the Sheep's speech to the end of the fable. Both seem reasonable, and they both produce the important effect of pathos.

20. Martin Stevens, 'The Royal Stanza in Early English Literature,' *PMLA* 94 (1979), 74.

21. Denton Fox, *The Testament of Cressid*, Introduction.

22. George Clark, 'Henryson and Aesop: The Fable Transfigured,' *ELH* 43 (1976), 1-18.

23. Ibid., p. 10.

24. See Howard Henry Roerecke, *The Integrity and Symmetry of Robert Henryson's Moral Fables*, Diss. Pennsylvania State University, 1969. The order differs radically only in the Bannatyne Manuscript. John MacQueen, in his *Robert Henryson: A Study of the Major Narrative Poems* (Oxford, 1967), has made a carefully reasoned argument in favor of the Bannatyne ordering, but the structural relationships I discuss here convince me of the efficacy of the more commonly accepted order.

25. The only work I have seen that treats the *Moral Fables* as a structurally integral whole is Howard Henry Roerecke's unpublished dissertation.

26. Roerecke, p. 126.

27. S. A. Handford, *The Fables of Aesop* (Baltimore: Penguin Books, 1970), p.xx.

28. Translation by Richard Schrader, from his unpublished dissertation, A

Critical and Historical Study of Robert Henryson's Morall Fabillis (The Ohio State University, 1968), p. 183.

29. Translation by Richard Schrader, p. 188.

30. R. T. Leneghan, *Caxton's Aesop* (Cambridge: Harvard University Press, 1967), p. 82.

31. Schrader, p. 189.

32. Ibid., p. 191.

33. Ibid., p. 194.

NOTE ON THE TEXTS
OF HENRYSON

The earliest extant texts of Henryson's *Morall Fabillis* date from almost
a century after its composition. Only four texts are of major importance:

1) The Bannatyne MS. (1568) in the National Library of
   Scotland; only ten of the thirteen fables appear, and these
   are interspersed with works by other authors. The order of
   the fables here differs from that of all other texts.

2) The text printed by Robert Lekpreuik for Henry Charteris,
   Edinburgh (1570). The only known copy today is in the
   British Library.

3) The Thomas Bassandyne print, Edinburgh (1571), the only
   known copy of which is now in the National Library of
   Scotland. This is the text which has formed the basis for
   the major modern editions.

4) The Harleian MS. (1571), now in the British Library.

Of somewhat lesser importance:

5) The Makculloch MS. (1477), now in the library of the
   University of Edinburgh. On the front leaves there is an
   autograph of no discernable date of the Prologue and the
   'Taill of the Cok and the Jasp.'

6) The early 16th century Asloan MS., unavailable to
   Henryson editors until 1925, now in the National Library
   of Scotland.

7) An "Englished" text printed by Richard Smith, London,
   1577, riddled with inaccuracies and not of much help in
   better understanding the original. The only known copy is
   in the National Library of Scotland.

8) An edition printed by Andro Hart, Edinburgh (1621), with
   Anglicized spellings. The only known copy is in the National Library of Scotland.

Until the Maitland Club reprinted Hart's edition in 1832, no other
edition seems to have appeared. No new work of any significance was
done on Henryson until David Laing undertook the task of resurrecting
the entire Henryson corpus (published 1865). His was followed in turn
by the complete editions of the German A. R. Diebler (1886), of G.
Gregory Smith for the Scottish Text Society (1914), of W. M. Metcalfe

(1917), of H. Harvey Wood (1933, second edition 1968), a nearly complete edition by Charles Elliott for the Oxford University Press (1963), and finally the excellent and thorough scholarly edition of Denton Fox, also for the Oxford University Press (1981).

I have based the present edition on the Bassandyne text and have noted the occasions when I have preferred variant readings.

NOTE ON THIS TRANSLATION

Henryson wrote the *Morall Fabillis* in Middle Scots, a literary language that was essentially a Northern dialect of Middle English. The Rhyme Royal stanza form he chose (with two brief excursions into eight-line stanzas) accounts for many of the work's effects. While recognizing the necessary and regrettable loss of those effects, I still decided to translate the work into prose stanzas, for two compelling reasons: (1) There is no way of duplicating the suffix rhymes of Henryson in modern English, which difficulty would necessitate in a poetic translation wholesale changes in word order and line content; and (2) since no complete translation of the work has been published to this date,[1] textual accuracy should be preferred to superior artistic effect wherever the two come into conflict.

I have done my utmost to maintain the artistry of the work, in particular by imposing a poetry-like restriction on the prose: for each five-stress line of Henryson's poetry, I have tried to limit the translation to five stresses of prose rhythm. Where Henryson switches to a four-stress line, the prose switches to four stresses as well. By this I hope to have accomplished two things: first, to maintain insofar as possible Henryson's balances and proportions, by making each line of the translation take about as much time to read as each line of the original; second, to retain some of the poetry's rhythmic effects.

In addition, I have attempted to reproduce the effects of Henryson's diction whenever possible, differentiating the passages in the formal, high style from those in the more prevalent middle style. Compare the high style of the Cock's rhetoric in the first tale:

> 'Thow hes na corne, and thairof haif I neid;
> Thy cullour dois bot confort to the sicht,
> And that is not aneuch my wame to feid;
> For wyfis sayis that lukand werk is licht.
> I wald have sum meit, get it geve I micht,
> For houngrie men may not weill leve on lukis;
> Had I dry breid, I compt not for na cukis.

> Of grain have you none, and thereof have I
> need. Your color satisfies only the sense of sight,
> and that is not sufficient to fill my stomach; for
> old wives say that looking on is hardly heavy
> work. I would have some food if only I could find
> some, for hungry men cannot live on looks. Had I
> but dry bread, I would not care a bit for a cook.

(Stanza 15)

to the middle style of the narrator when describing the widow in the third tale:

> Ane wedow dwelt, in till ane drop that dayis,
> Quhilk wan hir ffude off spinning on hir Rok,
> And na mair had fforsuth, as the Fabill sayis,
> Except off hennis scho had ane Lyttil flok;
> And thame to keip scho had ane Jolie Cok,
> Richt curageous, that to this wedow ay
> Devydit nicht and crew befoir the day.

> In those days there was a Widow, dwelling in a
> village, who won her food by spinning on a
> distaff; and truly that was all she had, the fable
> says, except she kept a little flock of hens; and to
> keep watch over them she had a lively Cock, full
> of spirit, who ever divided the night in half for
> the Widow, and crowed at break of day.

> (Stanza 59)

I have also tried to transfer to the prose significant changes or emphases in rhythm, syntax, and rhetorical trope that appear in the poetry. For example, the Wether in the eleventh tale speaks with an excess of alliteration, in pronounced rhythms, marked by strong caesuras and noticeable balances—but only as long as he remains confident of his own abilities:

> With that ane Wedder wichtlie wan on fute:
> 'Maister' (quod he), 'mak merie and be blyith;
> To brek your hart ffor baill it is na bute;
> For ane deid Dogge ye na cair on yow kyith.
> Ga ffeche him hither and fla his skyn off swyth;
> Syne sew it on me; and luke that it be meit,
> Baith heid and crag, bodie, taill, and feit.

> Just then a Wether walked up to him with confidence.
> 'Master' (he said), 'Be merry and of good cheer;
> to crack your heart will not cure your hurt; don't
> waste any worry over a Dog that is dead. Go fetch him
> hither, and straightaway flay off his skin; then
> sew it on me; and see that it be properly mea-
> sured, both head and neck, body, tail, and feet.

> (Stanza 354)

Once the Wolf has discovered the Wether's disguise and has captured him, the Wether's rhythms falter, the alliteration declines, and the confidence evaporates from his speech:

'Schir' (quod the Wedder), 'suppois I ran in hy,
My mynd wes never to do your persoun ill;
Ane flear gettis ane follower commounly,
In play or ernist, preif quha sa ever will.
Sen I bot playit, be gracious me till,
And I sall gar my freindis blis your banis;
Ane full gude servand will crab his Maister anis.'

'Sir' (said the Wether), 'although I ran so quickly,
I never intended your person any harm; he who
flees usually attracts a pursuer, either in play or
in earnest—test it for yourself. Since I but played
with you, be gracious unto me, and I shall have
my friends bless your bones; even the best
servant will cross his master once.'

(Stanza 368)

On occasion I have allowed a rhyme of Henryson's to remain in the
prose translation, but always with some distinct purpose. For example,
when the Fox advises the Wolf:

and be not afraid of any danger that may appear,
but keep yourself completely still when the Churl
comes near

(Stanza 305)

the rhyme might suggest that the Fox's plan sounds too pat. At the end
of the same tale, when the Fox has successfully robbed the Cadger and
cheated the Wolf, the rhyme that resolves the final stanza suggest a harshness in its finality:

the latter lacked the herring from his creels, and
the former's blood was running down to his
heels.

(Stanza 314)

At other times rhyme supports the harmony of the narrator's moral
resolutions:

The great Cheese may be called Covetice, which
abundantly grows in the eye of many a man.
Accursed be the well of that wicked vice! For it
is naught but fraud and fantasy, driving each man
to leap into the buttery that draws him downward
to the pains of Hell.—Christ keep all Christians
from that wicked well!

(Stanza 350)

NOTE

1. To my knowledge, there have been only three attempts made at translating the *Morall Fabillis*: (1) Richard Smith, *The Fabulous Tales of Esope the Phrygian* (London, 1577); (2) J. Ross, *The Book of Scottish Poems: Ancient and Modern*, Vol. I (Edinburgh, 1878), which includes about half of the *Morall Fabillis*; (3) David Joseph Fratus, *Robert Henryson's Moral Fables: Tradition, Text, and Translation*, (Diss., University of Iowa, 1971).

The Moral Fables of Aesop

The Prologue

1   Though the fabulous tales of old poetry are not
    all grounded in truth, still their polished terms
    of delightful rhetoric are most pleasing to the
    ear of man. Moreover, the reason they first
    were written was to reprove man's evil-living by
    representing it in terms of another thing.

2   In the same way that up through the rough
    earth (so long as it be worked with great dili-
    gence) spring the flowers and the first shoots of
    grain, wholesome and good for the sustenance
    of man, so springs a Moral of pleasant meaning
    out of the ingenious language of poetry, to good
    purpose for those who can apply it wisely.

3   The shell of a nut, though it be hard and tough,
    affords delight because it holds the kernel; in the
    same way there lies a doctrine of substantial wis-
    dom, full of fruit, within a ficticious fable. More-
    over, scholars think it most profitable to include
    a merry sport in their earnest teachings, to
    lighten the spirit and make the time seem short.

4   For as we see, a bow that is always bent even-
    tually warps, and its string will lose its snap; so
    it is with the mind that is constantly diligent,
    ever in earnest thoughts and ever studying. It
    makes good sense to mix some merriness with
    matters that are sober; that is surely why Aesop
    said, *Dulcius arrident seria picta Iocis.*

5   With your permission, my Masters, I would at-
    tempt to make a kind of translation of this
    author, from Latin to our mother tongue, submit-
    ting my efforts to your correction. I write not of
    my own accord, in presumptuous vanity, but at
    the request and command of a particular Lord,
    the name of whom needs not be recorded.

The Prolog

1   Thocht feinyeit fabils of ald poetre
Be not al grunded upon truth,° yit than
Thair polite termes° of sweit Rhetore
Richt plesand ar Unto the eir of man;
And als the caus that thay first began   5
Wes to repreif the haill misleving
Off man be figure of ane uther thing.°

2   In lyke maner as throw the bustious eird,
(Swa it be laubourit with grit diligence)
Springis the flouris, and the corne abreird,   10
Hailsum and gude to mannis sustenence,
Sa dois spring ane Morall sweit sentence,
Oute of the subtell dyte of poetry:
To gude purpois quha culd it weill apply.

3   The nuttes schell, thocht it be hard and teuch,   15
Haldis the kirnill, and is delectabill.
Sa lyis thair ane doctrine wyse aneuch,
And full of fruit, under ane fenyeit Fabill.
And Clerkis sayis it is richt profitabill
Amangis ernist to ming ane merie sport,   20
To light the spreit, and gar the tyme be schort.

4   For as we se, ane Bow that is ay bent
Worthis unsmart, and dullis on the string;
Sa dois the mynd that is ay diligent,
In ernistfull thochtis and in studying.   25
With sad materis sum merines to ming,
Accordis weill; thus Esope said, I wis,
Dulcius arrident seria picta Iocis.°

5   Of this Authour, my Maisteris, with your leif
Submitting me to your correctioun,   30
In Mother toung of Latyng I wald preif
To mak ane maner of Translatioun°—
Nocht of my self, for vane presumptioun,
Bot be requeist and precept of ane Lord,°
Of quhome the Name it neidis not record.   35

6   I have to write in homely language and in terms
     that are rude, for never have I understood the
     mysteries of Eloquence and Rhetoric. Therefore
     meekly I pray your Reverences: if you find ought
     that through my negligence has fallen short or
     overshot the mark, please correct me by your
     gracious wills.

7   My author in his fables tells how dumb beasts
     could speak and perceive, and knew how to dis-
     pute to good purpose and to argue, to construct a
     syllogism and also make conclusions—demon-
     strating through examples and stories how many
     men in their actions behave as if they were
     beasts.

8   Do not marvel that a man can come to resemble
     a beast, which ever loves carnal and foul delights;
     for in despite of shame, which can neither restrain
     nor arrest him, he grasps at every pleasure and in-
     dulges his appetite; and thus through habituation
     and daily rite, sin roots itself so firmly in his mind
     that he becomes transformed into a brute beast.

9   As I have said, this noble scholar Aesop, in
     splendid eloquence and in delightful metre, wrote
     his book in metaphorical terms, for he wished to
     criticize both the high and the lowly. And to
     begin with, he wrote at first of a Cock who while
     searching for his food found a beautiful Gem, the
     fable of which you shall hear at once.

The Cock and the Jasper

10   One day, early in the morning, a Cock with bright
     and colorful feathers, high spirited and cocky, de-
     spite his being poor, flew out and landed on a dung-
     hill; his only care was to find his dinner. While
     scratching about among the rubbish, he happened
     upon a gorgeous Jasper, a most precious gem, which
     had been swept from the house in the daily cleaning.

6   In hamelie language and in termes rude
       Me neidis wryte, for quhy of Eloquence
       Nor Rethorike I never Understude.
       Thairfoir meiklie I pray your reverence,
       Gif ye find ocht that throw my negligence   40
       Be deminute or yit superfluous,
       Correct it at your willis gratious.

7   My Author in his Fabillis tellis how
       That brutal beistis spak and Understude,
       And to gude purpois dispute and argow,   45
       Ane Sillogisme propone, and eik conclude;°
       Putting exempill and similitude
       How mony men in operatioun
       Ar like to beistis in conditioun.

8   Na mervell is, ane man be lyke ane Beist,   50
       Quhilk lufis ay carnall and foull delyte;
       That schame can not him renye nor arreist,
       Bot takis all the lust and appetyte;°
       And that throw custum and daylie ryte
       Syne in the mynd sa fast is Radicate,   55
       That he in brutal beist is transformate.

9   This Nobill Clerk, Esope, as I haif tauld,
       In gay metir, as poete Lawriate,
       Be figure wrait his buke; for he nocht wald
       Lak the disdane off hie nor low estate.   60
       And to begin, first of ane Cok he wrate,
       Seikand his meit, quhilk fand ane Jolie stone,
       Of quhome the Fabill ye sall heir anone.

The Taill of the Cok and the Jasp

10   Ane cok sum tyme with feddram fresch & gay,
       Richt cant and crous, albeit he was bot pure,   65
       Flew furth upon ane dunghill sone be day;
       To get his dennar set was al his cure.
       Scraipand amang the as, be aventure
       He fand ane Jolie Jasp,° richt precious,
       Wes castin furth in sweping of the hous.   70

11   Since careless and insolent chambermaids love to
        be dallying and to be seen on the street, they pay
        little attention when they are sweeping out the
        house; they only check to see that the floor is clean.
        Jewels are lost, as so often happens, by being dropped
        on the floor and then swept out of the house. Perhaps
        such was the case with this very stone.

12   Thus gazing upon the stone with wonder he said,
        'O worthy Jasper! O rich and noble thing! Though
        I have found you, of little value are you to me.
        You are a jewel fit for a Lord or a King. What a
        pity you should lie on this dungheap, buried thus
        among this muck on the ground, and you so fair
        and worth such a deal of gold.

13   'Pity it is that I should be the one to find you,
        for neither your great power nor your bright color
        can make me the more worthy of praise or glory;
        and you to me can bring but little joy. Although
        great Lords would consider you lovely and precious,
        I love far better things of lesser value, such as chaff
        or grain to fill my empty stomach.

14   Better for me to be scraping here with my nails in
        all this mud, searching for my sustenance, as chaff
        or grain or small worms or snails or any food that
        would do my stomach good, than to find a mighty
        multitude of gems. And you, in turn, by much
        the same reasoning, may condescend to me for
        fulfilling none of your needs.

15   'Of grain have you none, and thereof have I
        need. Your color satisfies only the sense of sight,
        and that is not sufficient to fill my stomach; for
        old wives say that looking on is hardly heavy
        work. I would have some food if only I could find
        some, for hungry men cannot live on looks. Had I
        but dry bread, I would not care a bit for a cook.

16   'Where is the home in which you are fit to dwell?
        Where should you live, but in a Royal Tower?
        Where should you sit, but on the crown of a
        King, exalted in worship, and in honor great?
        Gentle Jasper, of all stones the flower, arise from

11   As Damisellis wantoun and Insolent,
      That fane wald play, and on the streit be sene,
      To swoping of the hous thay tak na tent;
      Thay cair na thing, swa that the flure be clene.
      Jowellis ar tint, as oftymis hes bene sene,   75
      Upon the flure, and swopit furth anone—
      Peradventure, sa wes the samin stone.

12   Sa mervelland Upon the stane (quod he)
      'O gentill Jasp! O riche and Nobill thing!
      Thocht I the find, thow ganis not for me.   80
      Thow art ane Jowell for ane Lord or King.
      Pietie it wer, thow suld ly in this mydding,
      Be buryit thus amang this muke on mold,
      And thow so fair, and worth sa mekill gold.

13   'It is pietie I suld the find, for quhy   85
      Thy grit vertew,° nor yit thy cullour cleir,
      It may me nouther extoll nor magnify;
      And thow to me may mak bot lyttill cheir.
      To grit Lordis thocht thow be leif and deir,
      I lufe fer better thing of les availl,   90
      As draf, or corne, to fill my tume Intraill.

14   'I had lever ga scrapit heir with my naillis
      Amangis this mow, and luke my lifys fude,
      As draf or corne, small wormis or snaillis,°
      Or ony meit wald do my stomok gude,   95
      Than of Jaspis ane mekill multitude.
      And thow agane, Upon the samin wyis,
      May me as now for thyne availl dispyis.

15   'Thow hes na corne, and thairof haif I neid;
      Thy cullour dois bot confort to the sicht,   100
      And that is not aneuch my wame to feid;
      For wyfis sayis that lukand werk is licht.
      I wald have sum meit, get it geve I micht,
      For houngrie men may not weill leve on lukis;
      Had I dry breid, I compt not for na cukis.   105

16   'Quhar suld thow mak thy habitatioun?
      Quhar suld thow dwell, bot in ane Royall Tour?
      Quhar suld thow sit, bot on ane Kingis Croun,
      Exaltit in worschip and in grit honour?
      Rise, gentill Jasp, of all stanis the flour,   110

out this dungheap and go where you belong. You
are not fit for me, nor I for you.'

17   Leaving this jewel lying on the ground, this Cock
went on his way to seek his food. But when or
how or by whom it was found, at present I intend
to discuss no further. But the deeper meaning and
intent of this fable (and following still what my
author has written) I shall now set forth in rude
and homely terms.

18   This beautiful Gem has seven properties: To
begin with, its color would make one marvel, part
like the fire and part like the heaven. It
strengthens a man and makes him victorious; it
preserves him as well from perilous happenings.
Whoever owns this stone shall speed with good
luck; neither fire nor water would he need to fear.

MORALITAS

19   This noble Jasper, so distinctive in color, betokens perfect wisdom and learning, adorned with
the power of many virtuous deeds, more excellent
than any earthly thing. It enables men to rule
forever in honor and good fortune, sturdy enough
to gain the victory over all vices and over our
spiritual enemy.

20   Who may be hardy, rich, and gracious? Who can
overcome both peril and chance? Who can
govern a realm or city or house without
knowledge? No man, I assure you. Knowledge is
the wealth that shall ever endure, which neither
worms nor mould nor rust can destroy; to the soul
of man it is eternal sustenance.

21   This Cock, desiring more the simple grains than
any Gem, may be compared to a Fool, who only
makes a mock and scorns at knowledge, knowing
nothing good; and little will he learn. His heart
would turn to notice words of wisdom as would a
sow to notice precious stones that men have
dropped into her trough of swill.

22   Who is an enemy to knowledge and learning but
ignorant people, who understand nothing that is

Out of this midding, and pas quhar thow suld be;
Thow ganis not for me, nor I for the.'

17   Levand this Jowell law upon the ground,
      To seik his meit this Cok his wayis went.
      Bot quhen or how or quhome be it wes found,   115
      As now I set to hald no Argument.
      Bot of the Inward sentence and Intent
      Of this fabill (as myne Author dois write)
      I sall reheirs in rude and hamelie dite.

18   This Jolie Jasp hes properteis sevin:°   120
      The first, of cullour it is mervelous,
      Part lyke the fyre, and part lyke to the hevin.
      It makis ane man stark and victorious;
      Preservis als fra cacis perrillous.
      Quha hes this stane sall have gude hap to speid,   125
      Of fyre nor water him neidis not to dreid.

      MORALITAS°

19   This gentill Jasp, richt different of hew,
      Betakinnis perfite prudence and cunning,
      Ornate with mony deidis of vertew,
      Mair excellent than ony eirthly thing;   130
      Quhilk makis men in honour ay to Ring,
      Happie, and stark to wyn the victorie
      Of all vicis and Sprituall enemie.

20   Quha may be hardie, riche, and gratious?
      Quha can eschew perrell and aventure?   135
      Quha can Governe ane Realme, Cietie, or hous
      Without science?° No man, I yow assure.
      It is riches that ever sall Indure,
      Quhilk Maith, nor moist, nor uther rust can freit:
      To mannis saull it is eternall meit.   140

21   This Cok, desyrand mair the sempill corne
      Than ony Jasp, may till ane fulè be peir,
      Quhilk at science makis bot ane moik and scorne,
      And na gud can: als lytill will he leir.
      His hart wammillis wyse argumentis to heir,   145
      As dois ane Sow to quhome men for the nanis
      In hir draf troich wald saw precious stanis.°

22   Quha is enemie to science and cunning
      Bot Ignorants, that understandis nocht

so noble, so precious, and so worthy that one cannot buy it with anything on earth? Wealthy is
that man over all others who may spend the days
of his life in perfect study to further his knowledge; he needs no more than that.

23   But now, alas, this Gem is lost and hidden; we
seek it not, nor prize it once it is found. If we
have riches, no better life we seek, not even
knowledge, though the soul be bare and blind. To
speak of this matter turns words into mere wind.
Therefore I cease and will say nothing further.
Go seek the Jasper, you who will, for there it lies.

The Tale of the Country Mouse
and the City Mouse

24   Aesop, my authority, tells us of two Mice who
were loving sisters, the elder of whom dwelt in a
Borough town, while the other dwelt in the
country close by; alone, sometimes in the bushes,
sometimes in the briar, sometimes in the grain
she lived as outlaws do, on what they can pilfer
from other men.

25   This Country Mouse in the winter-time suffered
hunger, cold, and great distress; the other Mouse,
that lived in the town, was a member of the Guild
and made a free Burgess, also free from tolls, exempt
from both the Great and Little Customs, and with
freedom to go wherever she wished, among the
cheese in the cupboard and the meal in the chest.

26   Once, when she felt comfortable and was not sore
of foot, she thought upon her sister in the country, and longed to hear of her welfare, to see what
life she lived out in the greenwood. Barefoot,
alone, with pikestaff in her hand, as a poor
pilgrim she left the town to seek her sister over
both dale and down.

Quhilk is sa Nobill, sa precious, and sa ding, 150
That it may not with eirdlie thing be bocht.
Weill wer that man over all uther that mocht
All his lyfe dayis in perfite studie wair
To get science; for him neidis na mair.

23 But now (allace) this Jasp is tynt and hid: 155
We seik it nocht, nor preis it for to find.
Haif we richis, na better lyfe we bid,
Of science thocht the Saull be bair and blind.
Of this mater to speik, it wer bot wind.
Thairfore I ceis, and will na forther say. 160
Ga seik the Jasp, quha will, for thair it lay.°

*The Taill of the Uponlandis Mous
and the Burges Mous*

24 Esope, myn Author, makis mentioun
Of twa myis, and thay wer Sisteris deir,
Of quham the eldest dwelt in ane Borous toun,°
The uther wynnit uponland weill neir; 165
Soliter, quhyle° under busk, quhyle under breir,
Quhilis in the corne, and uther mennis skaith,
As outlawis dois, and levis on their waith.

25 This rurall mous in to the wynter tyde
Had hunger, cauld, and tholit grit distress; 170
The uther Mous, that in the Burgh can byde,
Was Gild brother° and made ane fre Burges;°
Toll fre als, but custom mair or les,°
And fredome had to ga quhair ever scho list,
Amang the cheis in ark, and meill in kist. 175

26 Ane tyme when scho was full and unfute sair,
Scho tuke in mynd hir sister uponland,
And langit for to heir of hir weilfair,
To se quhat lyfe scho had under the wand.
Bairfute, allone, with pykestaf in hir hand, 180
As pure pylgryme scho passit out off town,
To seik hir sister baith oure daill and down.

27   Forth through many wandering ways she walked,
      through swamp and mire, through banks, bush,
      and briar, from furrow to furrow, from ridge to
      ridge, crying 'Come forth to me, my own sweet
      sister dear! Cry "peep" once!' The Country
      Mouse heard the cry and knew her voice, as kins-
      men do by nature, and forth she went to meet her.

28   Would to God you had seen the heart-felt joy ex-
      pressed when these sisters met, and the great affec-
      tion they showed each other; for sometimes they
      laughed and sometimes wept for joy, sometimes
      sweetly kissed, and sometimes embraced each other.
      Thus they carried on until their mood became more
      sober; then step for step they went into the chamber.

29   I have heard it was a humble abode, poorly made
      of moss and fern, a simple cot under a heavy
      stone, the entrance of which was neither high
      nor broad. And without more delay they entered
      this house without fire or candle burning bright,
      for generally such pilferers do not love the light.

30   When they had settled in, these simple Mice, the
      younger sister went into her butterie and brought
      forth nuts and peas, instead of spice; I leave it for
      those at hand to decide how good a meal this
      was. The City Mouse spoke up in disdain and
      said, 'Sister, is this your daily diet?' 'Why not?'
      she said, 'Is this not a fine meal?'

31   'No, by my soul, I think it but a mockery.'
      'Madam,' said she, 'then you are the more to
      blame. My mother said, Sister, that when we
      were born, you and I lay both within one womb. I
      follow the fashion and traditions of my mother
      and my father, living in poverty; for we own no
      real estate.'

32   'My fair Sister,' said she, 'you must excuse me.
      This rude diet does not agree with me. My
      stomach is used to tender food, for nowadays I eat
      as well as any Lord. These withered peas and
      nuts, ere they be cracked, will break my teeth and

27   Furth mony wilsum wayis can scho walk,
        Throw mosse and mure, throw bankis, busk & breir,
        Fra fur to fur, cryand fra balk to balk,   185
        'Cum furth to me, my awin sueit sister deir!
        Cry peip anis!' With that the Mous culd heir,
        And knew hir voce as kinnisman will do,
        Be verray kynd;° and furth scho come hir to.

28   The hartlie joy, God! geve ye had sene,   190
        Beis kith quhen that thir Sisteris met;
        And grit kyndnes wes schawin thame betwene;
        For quhylis thay leuch, and quhylis for joy thay gret,
        Quhyle kissit sweit, quhylis in armis plet.
        And thus thay fure quhill soberit wes thair mude;   195
        Syne ffute ffor ffute unto the chalmer yude.

29   As I hard say, it was ane sober wane,
        Off fog & farne ffull febilie wes maid,
        Ane sillie scheill under ane steidfast stane,
        Of quhilk the entres wes not hie nor braid.   200
        And in the samin thay went but mair abaid,
        Without fyre or candill birnand bricht,
        For comonly sic pykeris luffis not lycht.

30   Quhen thay wer lugit thus, thir sely Myse,
        The youngest sister into hir butterie glyde,   205
        And brocht furth nuttis & peis in steid off spyce;
        Giff this wes gude ffair I do it on thame besyde.
        The Burges Mous prompit forth in pryde,
        And said, 'Sister, is this your dayly fude?'
        'Quhy not,' quod scho, 'is not this meit rycht gude?'   210

31   'Na, be my saull, I think it bot ane scorne.'
        'Madam,' (quod scho), 'ye be the mair to blame;
        My mother sayd, sister, quhen we wer borne,
        That I and ye lay baith within ane wame.
        I keip the rate and custome off my dame,   215
        And off my syre, levand in povertie,
        For landis have we nane in propertie.'

32   'My fair sister' (quod scho), 'have me excusit.
        This rude dyat and I can not accord.
        To tender meit my stomok is ay usit,   220
        For quhylis I fair alsweill as ony Lord.
        Thir wydderit peis and nuttis, or they be bord,

reduce the size of my stomach, which till now
was used to food more tender.'

33   'Well, well, Sister,' (said the Country Mouse), 'if
it please you, such things as you see here, both
food and drink, lodging and household, shall be
your own, even if you remain all year. You shall
have it with blithe and merry cheer, and that
should make foods that are coarse most tender
and remarkably good, being eaten among friends.

34   'What pleasure is there in delicate feasts which
are given with a gloomy brow? A gentle heart is
better entertained with gay spirits than it would
be with a boiled cow. A modicum is more to be
praised, as long as Good Will is carver at the
table, than ill-tempered expressions with lots of
spicy food.'

35   For all this merry exhortation, the City Mouse
had little will to sing; but heavily she cast down
her brows, despite all the 'dainties' that her sister
brought her. Yet at the last she said, half in
mockery, 'Sister, these victuals and all your royal
feast may well suffice for a country beast.

36   'Leave this hole and come to my place; I shall
show you by experience that my Good Friday is
better than your Easter; the crumbs I leave
behind on my dish are equal to your whole expense. I have several houses that are perfectly
safe; I need fear neither Cat nor traps.' 'I am willing,' she said, and off they went together.

37   Ever by secret ways, through thickest grass and
grain and under bushes, stealthily they crept; the
elder was the guide and went before, and the
younger took good care to follow her. At night
they ran, by day they slept; until one morning,
before the lark had sung, they found the town
and entered in good cheer.

38   It was not far from there to a worthy house, the
destination to which the City Mouse soon
brought them. Without Godspeed they took their
shelter in a larder filled with great plenty of food;
both cheese and butter upon its high shelves, and

      Wil brek my teith and mak my wame fful sklender,
      Quhilk wes before usit to meitis tender.'°

33   'Weil, weil, sister' (quod the rurall Mous),   225
      'Geve it pleis yow, sic thing as ye se heir,
      Baith meit and dreink, harberie and hous,
      Salbe your awin, will ye remane al yeir.
      Ye sall it have wyth blyith and mery cheir,
      And that suld mak the maissis that are rude,   230
      Amang freindis, rich tender and wonder gude.

34   'Quhat plesure is in the ffeistis delicate,
      The quhilkis ar gevin with ane glowmand brow?
      Ane gentill hart is better recreate
      With blyith curage, than seith to him ane Kow.   235
      Ane modicum is mair ffor till allow,
      Swa that gude will be kerver at the dais,
      Than thrawin vuit and mony spycit mais.'

35   For all this mery exhortatioun,
      This Burges Mous had littill will to sing.   240
      Bot hevilie scho kest hir browis doun,
      For all the daynteis that scho culd hir bring.
      Yit at the last scho said, halff in hething,
      'Sister, this victuall and your royall feist,
      May weill suffice unto ane rurall beist.   245

36   'Lat be this hole and cum into my place;
      I sall to you schaw be experience
      My gude friday is better nor your pace;
      My dische likingis is worth your haill expence.
      I have housis anew off grit defence;   250
      Off Cat, na fall, na trap,° I have na dreid.'
      'I grant,' quod scho; and on togidder thay yeid.

37   In skugry ay, throw rankest gers and corne,
      And under buskis prevelie couth thay creip;
      The eldest wes the gyde and went beforne,   255
      The younger to hir wayis tuke gude keip.
      On nicht thay ran, and on the day can sleip,
      Quhill in the morning, or the Laverok sang,
      Thay fand the town, and in blythlie couth gang.

38   Not fer fra thyne unto ane worthie Wane,   260
      This Burges brocht thame sone quhare thay suld be.
      Without God speid thair herberie wes tane,
      In to ane spence with vittell grit plentie;
      Baith Cheis and Butter upon thair skelfis hie,

meat and fish enough, both fresh and salt, and
sacks full of meal and also of malt.

39   Later, when they were disposed to dine, without
saying grace they washed and went to their food,
with all the courses that cooks could dream up,
mutton and beef, sliced into great strips. A lord's
fare thus did they mimick, except for one thing:
they drank clear water instead of wine; but even
so they made good cheer.

40   With merry looks and a smiling face, the eldest
sister asked her guest if she perceived any difference between this chamber and her sorry nest.
'Yes, Dame' (said she), 'but how long will this
last?' 'Forevermore, I believe, and longer, too.' 'If
that is true, then you are fortunate indeed,' she
replied.

41   To add to all that good cheer she brought forth
an extra course, a plate of groats and a dish full of
meal; in addition she did not spare the un-
leavened cakes, I believe, but spread them around
abundantly. And the finest bread she produced
instead of jelly, and a white candle out of a coffer
stall instead of seasoning to delight the palate.

42   Thus they made merry until they could eat no
more, and 'Hail, Yule, hail' they cried on high;
yet after joy oftentimes comes care, and trouble
after great prosperity. Thus as they sat in all their
jollity, the Steward came with keys in his hand,
opened the door, and found them at dinner.

43   They did not pause to wash up, I believe, but ran
off, each on her own. The City Mouse had a
hole, and in she went; but her sister had no hole
in which to hide; it was a great shame to see that
poor Mouse, so desolate and not knowing what to
do; for very fear she fell into a swoon, near dead.

44   But as God willed, it just so happened that the
Steward had no time to stop, neither to seek nor

And flesche and fische aneuch, baith fresche and salt,   265
And sekkis full off meil and eik of malt.

39   Eftir quhen thay disposit wer to dyne,
Withowtin grace thay wesche° and went to meit,
With all coursis that Cukis culd devyne,
Muttoun and beif, strikin in tailyeis greit.   270
Ane Lordis fair thus couth thay counterfeit,
Except ane thing: thay drank the watter cleir
In steid off wyne; bot yit thay maid gude cheir.

40   With blyith upcast and merie countenance,
The eldest Sister sperit at hir gest   275
Giff that scho be ressone fand difference
Betwix that chalmer and hir sarie nest.
'Ye, dame' (quod scho), 'bot how lang will this lest?'
'For evermair, I wait, and langer to.'
'Giff it be swa, ye ar at eis' (quod scho).   280

41   Till eik thair cheir ane subcharge° furth scho brocht,
Ane plait off grottis, and ane dische full off meill;
Thraf cakkis als I trow scho spairit nocht,
Aboundantlie about hir for to deill.
And mane full fyne scho brocht in steid off geill,   285
And ane quhyte candell out off ane coffer stall,
In steid off spyce to gust thair mouth withall.

42   This maid thay merie quhill thay micht na mair,
And 'Haill, Yule, haill,' cryit upon hie;
Yit efter joy oftymes cummis cair,   290
And troubill efter grit prosperitie.
Thus as thay sat in all thair jolitie,
The Spenser come with keyis in his hand,
Oppinnit the dure, and thame at denner fand.

43   Thay taryit not to wesche, as I suppose,   295
Bot on to ga quha that micht fformest win.
The Burges had ane hole, and in scho gois;
Hir sister had na hole to hyde hir in.
To se that selie Mous it wes grit sin,
So desolate and will off ane gude reid;   300
For verray dreid scho fell in swoun neir deid.

44   Bot as God wald, it fell ane happie cace:
The Spenser had na laser for to byde,

search, neither to scare them nor chase them; but
on he went and left the door wide open. The
brave City Mouse, having made sure that he was
gone, came out of her hole and cried aloud, 'How
fare you, Sister? Cry "peep," wherever you are.'

45   This Country Mouse lay flattened on the ground,
fearing every minute that she would be killed; for
her heart was pounding with strokes of fear, and
feverishly she trembled hand and foot. And when
her sister found her in such straits, for the sake of
pity first she grieved a bit, then comforted her
with words as sweet as honey.

46   'Why do you lie there so? Rise up, my Sister dear,
and come to your dinner; this peril is past.' The
other answered her with heavy cheer, 'I cannot
eat, I am so badly frightened. I had rather fast
these forty days with plain soup, with beans or
peas to gnaw upon, than have all your feast in
such dread and discomfort.'

47   Yet with eloquent pleas she convinced her to get
up, and they went back to the table and sat down
together; but hardly had they taken a drink or two
when in came Gib the hunter, our jolly Cat, and
bade them Godspeed. At that up jumped the City
Mouse and scurried into her hole as fast as fire
from flint; but Puss caught the other one by the back.

48   From paw to paw he cast her to and fro, sometimes
up, sometimes down, as playful as any kid; sometimes he would let her run under the straw, sometimes
he would shut his eyes and play Blind-Man's-
Buff with her. Thus he managed to torment this
poor Mouse, until at last, through fortune and good
luck, between a baseboard and the wall she crept.

49   Then up in haste behind the partition wall she
climbed high enough so that Gilbert might not
get at her; and skillfully she hung there by her
claws until he left, which greatly improved her
spirits. Then down she leapt, when there was none
to prevent her, and loudly to the City Mouse she
cried, 'Farewell, Sister, your feast I here renounce!

  Nowther to seik nor serche, to sker nor chace;
  But on he went and left the dure up wyde.   305
  The bald Burges his passing weill hes spyde,
  Out off hir hole scho come and cryit on hie,
  'How fair ye, Sister? cry peip, quhair ever ye be.'

45 This rurall Mous lay flatling on the ground,
  And for the deith scho wes full sair dredand,   310
  For till hir hart straik mony wofull stound,
  As in ane fever scho trimbillit fute and hand.
  And quhan her sister in sic ply hir fand,
  For verray pietie scho began to greit,
  Syne confort hir with wordis hunny sweit.   315

46 'Quhy ly ye thus? ryse up, my sister deir,
  Cum to your meit, this perrell is overpast.'
  The uther answerit hir with hevie cheir,
  'I may not eit, sa sair I am agast.
  I had lever thir fourty dayis fast   320
  With watter caill,° and to gnaw benis or peis,
  Than all your feist in this dreid and diseis.'

47 With fair tretie yit scho gart hir upryse,
  And to the burde thay went and togidder sat;
  And scantlie had thay drunkin anis or twyse, 325
  Quhen in come Gib° hunter, our Jolie Cat,
  And bad God speid;° the Burges up with that,
  And till her hole scho went as fyre on flint;
  Bawdronis the uther be the bak hes hint.

48 Fra fute to fute he kest hir to and ffra,   330
  Quhylis up, quhylis doun, als cant as ony kid;
  Quhylis wald he lat hir rin under the stra,
  Quhylis wald he wink, and play with hir buk heid.°
  Thus to the selie Mous grit pane he did,
  Quhill at the last, throw fortune and gude hap, 335
  Betwix ane burde and the wall° scho crap.

49 Syne up in haist behind the parraling
  Scho clam so hie that Gilbert° micht not get hir;
  And be the clukis craftelie can hing,
  Till he wes gane; hir cheir wes all the better. 340
  Syne doun scho lap quhen thair wes nane to let hir,
  And to the Burges Mous loud can scho cry,
  'Fairweill, Sister, thy feist hier I defy!

50   'Your meal in mingled all with care; your goose is
      good, but your garlic sauce is bitter as gall. The
      final course you serve is full of pain, as you shall
      discover hereafter, without fail. I thank that wall
      and that partition for my defense just now from
      yon cruel beast. Almighty God, keep me free
      from such a feast!

51   'Were I back in the home where I came from, there
      is nothing could persuade me to come here again.'
      With that she took her leave and started out, some-
      times through the grain, sometimes through the open
      field; and when she was away from there and free she
      was well pleased, and merrily made her way to the
      moor. I cannot tell how well she managed thereafter.

52   But I have heard tell she made her way back to
      her den, as warm as wool, although not a grand
      place, but well supplied, both inner and outer
      rooms, with beans and nuts, peas, rye, and wheat.
      Whenever she wanted she had enough to eat, in
      quiet and ease, without any fear; but to her
      sister's feast she returned no more.

      MORALITAS

53   Friends, if you will take heed, you may find in
      this fable a good morality. As vetches are mixed
      in with wholesome seed, so intermingled is adver-
      sity with earthly joy, so that no estate is free,
      without trouble and some vexation, especially for
      those who climb most high and are not content
      with few possessions.

54   Blessed be the simple life without fear; blessed be
      the humble feast in quiet. He who has enough, of
      no more does he need, though it be little in
      quantity. Great abundance and blind prosperity
      ofttimes make for an evil conclusion. The
      sweetest life, therefore, in this land of ours, is
      security with few possessions.

55   O wanton man! accustomed to feeding your
      stomach, making it into a god, look to yourself. I

50   'Thy mangerie is mingit all with cair;
       Thy guse is gude, thy gansell sour as gall.   345
       The subcharge off thy service is bot sair;
       Sa sall thow find heir efterwart na ffall.
       I thank yone courtyne and yone perpall wall
       Of my defence now ffra yone crewall beist.
       Almichtie God, keip me fra sic ane ffeist!   350

51   'Wer I into the kith I come ffra,
       For weill nor wo, suld I never cum agane.'
       With that scho tuke her leif and furth can ga,
       Quhylis throw the corne and quhylis throw the plane;
       Quhen scho wes furth and fre scho wes full fane,   355
       And merilie markit unto the mure.
       I can not tell how weill thairefter scho fure.

52   Bot I hard say scho passit to hir den,
       Als warm as woll, suppose it wes not greit,
       Full beinly stuffit, baith but and ben,°   360
       Off beinis and nuttis, peis, ry, and quheit.
       Quhen ever scho list, scho had aneuch to eit,
       In quyet and eis withoutin ony dreid;
       Bot to hir sisteris feist na mair scho yeid.

MORALITAS°

53   Friendis, ye may find, and ye will tak heid,   365
       In to this fabill ane gude moralitie.
       As fitchis myngit ar with nobill seid,
       Swa interminglit is adversitie
       With eirdlie joy, swa that na estate is frie,
       Without trubill and sum vexatioun: 370
       And namelie thay quhilk clymmis up maist hie,
       That ar not content with small possessioun.

54   Blissed be sempill lyfe withoutin dreid;
       Blissed be sober feist in quietie;
       Quha hes aneuch, of na mair hes he neid,   375
       Thocht it be littill into quantatie.
       Grit aboundance and blind prosperitie
       Oftymes makis ane evill conclusioun:
       The sweitest lyfe thairfoir, in this cuntrie,
       Is sickernes with small possessioun.   380

55   O wanton man! that usis for to feid
       Thy wambe, and makis it a God to be,

warn you well, without a doubt: the Cat comes
and has his eye on the Mouse. What avails then
thy feast and thy royalty, with fearful heart and
tribulation? Therefore the best thing on earth for
me, I say, is happiness in heart with few possessions.

56   Your own fire, my friend, even though it be but
an ember, warns well and is worth gold to you. And
Solomon says, if you will but read, 'under the heaven
there cannot be a better life than to be content and
live in honesty.' Wherefore I may conclude with this
pronouncement: of earthly joy, the highest degree is
to have happiness in heart with few possessions.

The Tale of Sir Chanticlere and the Fox

57   Though brute beasts are irrational, that is to say,
wanting powers of discretion, yet each one
naturally possesses many diverse characteristics:
the Bear so strong, the Wolf, the Lion wild, the
treacherous Fox, crafty and cunning, the Dog
which barks at night and guards the house.

58   So different are their traits, a mystery to man,
and so numerous, and demonstrating such diver-
sities in nature, that it exceeds my powers of
description. That is the reason I intend to write
about a particular case I came across, which happened just last year to a Fox and noble
Chanticlere.

59   In those days there was a Widow, dwelling in a
village, who won her food by spinning on a
distaff; and truly that was all she had, the fable
says, except she kept a little flock of hens; and to
keep watch over them she had a lively Cock, full
of spirit, who ever divided the night in half for
the Widow, and crowed at break of day.

Lieke to thy self; I warne the weill but dreid,
The Cat cummis, and to the Mous hes Ee.
Quhat vaillis than thy feist and royalitie,   385
With dreidfull hart and tribulatioun?
Best thing in eird, thairfoir, I say, for me,
Is blyithnes in hart, with small possessioun.

56 Thy awin fyre, my freind, sa it be bot ane gleid,
It warmis weill and is worth gold to the.   390
And Solomon sayis,° gif that thow will reid,
'Under the hevin thair can not better be
Than ay be blyith and leif in honestie.'
Quhairfoir I may conclude be this ressoun:
Of eirthly joy it beiris mais degre,   395
Blyithnes in hart, with small possessioun.

The Taill of Schir Chantecleir and the Foxe

57 Thocht brutall beistis be Irrationall,
That is to say, wantand discretioun,
Yit ilk ane in thair kynd naturall
Hes mony divers inclinatioun.   400
The Bair busteous, the Wolff, the wylde Lyoun,
The Fox fenyeit, craftie and cawtelous,
The Dog to bark on nicht and keip the hows.

58 Sa different thay ar in properteis,°
Unknawin to man, and sa infinite,   405
In kynd havand sa ffell diversiteis,
My cunning it excedis ffor to dyte.
For thy as now I purpose ffor to wryte
Ane cais I ffand, quhilk ffell this ather yeir,
Betwix ane Foxe and ane gentill Chantecleir.   410

59 Ane wedow dwelt, in till ane drop that dayis,
Quhilk wan hir ffude off spinning on hir Rok,
And na mair had fforsuth, as the Fabill sayis,
Except off hennis scho had ane Lyttil flok;
And thame to keip scho had ane Jolie Cok,   415
Richt curageous, that to this wedow ay
Devydit nicht° and crew befoir the day.

60   A little way from this particular Widow's house
      there was a thorny copse of great thickness,
      wherein a Fox, crafty and cunning, made his
      dwelling and daily residence. This Fox did great
      harm to this Widow by poaching her poultry in
      daylight and in darkness, and no way could she
      find to be revenged on him.

61   Just when the Lark had begun his song, this wily
      Fox, being plagued by hunger, went to the farm-
      house where Chanticlere, weary from the night,
      had flown from his nest into the grey dawning.
      Lawrence noted this, and in his mind he planned
      the stratagem, the methods, and the wiles
      through which he might this Cock beguile.

62   Feigning a friendly countenance and good cheer,
      he fell to his knees, and dissembling thus he said:
      'Good morning, my master, noble Chanticlere.'
      At that the Cock gave a start backwards in alarm.
      'Sir, by my soul, you need not be afraid, nor start
      back from me, nor flee; I come here but to do you
      service.

63   'I would be much to blame if I did not serve you
      as I have served your progenitors; your father full
      oft has filled my stomach and sent me food from
      his dungpile to the moors. And at his death I
      carefully did my duty, holding his head and giv-
      ing him warm drinks, until in the end the dear
      one died in my arms.

64   'Knew you my father?' Chanticlere said, and
      laughed. 'Yea, my fair son, I held up his head
      when he died under a birchen bough; and I said
      the *Dirigie* when he was gone. So how can there
      be a feud between us two? Whom should you
      trust but me, your servant, that did such great
      honor to your father?

65   'When I behold your feathers fair and fine, your
      beak, your breast, your hackle, and your comb,
      Sir, by my soul and the blessed Sacrament, it
      warms my heart; I feel I am at home. To serve
      you I would crawl upon my stomach through frost

60   Ane lyttil ffra this fforsaid wedowis hows,
     Ane thornie schaw thair wes off grit defence,
     Quhairin ane Foxe, craftie and cautelous,   420
     Maid his repair and daylie residence;
     Quhilk to this wedow did grit violence,
     In pyking off pultrie baith day and nicht,
     And na way be revengit on him scho micht.

61   This wylie Tod, quhen that the Lark couth sing,   425
     Full sair hungrie unto the Toun him drest,
     Quhair Chantecleir in to the gray dawing,
     Werie for nicht,° wes flowen ffra his nest.
     Lowrence this saw, and in his mynd he kest
     The Jeperdie, the wayis, and the wyle,   430
     Be quhat menis he micht this Cok begyle.

62   Dissimuland in to countenance and cheir,
     On kneis fell, and simuland thus he said:
     'Gude morne, my maister, gentill Chantecleir!'°
     With that the Cok start bakwart in ane braid.   435
     'Schir, be my Saull, ye neid not be effraid,
     Nor yit ffor me to start nor fle abak;
     I come bot heir service to yow to mak.

63   'Wald I not serve to yow, it wer bot blame,
     As I have done to your progenitouris;   440
     Your father full oft fillit hes my wame,
     And send me meit ffra midding to the muris.
     And at his end I did my besie curis,
     To hald his heid, and gif him drinkis warme,
     Syne at the last the Sweit swelt in my arme.'   445

64   'Knew ye my ffather?' (quod the Cok) and leuch.
     'Yea, my ffair Sone, I held up his heid,
     Quhen that he deit under ane birkin beuch;
     Syne said the Dirigie° quhen that he wes deid.
     Betwix us twa how suld thair be ane feid?   450
     Quhame suld ye traist bot me, your Servitour,
     That to your ffather did sa grit honour?

65   'Quhen I behald your ffedderis ffair and gent,
     Your beik, your breist, your hekill, and your kame,
     Schir, be my Saull, and the blissit Sacrament,   455
     My hart is warme; me think I am at hame.
     Yow for to serve, I wald creip on my wame,

and snow, in weather dank and wet, and lay my
silver-grey locks at your feet.

66   This crafty, false, and feigning Fox played a trick
on Chanticlere: 'You are, I think, quite changed
and fallen away from the high condition of your
father; he could have born the prize for skill in
crowing, for he could crow while standing on his
toes. This is no lie; I witnessed it myself.'

67   With that the Cock stood high upon his toes,
cast up his beak, and sang with all his might. Sir
Lawrence said, 'Well done, so might I prosper;
you are your father's son and proper heir. But yet
you lack one special skill of his.' 'What?' asked
the Cock. 'Have no doubt about it, he would close
his eyes and crow and three times turn about.'

68   The Cock, then, inflated by conceit and vanity,
which throw so many into confusion, trusting
thereby to win great admiration, shutting his eyes
unwarily and walking up and down, braced himself to sing and crow. But suddenly, before he had
crowed a single note, the Fox was ready and
grabbed him by the throat.

69   Then without delay he hastened with him to the
wood, having little fear of his misdeed. Then Pertock, Sprutock, and Toppock cried aloud. The
Widow heard, and with a shriek came out. Seeing
what had happened, she gasped and gave a shout:
'How now, murder, robbery!' with a hideous
clamor. 'Alas, now lost is noble Chanticlere.'

70   As if she were mad, with many a yell and cry,
tearing her hair, she beat upon her breast; then,
pale of countenance, half in a frenzy, collapsed
for grief in a swoon and a sweat. Seeing that, the
helpless hens left their food, and while the
Widow lay there in her swoon, they fell to
disputing the situation.

71   'Alas,' said Pertock, sorely moaning, with great
tears falling down about her cheeks; 'Yon Cock

In ffroist and snaw, in wedder wan and weit,
And lay my lyart loikkis under your feit.'

66   This fenyeit Foxe, ffals and dissimulate,   460
      Maid to this Cok ane cavillatioun:
      'Ye ar, me think, changit and degenerate
      Fra your ffather off his conditioun.
      Off craftie crawing he micht beir the Croun,
      For he wald on his tais stand and craw.   465
      This wes na le; I stude beside and saw.'

67   With that the Cok upon his tais hie
      Kest up his beik and sang with all his micht.
      (Quod Schir Lowrence) 'weill said, sa mot I the,
      Ye ar your ffatheris Sone and air upricht.   470
      Bot off his cunning yit ye want ane slicht:
      'Quhat?' quod the Cok. 'He wald, and haif na dout,
      Baith wink and craw and turne him thryis about.'

68   The Cok, infect with wind and fals vanegloir,
      That mony puttis unto confusioun,   475
      Traisting to win ane grit worschip thairfoir,
      Unwarlie winkand walkit up and down,
      And syne to chant and craw he maid him boun.
      And suddandlie, be he had crawin ane note,
      The Foxe wes war and hint him be the throte.   480

69   Syne to the woid but tarie with him hyit,
      Off that cryme haifand bot lytill dout.
      With that Pertok, Sprutok, and Toppok° cryit.
      The wedow hard, and with ane cry come out.
      Seand the cace, scho sichit and gaif ane schout: 485
      'How, murther, reylok!' with ane hiddeous beir,
      'Allace, now lost is gentill Chanticleir!'

70   As scho wer woid, with mony yell and cry,
      Ryvand hir hair, upon hir breist can beit;
      Syne, paill off hew, half in ane extasy,   490
      Fell doun ffor cair in swoning and in sweit.
      With that the selie hennis left thair meit,
      And, quhill this wyfe wes lyand thus in swoun,
      Fell in that cace in disputatioun.

71   'Allace,' quod Pertok, makand sair murning,   495
      With teiris grit attour hir cheikis fell;

was our great love and our day's darling, our
nightengale and also our morning bell, our
wakeful watch to warn us and tell when Aurora
with her grey kerchief put up her head betwixt
the night and the day.

72   'Who shall be our lover? Who shall lead us?
When we are sad, who shall sing to us? With his
dear bill he would break our bread for us—in all
this world was there a deed more thoughtful? In
loving he would satisfy us well, within his power,
as much as Nature allowed him. Now that he is
gone, alas, how shall we live?'

73   Then up spoke Sprutock: 'Sister, cease your sorrow. You are demented to mourn for him like
this; we shall fare well. St. John be my surety, I
find the proverb says, 'As good love comes as
goes.' I will dress myself in my Sunday best, and
freshen myself to greet this jolly May, and then
sing this song: 'Never was widow so gay!'

74   'He was so irritable, and kept us all in awe of him,
and he was wounded with the spear of jealousy.
As for his capacity in love-making, Pertock as you
will know, he was wasted, by nature cold and dry;
therefore, Sister, since he is gone, I say: Rejoice
in your sorrow, for that is the best solution; let the
living be for the living, the dead be for the dead.'

75   Then Pertock spoke, who had but feigned her
faith before and took all her delight in lust
without love, 'Sister, you know a score like him
would hardly suffice to satisfy our appetite. Since
he is departed, I swear by this hand within a week
(if I dare speak it for modesty) to find a man better able to claw our breach.

76   The Toppock spoke up boldly, like a Curate: 'What
we have seen was just vengeance from heaven; he
was so immoral, so lecherous; he could not stay
away from his wenches, more than seven of them.
But the righteous God, though He be patient, in
balancing his scales smites most painfully
adulterers who will not choose to repent.

'Yone wes our drowrie, and our dayis darling,
Our nichtingall, and als our Orloge bell,
Our walkryfe watche, us for to warne and tell
Quhen that Aurora with her curcheis gray   500
Put up hir heid betwix the nicht and day.

72   'Quha sall our lemman be? quha sall us leid?°
Quhen we are sad, quha sall unto us sing?
With his sweit Bill he wald brek us the breid,
In all this warld wes thair ane kynder thing?   505
In paramouris he wald do us plesing,
At his power, as nature did him geif.
Now efter him, allace, how sall we leif?

73   Quod Sprutock than, 'Ceis sister off your sorrow;
Ye be to mad ffor him sic murning mais.   510
We sall ffair weill; I find, Sanct Johne to borrow,°
The prouerb sayis, 'als gude lufe cummis as gais.'
I will put on my haly dais clais,
And mak me fresch agane this Jolie may,
Syne chant this sang, 'wes never wedow sa gay!'°   515

74   'He wes angry and held us ay in aw,
And woundit with the speir off Jelowsy.
Off chalmerglew, Pertock, full weill ye knaw,
Waistit he wes, off Nature cauld and dry.°
Sen he is gone, thairfoir, Sister, say I: 520
Be blyith in baill, ffor that is best remeid;
Let quik to quik, and deid ga to the deid.'

75   Than Pertock spak, that feinyeit faith befoir,
In lust but lufe that set all hir delyte:
'Sister, ye wait, off sic as him ane scoir   525
Wald not suffice to slaik our appetyte.
I hecht be my hand, sen that he is quyte,
Within ane oulk, ffor schame and I durst speik,
To get ane berne suld better claw oure breik.'°

76   Than Toppok lyke ane Curate spak full crous: 530
'Yone wes ane verray vengeance from the hevin;
He wes sa lous and sa lecherous;
Seis coud he nocht with kittokis ma than sevin.°
Bot rychteous God, haldand the balandis evin,
Smytis rycht sair, thocht he be patient,   535
Adulteraris that list thame not repent.

77   'He was prideful, and took great joy in his sin,
        and counted as naught God's favor or enmity, but
        trusted ever to do his will and then flee; until at
        the last he was led by his sins to an end full of
        shame, to yonder sudden death. And thus it was
        the very hand of God that cause him to be
        murdered by the Fox.'

78   When they had finished, the widow awoke from
        her swoon, jumped to her feet, and called for all
        her hunting dogs: 'Hey! bark Berry, Bell, Bawsy
        Brown, search the wood, come running, Curtis,
        Brown Clyde, come forth together at once with no
        complaining! Rescue my noble Cock before he is
        killed, or else see that you never come back to me.'

79   Then, without delay, they hurried off over the heath;
        over the fields they flew as quickly as fire from flint;
        full stoutly they went through the wood and the
        waters, and did not cease until they caught sight of Sir
        Lawrence. But when he spied the hounds coming in a
        pack, he said to himself, addressing the Cock in his
        mind, 'God grant that you and I make it safely
        home to my den.'

80   Then said the Cock, inspired by some good spirit,
        'Trust me and I shall guarantee you success. You are
        hungry, and tired from travelling so much, so lacking
        in strength you may not flee much further. There-
        fore turn about and say that you and I have be-
        come good friends and fellows for a year; then, take
        my word, they will stop and stir not another foot.'

81   This Fox, though he was false and not to be trusted,
        and had tricks enough to help him out of a cor-
        ner, was himself deceived by means most mirac-
        ulous; for falseness always will fail in the end. He
        started about and cried as he was instructed; but
        when he did so, the Cock flew up to a branch.
        Now you can judge if Lawrence had reason to laugh.

82   Thus beguiled, the Fox fell on his knees under
        the tree and said, 'Good Chanticlere, come down
        again, and I, without food or pay, shall be your
        man and servant for a year.' 'Nay, false thief and
        robber, stay away from me. My bloody hackle and

77   'Prydefull he wes, and joyit off his sin,
        And comptit not for Goddis favour nor feid,
        Bot traistit ay to rax and sa to rin,
        Quhill at the last his sinnis can him leid   540
        To schamefull end, and to yone suddand deid.
        Thairfoir it is the verray hand off God
        That causit him be werryit with the Tod.'

78   Quhen this wes said, this wedow ffra hir swoun
        Start up on fute, and on hir kennettis cryde,   545
        'How! berk, Berrie, Bell, Bawsie Broun,
        Rype schaw, Rin weil, Curtes, Nutticlyde,°
        Togidder all but grunching furth ye glyde!
        Reskew my Nobill Cok, or he be slane,
        Or ellis to me se ye cum never agane.'°   550

79   With that but baid thay braidet over the bent;
        As fyre off flint thay over the feildis flaw;
        Full wichtlie thay throw wood and wateris went,
        And ceissit not schir Lourence quhill thay saw.
        Bot quhen he saw the raches cum on raw,   555
        Unto the Cok in mynd he said, 'God sen,
        That I and thow wer fairlie in my den.'

80   Then said the Cok, with sum gude Spirit inspyrit,
        'Do my counsall and I sall warrand the;
        Hungrie thow art, and ffor grit travell tyrit,   560
        Richt faint off force, and may not ferther fle.
        Swyith turne agane, and say that I and ye
        Freindis ar maid, and fellowis ffor ane yeir;°
        Than will thay stint, I stand ffor it, and not steir.'

81   This Tod, thocht he wes fals and frivolus,   565
        And had frawdis his querrell to defend,
        Desauit wes be menis richt mervelous;
        For falset failyeis ay at the latter end.
        He start about, and cryit as he wes kend:
        With that the Cok he braid unto a bewch.   570
        Now Juge ye all quhairat Schir Lowrence lewch.

82   Begylit thus, the Tod under the tre
        On kneis fell, and said, 'gude Chantecleir,
        Cum doun againe, and I, but meit or fe,
        Salbe your man and servand ffor ane yeir.'   575
        'Na, fals theif and revar, stand not me neir.

my neck turned blue have destroyed forever any
friendship between us.

83   'I was unwise to close my eyes at your bidding,
whereby I nearly forfeited my head.' 'But more the
fool was I,' said he, 'who could not keep my peace,
but spoke, and thereby lost my prey.' 'On your
way, false thief, and God save me from ever being
your dinner.' And saying that, the Cock flew over
the fields until he alighted inside the Widow's louver.

MORALITAS

84   Now, worthy folk, although this is a fable, endowed with allegorical representations, still you
may find a meaning most fitting under potentially
misleading language. For our purposes we well
may call this Cock proud and foolish men, ar-
rogant and vain, presumptuous both in nature
and character.

85   Fie! Puffed-up pride, you are so poisonous;
whoever favors you is bound to have a fall. Your
strength is naught; your footstool stands unstable.
Take good note of the Infernal Fiends, who were
hounded out of that heavenly hall down to Hell's
hole and to that hideous house, because in pride
they were so presumptuous.

86   This treacherous Fox may well correspond to flat-
terers with specious, pleasing words, with meanings false and a poisonous mind, whose whole
delight is but to flatter and lie. All worthy folk
should have disdain for these, for what can be
more dangerous a plague than to give too hasty
credence to liars?

87   An evil-thinking mind and flattery have the
outward show of sugar sweet, but they are bitter
as gall and full of poison to the taste of those
who have clear understanding. Thus (and now I
shortly will conclude) these sins of flattery and
vanity are venomous; therefore, good folks, flee
them both.

My bludy hekill and my nek sa bla
Hes partit freindschip ffor ever betwene us twa.

83   'I wes unwyse that winkit at thy will,   580
      Quhairthrow almaist I loissit had my heid.'
      'I was mair fule,' quod he, 'coud nocht be still,
      Quhairthrow to put my pray in to pleid.'
      'Fair on, fals theif, God keip me ffra thy feid.'
      With that the Cok over the feildis tuke his flicht,
      And in at the Wedowis Lewer° couth he licht.   585

MORALITAS

84   Now, worthie folk, suppose this be ane Fabill,
      And overheillit wyth typis figurall,
      Yit may ye find ane sentence richt agreabill,
      Under thir fenyeit termis textuall:
      To our purpose this Cok weill may we call   590
      Nyse proud men, woid and vaneglorious,
      Of kind and blude quhilk ar presumpteous.

85   Fy! puft up pryde, thow is full poysonabill;
      Quha favoris the on force man haif ane fall.
      Thy strenth is nocht, thy stule standis unstabill;   595
      Tak witnes of the Feyndis Infernall,
      Quhilk houndit doun wes fra that hevinlie hall
      To Hellis hole, and to that hiddeous hous,
      Because in pryde thay wer presumpteous.

86   This fenyeit Foxe may weill be figurate   600
      To flatteraris with plesand wordis quhyte,
      With fals mening and mynd maist toxicate,
      To loif and le that settes thair haill delyte.
      All worthie folk at sic suld haif despyte;
      For quhair is thair mair perrellous pestilence   605
      Nor gif to learis haistelie credence?

87   The wickit mynd and Adullatioun
      Of sucker sweit haifand the similitude,
      Bitter as gall and full of poysoun,
      To taist it is quha cleirlie understude.   610
      For thy, as now schortlie to conclude,
      Thir twa sinnis, flatterie and vaneglore,
      Ar vennomous; gude folk, fle thame thairfoir.

The Tale of How This Same Fox Made His
Confession to Friar Wolf-Who-Lies-in-Wait

88   We leave this Widow happy, I assure you, rejoicing over Chanticlere more than I can tell, and let us speak of the strange adventure and fate that fell upon this Fox, who dared no longer meddle with poaching while a glimmer of the light of day remained, but lay there lurking, waiting for the night.

89   When Thetis, goddess of the sea, had summoned Phoebus to his resting place, and Hesperus had raised his cloudy hood, showing his bright-hued countenance in the sky, then Lawrence looked up from where he lay, and shielding his eyes he looked on high, merry and glad that night had come.

90   He left the wood and went to a hill from where he might clearly see the twinkling stars and all the planets that were in the firmament, their course, and also their movement in their sphere, some in retrograde and others stationary, and in what degree of the Zodiac they were, each one, as Lawrence has instructed me.

91   At that time, old Saturn was entered into Capricorn, and Jupiter moved in Sagittarius, and Mars was borne up into the Ram's head, and Phoebus had gone forth into the Lion; Venus was in the Crab, and the Moon in Aquarius; Mercury, the God of eloquence, made his residence in the sign of the Virgin.

92   Without astrolabe, quadrant, or almanac, having learned much about Nature by instruction, this Fox understood the movings of the heavens, and what influence the constellations were likely to visit upon the earth. And he said to himself, without more ado, 'Blessed be my father for sending me to school.

93   'My destiny and also my fate I understand; my future is clearly revealed to me. My fate will be

88   Leif we this wedow glaid, I yow assure,
       Off Chantecleir mair blyith than I can tell,   615
       And speik we off the subtell aventure
       And destenie that to this Foxe befell,
       Quhilk durst na mair with miching Intermell,
       Als lang as Leme or Licht wes off the day,
       Bot, bydand nicht, full styll Lurkand he Lay.   620

89   Quhill that Thetes, the Goddess off the flude,
       Phebus had callit to the harbery,
       And Hesperous put up his cluddie hude,
       Schawand his Lustie Visage in the sky.
       Than Lowrence luikit up, quhair he couth ly,   625
       And kest his hand upon his Ee on hicht,
       Merie and glade that cummit wes the nicht.

90   Out off the wod unto ane hill he went,
       Quhair he micht se the twinkling sternis cleir,
       And all the planetis off the firmament,   630
       Thair cours, and eik thair moving in the Spheir,°
       Sum retrograde and sum stationeir,
       And off the Zodiak, in quhat degre
       Thay wer ilk ane, as Lowrence leirnit me.°

91   Than Saturne auld wes enterit in Capricorne,°   635
       And Juppiter movit in Sagittarie,
       And Mars up in the Rammis heid wes borne,
       And Phebus in the Lyoun furth can carie;
       Venus the Crab, the Mone wes in Aquarie;
       Mercurius, the God off Eloquence,   640
       Into the Virgyn maid his residence.

92   But Astrolab, Quadrant, or Almanak,
       Teichit off nature be Instructioun,
       The moving off the hevin this Tod can tak,
       Quhat influence and constellatioun   645
       Wes lyke to fall upon the eirth adoun.
       And to him self he said, withoutin mair,
       'Weill worth my ffather, that send me to the Lair.

93   'My destenie and eik my weird I watt,
       My aventure is cleirlie to me kend,   650

mixed with misfortune unless I soon mend my
evil way of living; for the reward of Sin is death
and a shameful end. Therefore I will go seek some
Confessor and shrive me clean of my sins to this
hour.

94   'Alas,' he said, 'so cursed are we thieves, who
nightly put our lives in jeopardy. Our cursed trade
injures many a man; for always we are stealing,
but always we are poor. We live out our days in
fear and shame; then we are called Withy-neck
and Gallows-bird and as a reward are hung up the
neck.'

95   Thus challenging his cankered conscience, he
looked all around him from the top of a hill; so
he saw, coming from a little distance, a worthy
Doctor of Divinity, Friar Wolf Waitskaith, a
wonderfully clever scholastic, fresh come from
the cloister in order to teach and pray, with beads
in hand, saying his *Pater Noster*.

96   Seeing this Wolf, this crafty traitor Fox fell on his
knees, his hood drawn back upon his neck: 'Welcome, my spiritual father under God' (he said),
with a great deal of cringing and bowing. 'Ha'
(said the Wolf), 'Sir Fox, for what reason do you
carry on so? Rise up and put on your hood.' 'Father'
(said the Fox), 'great cause have I for this behavior.

97   'You are the Mirror, the Lantern, the Sure Way,
and should guide such simple folk as me to grace.
Your bare feet, your gray russet cowl, your lean
cheek, your pale face full of pity, reveal to me
your perfect holiness. Happy the man who once
in his life has had the good fortune to be shriven
of his sins by you.'

98   'Nay, poor Lawrence' (the Wolf said, and laughed),
'it pleases me that you are penitent.' 'I am all too
well acquainted, Sir, with robbery and theft,
which gives me great cause to repent. But,
Father, stay awhile here on the grass, I beseech
you, and hear me declare my innermost thoughts,
which trouble me so deeply.'

With mischeif myngit is my mortall fait
My misleving the soner bot I mend;
Deid is reward off sin and schamefull end.
Thairfoir I will ga seik sum confessour
And schryiff me clene off all sinnis to this hour.   655

94   'Allace' (quod he), 'richt waryit ar we thevis,
Our lyfis set ilk nicht in aventure;
Our cursit craft full mony man mischevis;
For ever we steill and ever alyk ar pure.
In dreid and schame our dayis we Indure;   660
Syne Widdinek° and Crakraip callit als,
And till our hyre ar hangit be the hals.'

95   Accusand thus his cankerit conscience,
In to ane Craig he kest about his Ee;
So saw he cummand ane lyttill from thence   665
Ane worthie Doctour of Divinitie,
Freir Wolff Waitskaith,° in science wonder sle,
To preich and pray wes new cum ffra the Closter
With Beidis in hand, sayand his Pater Noster.

96   Seand this Wolff, this wylie tratour Tod   670
On kneis fell, with hude in to his nek;°
'Welcome, my Gostlie ffather under God'
(Quod he), with mony binge and mony bek.
'Ha' (quod the Wolff), 'Schir Tod, for quhat effek
Mak ye sic feir? Ryse up, put on your hude.'   675
'Father' (quod he), 'I haif grit cause to dude.

97   'Ye ar Mirrour, Lanterne, and sicker way,
Suld gyde sic sempill folk as me to grace.
Your bair feit and your Russet° Coull off gray,
Your lene cheik, your paill and pietious face,   680
Schawis to me your perfite halines.
For weill wer him that anis in his lyve
Had hap to yow his sinnis ffor to schryve.'

98   'Na, selie Lowrence' (quod the Wolf) and leuch:
'It plesis me that ye ar penitent.'   685
'Off reif and stouth, Schir, I can tell aneuch,
That causis me full sair for to repent.
Bot, ffather, byde still heir upon the bent,
I you beseik, and heir me to declair
My conscience, that prikkis me sa sair.'   690

99   'Well' (said the Wolf), 'kneel down upon your
       knee.' And he, bare-headed, knelt down very
       humbly and then began with *Benedicite*. When I
       saw this, I stood a little further off, for it is im-
       proper to hear, see, or reveal anything said in
       such a privileged communication. In the follow-
       ing manner the Wolf spoke to the Fox:

100   'Art thou contrite and sorry in thy soul for thy
       trespasses?' 'No, Sir, I cannot say that I am; for
       hens to me are so honey sweet, as is lamb's flesh
       newly drained of blood, that my mind cannot
       resolve to repent, except for this one thing—that
       I have slain so few.' 'Well' (said the Wolf), 'in
       faith, you are a rascal.'

101   'Since you cannot repent of your wickedness, will
       you at least forbear these things in times to come, and
       mend yourself?' 'Alas, if I forbear, the how shall I live,
       having no other profession to sustain me? It is
       Necessity that forces me to steal wherever I go. I
       consider it shameful to beg, and I cannot work, as you
       know; yet still would I aspire to a state of gentility.'

102   'Well,' (said the Wolf), 'you are lacking on two of
       the points necessary to perfect Confession. Let us
       proceed to the third part of Penitence: Are you
       willing to suffer pains for your transgression?' 'No,
       Sir; consider my constitution, so fragile and weak,
       and my tender nature. Lo, you can see, I am both
       lean and slight.

103   'Yet, nevertheless, I would—so long as it were
       light, brief, and not harmful to my frail condition—
       do some penance, if I could bear it, to put my
       poor soul in the way of grace.' 'You must' (said
       the Wolf) 'forbear to eat meat until Easter, in
       order to subdue your body, that faulty flesh; and I
       hereby will grant you full remission of your sins.'

104   'I will agree to that, so long as you grant me leave
       to eat sausages, or lap up a little blood, or let me
       try a head or foot or paunch, in case I get no
       other meat in my diet.' 'In case of extreme need,
       I give you leave to do so twice a week, for

99 'Weill' (quod the Wolff), 'sit down upon thy kne.'
  And he doun bairheid sat full humilly,
  And syne began with 'Benedicitie.'°
  Quhen I this saw, I drew ane lytill by,
  For it effeiris nouther to heir, nor spy,   695
  Nor to reveill thing said under that seill.
  Unto the Tod this gait the Wolf couth mele:

100 'Art thow contrite and sorie in thy Spreit
  For thy trespas?' 'Na, Schir, I can not duid:
  Me think that hennis ar sa honie sweit,   700
  And Lambes flesche that new ar lettin bluid,
  For to repent my mynd can not concluid
  Bot off this thing, that I haif slane sa few.'
  'Weill' (quod the Wolff), 'in faith thow art ane schrew.'

101 'Sen thow can not forthink thy wickitnes,   705
  Will thow forbeir in tyme to cum, and mend?'
  'And I forbeir, how sall I leif, allace,
  Haifand nane uther craft me to defend?
  Neid causis me to steill quhair evir I wend.
  I eschame to thig, I can not wirk, ye wait,   710
  Yit wald I fane pretend to gentill stait.'

102 'Weill' (quod the Wolff) 'thow wantis pointis twa,
  Belangand to perfyte Confessioun.
  To the thrid part off penitence° let us ga:
  Will thow tak pane for thy transgressioun?'   715
  'Na, Schir, considder my Complexioun,
  Selie and waik, and off my Nature tender;
  Lo, wil ye se, I am baith lene and sklender.'

103 'Yit, neuertheles, I wald, swa it wer licht,
  Schort, and not grevand to me tendernes,   720
  Tak part off pane, fulfill it gif I micht,
  To set my selie Saull in way off grace.'
  'Thou sall' (quod he) 'forbeir flesch untill pasche,
  To tame this Corps, that cursit Carioun;
  And heir I reik the full remissioun.'   725

104 'I grant thairto, swa ye will giff me leif
  To eit puddingis, or laip ane lyttill blude,
  Or heid, or feit, or paynches let me preif,
  In cace I falt of flesch in to my fude.'
  'For grit mister I gif the leif to dude   730

Necessity knows no Law.' 'God reward you, Sir,
for well I know that text.'

105   When this was said, the Wolf went on his way.
       The Fox, on foot, fared towards the sea; to find
       some fish was his whole intent. But when he saw
       the surging stormy waves, he stood stock still,
       astonished, staring, and said, 'It would have been
       better had I stayed at home and never been a
       fisherman in the Devil's name.

106   'Now may I dig in the sand for my food, for I
       have neither boat nor net nor bait.' As he was
       complaining thus for lack of food, searching
       about to find a bit to eat, he spied a flock of
       Goats under a tree. Then he rejoiced; and he hid
       himself in a ravine, and from the Goats he stole a
       little Kid.

107   Then over the ravine and to the sea he hurried,
       and taking hold of the Kid by the two horns, he
       dunked him in the water either two or three
       times, saying to him: 'Go down, Sir Kid; come up
       again Sir Salmon!' He continued until the Kid
       was dead; then he dragged him to land, and of
       that newly-created Salmon he ate his fill.

108   When he was finally filled with young and tender
       meat, he took himself in fear to a secret place by
       a bush, where the sun shone down hard. He thought
       it best to warm his belly and his breast; and reck-
       lessly he said, on the spot where he rested, strok-
       ing his belly against the sun's heat, 'This stomach
       of mine would make a perfect target for an arrow.'

109   While he was saying this, the keeper of the Goats,
       heavy in his heart that his Kid had been stolen,
       was searching everywhere, until at last he found
       the spot where Lawrence lay. He bent his bow,
       and drew to his head an arrow with grey feathers;
       and before the Fox could stir, the keeper pinned
       him fast to the ground.

110   'Now' (said the Fox) 'alas and wellaway! I am
       struck down, and I can go no further. No man, I

Twyse in the oulk, for neid may haif na Law.'
'God yeild yow, Schir, for that Text weill I knaw.'

105   Quhen this wes said, the Wolff his wayis went.
The Foxe on fuit he fure unto the flude—
To fang him fisch haillelie wes his intent.   735
Bot quhen he saw the walterand wallis woude,
All stonist still in to ane stair he stude,
And said, 'Better that I had biddin at hame
Nor bene ane ffischar in the Devillis Name.

106   'Now may I scraip my meit out off the sand,   740
For I haif nouther boittis net nor bait.'
As he wes thus ffor ffalt of meit murnand,
Lukand about his leving ffor to lait,
Under ane tre he saw ane trip off Gait;
Than wes he blyith, and in ane heuch him hid,   745
And ffra the Gait he stall ane lytill Kid.

107   Syne over the heuch unto the see he hyis,
And tuke the Kid be the hornis twane,
And in the watter outher twyis or thryis
He dowkit him, and till him can he sayne: 750
'Ga doun, Schir Kid, cum up Schir Salmond agane!'
Quhill he wes deid; syne to the land him drewch,
And off that new maid Salmond eit anewch.

108   Thus fynelie fillit with young tender meit,
Unto ane derne ffor dreid he him addrest,   755
Under ane busk, quhair that the sone can beit,
To beik his breist and bellie he thocht best.
And rekleslie he said, quhair he did rest,
Staikand his wame aganis the sonis heit,
'Upon this wame set wer ane bolt full meit.'   760

109   Quhen this wes said, the keipar off the Gait,
Cairfull in hart his kid wes stollen away,
On everilk syde full warlie couth he wait,
Quhill at the last he saw quhair Lowrence lay.
Ane Bow he bent, ane flane with ffedderis gray   765
He haillit to the heid, and, or he steird,
The Foxe he prikkit fast unto the eird.

110   'Now' (quod the Foxe), 'allace and wellaway!
Gorrit I am, and may na forther gang.

think, can speak a word in jest, but nowadays it is
taken in earnest.' The keeper seized him and
drew out the arrow; and in compensation for the
Kid, and for other acts of violence, he skinned
him.

MORALITAS

111   This sudden death and unprepared-for end of this
      false Fox, without contrition, is an exmple to ex-
      hort folk to mend their ways, for fear of coming
      to a similar conclusion; for many now who go to
      confession do not repent, nor weep for their sins,
      because they think their pleasures in life so sweet.

112   Some people also through habitude and custom
      are overcome with carnal sensuality; even though
      they might be contrite for the moment, they can-
      not forbear, nor flee from their sins. Habitude has
      such power to dominate Nature in beast and
      man, that they act as they do out of necessity,
      since for so long it has been their custom.

113   Be wary, good folk, and fear this sudden arrow-
      shot, which smites so sorely and allows no resist-
      ance. Listen carefully, and note it well in your
      heart: no man may make defense against death.
      Cease your sinning; let your conscience feel re-
      morse; do willing penance here; and you shall go,
      after your death, to a state of bliss without end.

      The Tale of the Son and Heir of theAforementioned Fox,
      Called Worse-than-His-Father; Also of the Parliament
      of the Four-footed Beasts Held by the Lion

114   This aforementioned Fox, who died for his mis-
      deed, had not one son legitimately conceived
      that might become his heir by law; but he had a
      son begotten in adultery and secret bastardy,
      known by the appelation of 'Worse-than-his-
      father,' who greatly loved to sport and dally with
      the poultry.

Me think na man may speik ane word in play,   770
Bot now on dayis in ernist it is tane.'
The hird him hynt, and out he drew his flane;
And ffor his Kid, and uther violence,
He tuke his skyn and maid ane recompence.

MORALITAS

111   This suddand deith and unprovysit end   775
Of this fals Tod, without contritioun,°
Exempill is exhortand folk to mend,
For dreid of sic ane lyke conclusioun;
For mony gois now to confessioun
Can not repent, nor for thair sinnis greit,   780
Because thay think thair lustie lyfe sa sweit.

112   Sum bene also throw consuetude and ryte,
Vincust with carnall sensualitie;
Suppose thay be as for the tym contryte,
Can not forbeir, nor fra thair sinnis fle;   785
Use drawis Nature swa in propertie
Of beist and man, that neidlingis thay man do,
As thay of lang tyme hes bene hantit to.

113   Be war, gude folke, and feir this suddane schoit,
Quhilk smytis sair withoutin resistence.   790
Attend wyislie, and in your hartis noit,
Aganis deith may na man mak defence.
Ceis of your sin; remord your conscience;
Do wilfull pennance here; and ye sall wend,
Efter your deith, to blis withouttin end.   795

The Taill of the Sone & Air of the foirsaid Foxe,
callit Father wer: Alswa the Parliament of fourfuttit
Beistis, haldin be the Lyoun

114   This foirsaid ffoxe, that deit ffor his misdeid,
Had not ane barne wes gottin richteouslie,
That to his airschip micht of law succeid,°
Except ane Sone, quhilk in Adulterie
He gotten had in purches privelie,   800
And till his Name wes callit Father war,
That luifit weill with pultrie to tig and tar.

115   It follows well by natural reason, demonstrated
point by point in a reasonable analogy, that after
evil comes worse evil, and after worse comes the
worst of all; ill behavior generates a false succes-
sion. This Fox, illegitimate by birth, to be true to
his nature had to be false, just like his father and
grandfather before him.

116   While seeking food by his sense of smell, as Nature bid him do, he happened to find his father's
corpse, newly slain and skinned. He went to him
and lifted up the head; then he fell to his knees,
thanking God in his greatness for that event and
saying, 'Now, since I am your heir, I shall enjoy
the gain from all the lands you used to haunt.'

117   Fy! Covetice, unnatural and venomous; the son
was glad to find his father dead, struck down for
odious deeds by a sudden shot, for he might now
prevail and rule in his stead, fearing not at all to
lead a similar life of theft and robbery as his
father did before him; but he paid no more attention to what his end might be.

118   Yet nevertheless through instinctive pity, he
takes upon his back the lifeless body. 'I find the
proverb very true' (he said): 'The fox will run as
long as he has feet.' Then he takes the corpse to
a peat-hole, full of water, and casts it into the
depths, and gives his bones to the devil to keep.

119   O foolish man, steeped in worldliness! To acquire
worldly goods and gold and property you put your
soul in danger or in sorrow, only to enrich your
heir, who, after you are gone, will have your
goods and take but little interest in praying for
your salvation. The moment you are dead, the
prayers for you are finished.

120   To rest himself, this Fox went up to a small hill,
and there he heard a blaring bugle blow, which
he thought made all world to stir. He jumped
up when he heard this and saw a Unicorn come
leaping over the land, with horn in hand, bearing

115   It followis weill be ressoun naturall,
        And gre be gre, off richt comparisoun,
        Off euill cummis war, off war cummis werst of all,   805
        Off wrangus geir cummis wrang successioun.
        This ffoxe, Bastard of generatioun,
        Off verray kinde behuifit to be fals;
        Swa wes his Father, and his Grandschir als.

116   As Nature will, seikand his meit be sent,   810
        Off cace he fand his ffather is Carioun,
        Nakit, new slane; and till him is he went,
        Tuke up his heid, and on his kne fell doun,
        Thankand grit God off that conclusioun;
        And said, 'Now sall I bruke, sen I am air,   815
        The boundis quhair thow wes wont ffor to repair,'

117   Fy! Covetice, unkynd and venemous!
        The Sone wes fane he fand his ffather deid,
        Be suddand schot, ffor deidis odious,
        That he micht ringe and raxe in till his steid,   820
        Dreidand na thing the samin lyfe to leid
        In thift and reif as did his ffather befoir;
        Bot to the end attent he tuke no moir.

118   Yit nevertheless, throw Naturall pietie,
        The Carioun upon his bak he tais.   825
        'Now find I weill thie prouerb trew' (quod he),
        ' "Ay rinnis the ffoxe, als lang as he fute hais." '
        Syne with the Corps unto ane peitpoit gais,
        Off watter fful, and kest him in the deip,
        And to the Devill he gaif his banis to keip.   830

119   O fulsiche man! plungit in warldlynes,
        To conqueis warldlie gude and gold and rent,
        To put thy Saull in pane or hevines,
        To riche thy air, quhilk efter thow art went,
        Have he thy gude, he takis bot small tent   835
        To sing or say for thy saluatioun.
        Fra thow be dede, done is thy devotioun.

120   This Tod to rest him carit to ane craig,
        And thair he hard ane busteous Bugill blaw,°
        Quhilk, as he thocht, maid all the warld to waig.   840
        Than he start up, quhen he this hard, and saw
        Ane Unicorne come lansand over ane Law,

a message in a small case; he seemed a proper
Pursuivant, I assure you.

121   He hastened to a bank from where he might see
around him on every side, shouted out in the
shrillest of voices, and two or three times cried
'Oyez! Oyez!' At that the beasts in the field
nearby, all wondering what such a thing could
signify, in great amazement gathered on the
green.

122   Out of the case he soon produced a pronouncement and read the text without delay. Command-
ing silence, solemnly he spoke as follows: 'I, the
noble Lion, King of all the beasts, send Greetings
to God, and health everlasting to all beasts, irrational and brute, to all my subjects both great and
small.

123   'My loftiness and high maginificence thus informs
you that straightaway, indeed tomorrow morning,
I intend, with royal persistence, to hold a Parliament upon this hill. Urgently, therefore, I give
the commandment for everyone to appear before
my tribunal, failure in which will bring with it
pain and penalties.'

124   The morrow arrived, and Phoebus with his beams
of light dispelled the grey, misty clouds. The ground
was green and gleamed as if it were gold, with
grass thickly grown, abundant and pleasant. The
sunbeams scattered about on every sprig and spray
like spices; the Lark, the Thrush, and the Blackbird sweetly sang on high, darting from tree to tree.

125   Three Leopards came, bearing to the top of that
hill a crown of weighty gold, studded with jaspers,
encased with royal rubies, and adorned with
many diverse diamonds. With good, strong poles
they pitched a pavillion; and on that throne
there sat a fierce Lion in royal robes, with his
sceptre, sword, and crown.

126   Obeying the intent of the previous day's an-
nouncement, all the beasts on earth that go on

With horne in hand, ane bill in breist he bure;
Ane pursephant° semelie, I yow assure.

121   Unto ane bank, quhair he micht se about   845
On everilk syde, in haist he culd him hy,
Schot out his voce full schyll and gaif ane schout,
And 'Oyas! Oyas!'° twyse or thryse did cry.
With that the beistes in the feild thairby,
All mervelland quhat sic ane thing suld mene,   850
Gritlie agast, thay gaderit on ane grene.

122   Out off his buste ane bill sone can he braid
And red the Text withoutin tarying.
Commandand silence, sadlie thus he said:
'The Nobil Lyoun,° off all beistis the King,   855
Greting to God, helth everlestyng
To brutall beistis and Irrationall
I send, as to my subjectis grit and small.

123   'My celsitude and hie magnificence
Lattis yow to wait, that evin incontinent,   860
Thinkis the morne, with Royall deligence,
Upon this hill to hald ane Parliament.°
Straitlie thairfoir I gif commandement
For to compeir befoir my Tribunall,
Under all pane and perrell that may fall.'   865

124   The morrow come, and Phebus with his bemis
Consumit had the mistie cluddis gray.
The ground wes grene, and als as gold it glemis,
With gers growand gudelie, grit and gay;
The spyce thay spred to spring on everilk spray;   870
The Lark, the Maveis, and the Merll, full hie,
Sweitlie can sing, creippand ffra tre to tre.

125   Thre Leopardis° come, a Croun off massie gold
Beirand thay brocht unto that hillis hicht,
With Jaspis Jonit, and Royall Rubeis rold,   875
And mony diveris Dyamontis dicht,
With pollis proud ane Palyeoun doun thay picht;
And in that Throne thair sat ane wild Lyoun,
In Rob Royall, with Sceptour, Swerd, and Croun.

126   Efter the tennour off the cry befoir,   880
That gais on all fourfuttit beistis in eird,

four feet, without more ado and as they were
commanded, appeared before their lord the Lion;
and which they were, as Lawrence has instructed
me, I shall relate, one example of each kind, as
far as I can remember them.

127　　The Minotaur, a marvellous monster, Beller-
ephont the beast of Bastardy, the Werewolf, and
the dangerous Pegasus, transformed by the help of
sorcery. The Lynx, the Tiger full of tyranny; the
Elephant, and also the Dromedary; the Camel
carrying his crane-like neck before him.

128　　The Leopard, as I have told before, the Antelope,
the Sparth so quickly came; the spotted Panther,
and the Unicorn; the Reindeer ran through the
river, rushes, and reeds; the jolly Mare and the
gentle Steed, the Ass, the Mule, the Horses of
every kind; the Doe, the Roe, the antlered Hart,
the Hind.

129　　The Bull, the Bear, the Buffalo, and the Boar, the
tame Cat, the Wildcat, and the Wildwood
Swine, the Hardbacked Hedgehog, and the limping Hare, both Otter and Ape, and pinpointed
Porcupine; the foolish Goat, the innocent Sheep,
the Swine, the wild Lynx, the Buck, the clumsy
Badger, the Polecat, and the Beaver formed a flock.

130　　The sprightly Greyhound, the Bloodhound
smoothly approached, with Dogs of many different sorts; the little Rat ran, the Dormouse
glided forth, the whining Stoat with the Weasel
went, the Fitchew that has furred the borders of
robes, the Martin, along with the Rabbit and
Squirrel, the Bowranbane, and also the Lerioun.

131　　The Marmoset had to lead on the Mole, since
Nature had denied her sight. Thus they all came
forth, fearing the penalty of death; the Civet Cat
the little Mouse with all her might hurried in
haste to the top of that hill; and many kinds of
beast I did not know; before their lord the Lion
they made their low obeissance.

As thay commandit wer withoutin moir,
Befoir thair Lord the Lyoun thay appeird.
And quhat thay wer, to me as Lowrence leird,°
I sall reheirs ane part of everilk kynd,   885
Als fer as now occurris to my mynd.

127   The Minotaur, ane Monster mervelous,°
      Bellerophont,° that beist of Bastardrie,
      The Warwolff, and the Pegase° perillous,
      Transformit be assent of sorcerie.   890
      The Linx, the Tiger full off Tiranie;
      The Elephant, and eik the Dromedarie;°
      The Cameill with his Cran nek furth can carie.

128   The Leopard, as I haif tauld beforne,
      The Anteloip,° the Sparth° furth couth speid,   895
      The peyntit Pantheir, and the Unicorne;
      The Rayndeir° Ran throw Reveir, Rone, and Reid,
      The Jolie Gillet, and the gentill Steid,
      The Asse, the Mule, the Hors of everilk kynd;
      The Da, the Ra, the hornit Hart, the Hynd.   900

129   The Bull, the Beir, the Bugill, and the Bair,
      The tame Cat, Wildcat, and the Wildwod Swyne,
      The Hardbakkit Hurcheon, and the Hirpland Hair,
      Baith Otter and Aip, and pennit Porcupyne;
      The Gukit Gait, the selie Scheip, the Swyne,   905
      The wylde Once,° the Buk, the Welterand Brok,
      The Fowmart with the Fibert ffurth can flok.

130   The gay Grewhound, the Sleuthound furth can slyde,
      With Doggis all divers and different;
      The Rattoun ran, the Glebard° furth can glyde,   910
      The quhrynard Quhitret with the Quhasill went,
      The Feitho° that hes furrit mony fent,
      The Metrik, with the Cunning and the Con,
      The Bowranbane,° eik the Lerioun.°

131   The Marmisset the Mowdewart couth leid,   915
      Because that Nature denyit had hir sicht;
      Thus dressit thay all ffurth, ffor dreid of deid;
      The Musk, the lytill Mous with all hir micht
      With haist scho haikit unto that hill of hicht;
      And mony kynd of beistis I couth not knaw,   920
      Befoir thair Lord the Lyoun thay loutit law.

132   Seeing all these beasts ready at his bidding, he
gave a start and looked all about him; then they
all fell down flat at his feet; for dread of death
they all dropped down in fear. When he saw
them all showing the proper respect, he bade
them, with a kindly look, 'Be not afraid, but
stand up on your feet.

133   'I hereby inform you that my might is full of
mercy and punishes none that will lie prostrate
before me, but is full of anger, hostile, and harsh
to all that stand opposed to my estate. I rend and
tear to pieces all beasts that dare to contend
against the might of my Magnificence: so let
none dare be proud in my presence.

134   'My loftiness and my high Majesty shall ever be
entwined with might and mercy; the lowest here
I can raise on high in an instant and make him
master over you all, should I wish. The Dromedary, if he but make a disturbance, the great
Camel, though he were never so self-assured, I
can lower him to the status of a little Mouse.

135   'Within twenty miles of where I am the Kid goes
safely by the side of the Goat, and Lawrence the
Fox looks not upon the Lamb, and not a thieving
beast dares go on a raid.' After this was decreed,
they all lay down. The Justice bade the Court
come to order, the suits be called, and that all the
absentees be subject to forfeit.

136   The Panther, with his spotted coat of armor,
brought the Court to order, in the proper manner
according to Law. Then Lawrence the Fox looked
up from where he was crouching and jumped to his
feet, all amazed and alarmed, tearing his hair, he
cried with a moan; quaking in fear and heaving
sighs he said, 'Alas this hour, alas this doleful day!

137   'I know that this suddenly assembled group I see,
which seems in all respects a Parliament, is made
to deal with mis-doers like myself. Therefore if I
appear there, I will be undone; yet if I am read as
absent, I will be sought out. To stay, to flee—

132 Seing thir beistis all at his bidding boun,
  He gaif ane braid and luikit him about;
  Than flatlingis to his feit thay ffell all doun,
  For dreid off deith thay droupit all in dout.   925
  He lukit quhen that he saw thame lout,
  And bad thame, with ane countenance full sweit,
  'Be not efferit, bot stand up on your feit.

133 'I lat yow wit my micht is merciabill,°
  And steiris nane that ar to me prostrait,   930
  Angrie, austerne, and als unamyabill
  To all that standfray ar to myne estait.
  I rug, I reif all beistis that makis debait
  Aganis the micht off my Magnyficence:
  Se nane pretend to pryde in my presence.   935

134 'My Celsitude and my hie Maiestie
  With micht and mercie myngit sall be ay;
  The lawest heir I can ffull sone up hie,
  And mak him maister over yow all I may.
  The Dromedarie, giff he will mak deray,   940
  The grit Camell,° thocht he wer never sa crous,
  I can him law als lytill as ane Mous.

135 'Se neir be twentie mylis° quhair I am
  The Kid ga saiflie be the gaittis syde,
  The Tod Lowrie luke not to the lam,   945
  Na revand beistis nouther ryn nor ryde.'
  Thay couchit all efter that this wes cryde;
  The Justice bad the Court ffor to gar fence,°
  The sutis callit, and ffoirfalt all absence.

136 The Panther, with his payntit Coit Armour, 950
  Fensit the Court, as off Law effeird.
  Than Tod Lowrie luikit quhair he couth lour
  And start on fute, all stonist and all steird,
  Ryifand his hair, he cryit with ane reird,
  Quaikand ffor dreid and sichand couth he say: 955
  'Allace this hour, allace this dulefull day!

137 'I wait this suddand Semblie that I se,
  Haifand the pointis off ane Parliament,
  Is maid to mar sic misdoars as me;
  Thairfoir, geve I me schaw, I will be schent; 960
  I will be socht, and I be red absent;

neither serves me well; both are the same, and
nothing can follow but death.'

138   Troubled thus in his heart, he pondered how he
might defend himself through falsehood. He drew
his hood down low about his eyes, and closing
one eye, forth he went. Haltingly he came, so
that he might not be recognized; and for fear that
he should be arrested, he played hide-and-seek
behind the crowd from beast to beast.

139   O defiled and cankered conscience! arraigned
before a King in righteousness, with cheeks made
pale and guilty looks! Farewell to thy fame; now
all thy grace is gone. Thy physiognomy, the appearance of thy face, is foul and disfigured, not at
all helpful for your defense; and brought to the
light, it is sullied, stupid, and spiritless.

140   Lawrence, if you be legally charged with theft or
with treason because of your hurtful misdeeds and
faithlessness, your countenance changes; you
must look down; your worldy reputation vanishes.
Consider the examle of this Fox, how he was
frighted, and flee the filth of falsehood, as I
counsel you, whereafter there follows sin and
shameful death.

141   When all had appeared before their Lord and King
in the accustomed order according to each one's
estate, the Lion caused one of each kind to come
forth; and he spoke, inspiring great awe, and asked
them if any kind of beast on earth was absent,
and insisted they swear a deep oath in answering;
and they said, 'None, except a grey brood Mare.'

142   'Go, send a messenger now unto that Mare.' The
Court then cried: 'My Lord, who shall it be?'
'Come forth, Lawrence, hiding under your hood.'
'No, Sir, Mercy! Look, I have only one eye, and I
am lame in one leg; it's crooked, as you can see.
The Wolf is a far better ambassador and far more
learned in the Law than I.'

143   Rearing in anger, the Lion said, 'Go forth, both you
beggarly creatures!' and they departed without

To byde or fle, it makis no remeid;
All is alyke, thair ffollowis not bot deid.'

138 Perplexit thus in his hart can he mene
Throw ffalset how he micht himself defend; 965
His Hude he drew laich attour his Ene,
And winkand with ane Eye, furth he wend.
Clinschand he come, that he micht not be kend,
And for dreddour that he suld bene arreist,
He playit bukhude behind, ffra beist to beist. 970

139 O fylit Spreit! and cankerit Conscience!
Befoir ane Roy renyeit with richteounes,
Blakinnit cheikis and schamefull countenance!
Fairweill thy fame, now gone is all thy grace,
The Phisnomie,° the favour off thy face, 975
For thy defence is foull and diffigurate,
Brocht to the licht, basit, blunt, and blait.

140 Be thow atteichit with thift or with tressoun,
For thy misdeid wrangous and wickit fay,
Thy cheir changis, Lowrence; thow man luke doun; 980
Thy worschip of this warld is went away.
Luke to this Tod, how he wes in effray,
And fle the filth of falset, I the reid,
Quhairthrow thair followis syn and schamefull deid.

141 Compeirand thus befoir thair Lord and King, 985
In ordour set as to thair estait effeird,
Or everilk kynd he gart ane part furth bring,
And awfullie he spak, and at thame speird
Geve there wes ony kynd of beistis in eird
Absent, and thairto gart thame deiplie sweir; 990
And thay said, 'Nane, except ane Stude gray Meir.'

142 'Ga, mak ane message sone unto that Stude.'
The Court than cryit: 'My Lord, quha sall it be?'
'Cum furth, Lowrie, lurkand under thy hude.'
'Na, Schir, mercie! lo, I have bot ane Ee; 995
Hurt in the hoche, and cruikit as ye may se;
The Volff is better in Ambassatry,
And mair cunning in Clergie fer than I.'

143 Rampand° he said, 'ga furth, brybouris baith!
And thay to ga withoutin tarying. 1000

delay. Through thickets and roots they ran together in haste, and they found the Mare at her morning meal. 'Now' said the Fox, 'Madam, come unto
the King; the Court is called and you are *Contumax*.'
'O Lawrence' (said she), 'quit your lawyerly tricks.'

144   'Mistress' (said he), 'come to the Court you must;
the Lion has commanded so without question.' 'Sir
Fox, the jest is on you; I have Respite for a year, if
you will but read it.' 'I'm not much good, so help
me God, at dealing with spelling' (he said). 'Here
is the Wolf, a noble scholar of everything, and it
is he that has been put in charge of this embassy.

145   'He is fully qualified, and a man of years, and has
had great experience with legal documents. Let
him take a look and read your privilege, and I
shall stand by and act as witness for you.' 'Where
is your Respite?' (the Wolf said bruskly). 'Sir, it is
here, well hidden under my hoof.' 'Hold up your
heel' (said he); and so she did.

146   Though he was blinded with pride, yet he presumed to look down low where her letter was supposed to be. With that the Mare gave him a kick
in the chops and knocked off a piece of his
crown. Half dead, he fell to the ground: 'Alas'
(said Lawrence), 'O *Lupus*, thou art lost.' 'His
knowledge' (said the Mare) 'cost him dear.

147   'Lawrence' (said she), 'Would you like a look at
my letter, since the Wolf can make nothing of
it?' 'No, by St. Bride' (said he), 'I prefer to sleep
in a whole skin, not a hurt skin. I once found a
scroll, and this was written on it—and for five
shillings I would not part with it—*Felix quem
faciunt aliena pericula cautum.*'

148   With a broken head and bloody red cheeks, this
wretched Wolf wept as he went on his way, considering the means to revenge his injury; he intended to tell the King of the case. 'Sir' (said the
Fox), 'Stay awhile on this spot, and from your
brow wash away the blood; and take a drink, for
it will do you good.'

Over Ron and Rute thay ran togidder raith,
And fand the Meir at hir meit in the morning.
'Now,' quod the Tod, 'Madame, cum to the King,
The Court is callit, and ye ar *Contumax*.'°
'Let be, Lowrence' (quod scho) 'your Courtlie Knax.'   1005

144   'Maistres' (quod he), 'cum to the Court ye mon;
The Lyoun hes commandit so in deid.'
'Schir Tod, tak ye the Flyrdome and the Fon,
I have repite ane yeir, and ye will reid.'
'I can not spell' (quod he), 'sa God me speid.   1010
Heir is the Volff, ane Nobill Clerk at all,
And of this Message is maid principall.

145   'He is Autentik, and ane man of age,
And hes grit practik of the Chanceliary;
Let him ga luke and reid your Privilage,   1015
And I sall stand and beir witnes yow by.'
'Quhair is thy Respite?' (quod the Wolff) in hy.
'Schir, it is heir, under my hufe weill hid.'
'Hald up thy heill' (quod he); and so scho did.

146   Thocht he wes blindit with pryde, yit he presumis   1020
To luke doun law, quhair that hir letter lay.
With that the meir gird him upon the gumis,
And straik the hattrell off his heid away.
Halff out off lyif, thair lenand doun he lay:
'Allace' (quod Lowrence). *Lupus*,° thow art loist.'   1025
'His cunning' (quod the Meir) 'wes worth sum coist.

147   'Lowrence' (quod scho), 'will thow luke on my letter,
Sen that the Wolff na thing thairoff can wyn?'
'Na, be Sanct Bryde' (quod he), 'me think it better
To sleip in haill nor in ane hurt skyn.   1030
Ane skrow I ffand, and this wes writtin in,
—For ffyve schillingis I wald not anis fforfaut him—
Felix quem faciunt aliena pericula cautum.°

148   With brokin skap and bludit cheikis reid,
This Wolff weipand on his wayis went,   1035
Off his menye markand to get remeid,
To tell the King the cace wes his Intent.
'Schir' (quod the Tod), 'byde still upon this bent,
And ffra your browis wesche away the blude,
And tak ane drink, ffor it will do yow gude.'   1040

149   This false Fox went off to fetch some water; side-
       ways and backwards he went as he sought for a
       stream. Coming from the moor, by chance he
       found a flock of lambs, gambolling on a dyke.
       This traitor Fox, this tyrant, this thief, felled the
       very fattest of this flock and ate his fill; then back
       to the Wolf he went.

150   They drank together and then took to their
       journey; at last before the King they knelt upon
       their knees. 'Where is that Mare, Sir Fox, that
       was *Contumax*?' The Lawrence said, 'Put not that
       question to me! This new-made Doctor of Divin-
       ity, with his red cap, can tell you well enough.'
       At that the Lion and all the rest laughed.

151   'Tell us what happened, Lawrence; now let us
       hear.' 'This clever Wolf' (said he), 'This ancient
       scholar, demanded on your behalf that this Mare
       appear; but she alleged she had a privilege—
       "Come near and see, and you will get your
       reward." Because he read the Respite clear and
       well, yon red bonnet she gave him with her heel.'

152   The Lion said, 'By that red cap I know this tale is
       true, whoever pays it attention; the greatest
       Clerks are not the wisest men; the hurt of one
       will make another happy.' As they were chatter-
       ing about this case and joking, all the court in
       commotion and in sport, in came the Ewe, the
       mother of the Lamb.

153   She fell on her knees before the Justice and made
       her complaint woefully in this way: 'This
       whoreson harlot, this hound of Hell, most cruelly
       has devoured my Lamb within a mile of here,
       contrary to your decree. For the love of God, my
       Lord, give me legal remedy against this rogue.'
       Hearing that, Lawrence tried to slip away.

154   'Just a minute, rogue' (said the Lion); 'let us see if
       this innocent Ewe has spoken the truth.' 'Ah,
       sovereign Lord, God save your Mercy' (said he).
       'My purpose was but to have played with him;
       without cause he fled, as if he were afraid. In fear

149   To fetche watter this ffraudfull Fox furth fure,
     Sydelingis abak° he socht unto ane syke;
     On cace he meittis, cummand ffra the mure,
     Ane Trip of Lambis dansand on ane dyke.
     This Tratour Tod, this Tirrant, and this Tyke,   1045
     The fattest off this flock he ffellit hais,
     And eit his fill; syne to the Wolff he gais.

150   Thay drank togidder and syne thair journey takis;
     Befoir the King syne kneillit on thair kne.
     'Quhair is yone Meir, Schir Tod, wes *Contumax?*'   1050
     Than Lowrence said: 'My Lord, speir not at me!
     This new-maid Doctour off Divinitie,
     With his reid Cap,° can tell yow weill aneuch.'
     With that the Lyoun and all the laif thay leuch.

151   'Tell on the cais now, Lowrence, let us heir.'   1055
     'This wittie Wolff' (quod he), 'this Clerk off age,
     On your behalff he bad the Meir compeir,
     And scho allegit to ane privilage—
     "Cum neir and se, and ye sall haif your wage."
     Because he red his rispite plane and weill,   1060
     Yone reid Bonat scho raucht him with her heill.'

152   The Lyoun said, 'be yone reid Cap I ken
     This Taill is trew, quha tent unto it takis;
     The greitest Clerkis° ar not the wysest men;
     The hurt of ane happie the uther makis.'   1065
     As thay wer carpand in this cais, with knakis,
     And all the Court in garray and in gam,
     Swa come the Yow, the Mother off the Lam.

153   Befoir the Justice on hir kneis fell,
     Put out hir playnt in this wyis wofully: 1070
     'This harlet huresone, and this hound of hell,
     Devorit hes my Lamb full doggitly,
     Within ane myle, in contrair to your cry.
     For Goddis lufe, my Lord, gif me the Law
     Off this lurker:' with that Lowerence let draw.   1075

154   'Byde' (quod the Lyoun), 'Lymmer, let us se
     Giff it be suthe the selie yow hes said.'
     'Aa. Soverane Lord, saif your mercie' (quod he),
     'My purpois wes with him ffor to haif plaid;
     Causeles he fled, as he had bene effraid;   1080

of death he dashed over a dyke and broke his
neck.' 'You lie, false thief' (said she).

155   'His death may be easily proved by the evidence:
your gory gums and your bloody snout; the wool
and the flesh yet stick to your teeth; and that is
evidence enough, without doubt.' The Justice
ordered some to assemble an Assize; and so they
did, and found the Fox had lied and was guilty of
murder, theft, and treason too.

156   They bound him fast; the Justice gave the order for
the sentence to be pronounced immediately and for
the Fox to be stripped of all his clothes. The Wolf,
that new-made Doctor, was chosen to shrive him.
Then he led him forth, and on they went to the gallows; and at the ladder's foot he took his leave. The
Ape was executioner and ordered him immediately to
ascend; then he hanged him. Thus he met his end.

MORALITAS

157   Just as the Miner, plying his trade, by fire may
win fair gold from the lead, just the same under a
symbolic fable man may seek a serious meaning,
and after that, as daily do the Doctors of Divinity, fairly show its application to our lives and
present the matter through the means of Poetry.

158   The Lion's character represents the World, to
whom bow down both Emperor and King, as they
think to gain increased wealth from this world,
thinking daily to increase their living; some to
rule and some to dominate; some to gather possessions, some gold, some other things; to control
this world, some labor as if they were mad.

159   The Mare represents men of contemplation,
walking through the wilderness in penance, like
monks and other men of religion, who please
God by praising him everywhere, set apart from
the world's wretchedness, in voluntary poverty,
mortified in their minds from pomp and pride and
from this world.

For dreid of deith he duschit ouer ane dyke,
And brak his nek,' 'Thow leis' (quod scho), 'fals tyke.

155   'His deith be practik may be previt eith:
     Thy gorrie gumis and thy bludie snout,
     The woll, the flesche yit stikkis on thy teith,   1085
     And that is evidence aneuch, but dout.'
     The Justice bad ga cheis ane Assyis° about;
     And so thay did, and fand that he wes fals,
     Off Murther, thift, pyking,° and tressoun als.

156   Thay band him fast; the Justice bad belyif   1090
     To gif the dome° and tak off all his clais;
     The Wolff, that new maid Doctour, couth him schrif;
     Syne furth him led and to the Gallous gais,
     And at the ledder fute his leif he tais;
     The Aip was Basare and bad him sone ascend,   1095
     And hangit him; and thus he maid his end.

MORALITAS

157   Richt as the Mynour in his Minorall
     Fair Gold with fyre may fra the Leid weill wyn,
     Richt so under ane Fabill figurall
     Sad sentence man may seik, and efter syne,   1100
     As daylie dois the Doctouris of Devyne,
     That to our leving full weill can apply
     And paynt thair mater furth be Poetry.

158   The Lyoun is the warld be liknes,
     To quhom loutis baith Empriour and King,   1105
     And thinkis of this warld to get incres,
     Thinkand daylie to get mair leving;
     Sum for to reull, and sum to raxe and ring;
     Sum gadderis geir, sum Gold, sum uther gude;
     To wyn this warld, sum wirkis as thay wer wod.   1110

159   The Meir is men of contemplatioun,°
     Off pennance walkand in this wildernes,
     As monkis and othir men of religioun
     That presis God to pleis in euerilk place,
     Abstractit from this warldis wretchitnes,   1115
     In wilfull pouertee, fra pomp and pryde,
     And fra this warld in mynd ar mortyfyde.

160   This Wolf I liken to Sensuality, as when, like
        brute beasts, we set our mind only on the vanity
        of this world, choosing to take and love it as our
        Lord. Flee from it in haste, if you will rightly re-
        pent; then shall Reason rise, rule, and reign; and
        for thy Soul there is nothing better.

161   Her Hoof I liken to the thought of death. If you
        will remember, Man, that you must die, you may
        break sensuality's head, and fleshly lust away from
        you shall fly from the moment you begin to mor-
        tify your mind. Solomon's saying you might per-
        ceive herein: 'Think on thy end, and thou shalt
        not gladly sin.'

162   This Fox I liken to Temptations, which bring to
        the mind many thoughts that are vain, that daily
        beseige men of religion, crying to them 'Come
        back to the World!' Yet if they see Sensuality
        nearly slain, and sudden death draw near with
        pains so sore, they back away and tempt them-
        selves no more.

163   O Mary mild, meek mediator of Mercy, sit down
        before your heavenly Son, for we sinners beseech
        his loftiness to defend us from our perils and pain,
        and to help us up to thy heavenly hall in glory,
        where we may see the face of God—and thus ends
        the story of the Fox.

        The Tale of the Sheep and the Dog

164   Aesop recalls for us a tale concering a Dog who,
        because he was poor, called a Sheep before the
        Consistory to recover from him a certain loaf of
        bread. The Judge who bore the authority and
        jurisdiction at that time was a fraudulent Wolf;
        and he sent forth a binding summons to the
        Sheep.

160   This Wolf I likkin to Sensualitie,
As quhen lyke brutal beistis we accord
Our mynd to all this warldis vanitie,   1120
Lyking to tak and loif him as our Lord.
Fle fast thairfra, gif thow will richt remord;
Than sall Ressoun ryse, Rax and Ring,
And for thy Saull thair is na better thing.

161   Hir Hufe I likkin to the thocht of deid.°   1125
Will thow remember, Man, that thow man de,
Thow may brek sensualiteis heid;
And fleschlie lust away fra the sall fle,
Fra thow begin thy mynd to mortifie;
Salomonis saying° thow may persaif heirin: 1130
'Think on thy end, thow sall not glaidlie sin.'

162   This Tod I likkin to Temptationis,
Beirand to mynd mony thochtis vane,
That daylie sagis men of religiounis,
Cryand to thame, 'Cum to the Warld agane!'   1135
Yit gif thay se Sensualitie neir slane,
And suddand deith draw neir with panis sore,
Thay go abak, and temptis thame no moir.

163   O Mary myld, Mediatour of mercy meik,
Sitt doun before thy Sone Celestiall,   1140
For us synnaris His celsitude beseik
Us to defend fra pane and perrellis all,
And help us up unto thy hevinlie hall,
In gloir, quhair we may se the face of God.—
And thus endis the talking of the Tod.   1145

The Taill of the Scheip and the Doig

164   Esope ane Taill puttis in memorie
How that ane Doig, because that he wes pure,°
Callit ane Scheip unto the Consistorie,°
Ane certaine breid ffra him ffor to recure.
Ane fraudful Wolff wes Juge that tyme and bure   1150
Authoritie and Jurisdictioun;
And on the Scheip send furth ane strait summoun.

165   Following the accepted practice, procedure, and
style, he made the Citation in the following manner: 'I, the Honorable Wolf, guiltless of fraud and
guile, under the pains of High Suspension, of Excommunication, of Interdiction, charge thee, Sir
Sheep, in court to appear, before me here, to
answer to the charge of a Dog.'

166   Sir Corbie the Raven was chosen Summoner—he
who had pecked out many a dead Sheep's eye; he
undertook the responsibility and took up the
Citation, which summoned the Sheep before
Justice Wolf to appear without fail, within two
days or three, under the penalties listed in full,
'To hear what Shag the Dog to thee will say.'

167   Witnesses enough attested to the Summons; and
the Raven, well instructed as to his duties, en-
dorsed the writing and flew away. The poor
Sheep dared not stop for a mouthful of grass
before appearing in front of the awesome Judge,
who had set the hour of trial at the first dark
signs of Hesperus's face.

168   The Fox was Clerk and Notary in the case; the
Kite and the Vulture both stood at the bar; as
Advocates, experts in Law, they took in hand the
Dog's plea, banding together in close conspiracy
to procure a judgment against the Sheep. Though
the charge was false, they showed not a sign of
conscience.

169   The Clerk called the Sheep, and he appeared; the
Advocates stated the case as follows: 'A certain
loaf of bread, worth five shillings or more, you owe
the Dog, for which the term has expired.' Relying
on his wits, alone, without legal counsel, the Sheep
responded with prudence to the charge: 'I hereby
object to the Judge, the time, and the place.

170   'This, in brief, is the essence of my case: The Law
declares it most perilous to enter a plea before a
Judge suspect of prejudice; and you, Sir Wolf,
have been most hateful to me, for with your
ravenous teeth you have slain a great many of my

165   For by the use, and cours, and common style
       On this maner maid his Citatioun:°
       'I, Maister Wolff, parties off fraud and gyle,   1155
       Under the panis off hie Suspensioun,
       Off grit Cursing, and Interdictioun,°
       Schir Scheip, I charge the for to compeir
       And answer to ane Doig befoir me heir.'

166   Schir Corbie Rauin wes maid Apparitour,   1160
       Quha pykit had ffull mony Scheipis Ee;°
       The charge hes tane, and on the letteris° bure;
       Summonit the Scheip befoir the Wolff, that he,
       Peremptourlie,° within twa dayis or thre,
       Compeir under the panis in this bill,   1165
       'To heir quhat Perrie Doig will say the till.'

167   This summondis maid befoir witnes anew;
       The Rauin, as to his office weill effeird,
       Indorsat° hes the write, and on he flew.
       The selie Scheip durst lay na mouth on eird,   1170
       Till he befoir the awfull Juge appeird,
       The oure off cause, quhilk that the Juge usit than,
       Quhen Hesperus° to schaw his face began.

168   The Foxe wes Clerk and Noter in the Cause;
       The Gled, the Graip, up at the bar° couth stand;   1175
       As Advocatis expert in to the Lawis,
       The Doggis pley togidder tuke on hand,
       Quhilk wer confidderit straitlie in ane band,
       Aganis the Scheip to procure the sentence;
       Thocht it wes fals, thay had na conscience.   1180

169   The Clerk callit the Scheip, and he wes thair;
       The Advocatis on this wyse couth propone.
       'Ane certaine breid, worth fyve schilling or mair,°
       Thow aw the Doig, off quhilk the terme is gone.'
       Off his awin heid, but Advocate, allone,°   1185
       The Scheip avysitlie gave answer in the cace;
       'Heir I declyne the Juge, the tyme, the place.

170   'This is my cause, in motive and effect:
       The Law sayis it is richt perrillous
       Till enter in pley befoir ane Juge suspect;°   1190
       And ye, Schir Wolff, hes bene richt odious
       To me, for with your Tuskis ravenous

kinsmen. Therefore, on grounds of prejudice, I
challenge you as Judge.

171   'And in short, all the members of this court, both
       legal advisors, Clerk, and Advocate, are mortal
       enemies to me and mine, and always have been,
       as many a shepherd knows; the place is too distant,
       the time not within the Court's term and too late
       into the evening, when no Judge should sit in the
       Consistory; I challenge you for these reasons.'

172   Having been challenged in this way, the Judge
       ordered the parties to agree on a choice of two
       Arbitrators, as the Law provides, to consider the
       point and hand down a decision whether or not
       the Sheep should submit to be tried by the Wolf;
       and so the parties agreed on a choice, the names
       of whom you shall shortly hear.

173   The Bear and the Badger took the matter in
       hand, to decide whether the objection was with-
       out substance or might lawfully be sustained; and
       thereupon, as Judges, they sat down and disputed
       together a long while, combing through many a
       legal decision and many a gloss in search of the
       truth.

174   They searched through many a volume of Civil
       Law, the Codes and Digests, both Old Series and
       New; they analyzed the arguments both pro and
       con, some objecting and some supporting; for neither
       prayer nor money (you can believe) would they
       cease, but kept close to the gloss and the text of the
       Decrees, as true Judges; I curse those ever that lie.

175   In brief, to make an end of this debate: the Arbi-
       trators then swore the oath, gave the judgment,
       and issued the mandate: the Sheep must come
       again before the Wolf and complete his plea.
       With that the Sheep was not at all pleased, for
       from their judgment he had no appeal. I leave it
       to the scholars whether this decree was just.

176   Again the Sheep appeared before the Wolf and
       stood there humbly, without an attorney. Up rose

Hes slane full mony kinnismen off mine;
Thairfoir, as Juge suspect, I yow declyne.

171   'And schortlie, of this Court ye memberis all,   1195
       Baith Assessouris, Clerk, and Advocate,
       To me and myne ar ennemies mortall,
       And ay he bene, as mony Scheipheird wate.
       The place is fer,° the tyme is feriate,°
       Quhairfoir na juge suld sit in Consistory   1200
       Sa lait at evin,° I yow accuse ffor thy.'

172   Quhen that the Juge in this wyse wes accusit,°
       He bad the parteis cheis, with ane assent,
       Twa Arbeteris, as in the Law is usit,
       For to declair and gif Arbitriment,   1205
       Quhidder the Scheip suld answer in Jugement
       Befoir the Wolff; and so thay did but weir,
       Off quhome the Namis efterwart ye sall heir.

173   The Beire, the Brok, the mater tuke on hand,
       For to discyde gif this exceptioun   1210
       Wes of na strenth, nor lauchfully mycht stand;
       And thairupon, as Jugis, thay sat doun,
       And held ane lang quhyle disputatioun,
       Seikand full mony Decreitis off the Law,
       And Glosis als, the veritie to knaw.   1215

174   Of Civile many volum thay revolve,
       The Codies and Digestis new and ald;°
       Contra et pro, strait argumentis thay resolve,
       Sum objecting, and sum can hald;
       For prayer nor price, trow ye, thay wald fald,   1220
       Bot hald the glose and Text of the Decreis,°
       As trew Jugis; I beschrew thame ay that leis.

175   Schortlie to mak ane end off this debait:
       The Arbiteris than sweirand plane,
       The sentence gave, and process fulminait: 1225
       The Scheip suld pas befoir the Wolff agane
       And end his pley. Than wes he nathing fane,
       For ffra thair sentence couth he not appeill.°
       On Clerkis I do it, gif this sentence wes leill.

176   The Scheip agane befoir the Wolff derenyeit,   1230
       But Advocate, abasitlie couth stand.

the Dog, and he charged the Sheep thus: 'A sum
of money I paid in advance for a certain loaf of
bread.' He found a witness to testify that the
Sheep withheld the bread without cause; this the
Sheep denied, and there began to plead.

177   And when the Sheep had done contesting this
charge, the process of Justice further unfolded;
Lawrence recorded the acts and the procedure,
and thus they hurried the case to an end: this accursed Court, corrupted by a bribe, against good
faith, Law, and also conscience, awarded the
judgment to this false-speaking Dog.

178   And putting this judgment into execution, the
Wolf charged the Sheep, without delay and under
pains of Interdiction, either to pay the sum of
silver or to deliver the bread. What shall I say
(alas) of this judgment, which has condemned the
poor Innocent one and justified the wrongful
decision?

179   The Sheep, fearing yet further persecution, and
complying with the judgment of the court, made
his way to a Merchant of the Town and sold the
fleece he bore upon his back; then he purchased
the bread and made the Dog prompt payment, as
it had been commanded; then naked and shorn
he returned to the fields.

MORALITAS

180   This innocent Sheep may stand in allegory for
the poor Commoners that daily are oppressed by
tyrannous men, who direct all their energy towards gaining possessions by unjust means, trusting that this present life will last forever; but,
completely deceived, they soon will end their life
and go after death to everlasting pains.

181   This Wolf I liken to a stout Sheriff who purchases
the right to collect fines in the name of the King,
who has about him an accursed Assize and indicts
all the poor men in the land. For though one were
innocent as ever was St. John, when he comes

      Up rais the Doig, and on the Scheip thus plenyeit:
      'Ane soume I payit have befoir the hand
      For certane breid;' thairto and Borrow he fand,
      That wrangouslie the Scheip did hald the breid;   1235
      Quhilk he denyit; and thair began the pleid.

177   And quhen the Scheip this stryif had contestait,
      The Justice in the cause furth can proceid:
      Lowrence the actis and the proces wrait,
      And thus the pley unto the end thay speid.   1240
      This Cursit Court, corruptit all ffor meid,
      Aganis gude faith, Law, and eik conscience,
      For this fals Doig pronuncit the sentence.

178   And it till put to executioun
      The Wolff chargit the Scheip, without delay,   1245
      Under the panis off Interdictioun,
      The soume off silver or the breid to pay.
      Off this sentence (allace) quhat sall I say,
      Quhilk dampnit hes the selie Innocent,°
      And Justifyit the wrangous Jugement?   1250

179   The Scheip, dreidand mair persecutioun,
      Obeyand to the sentence, he couth tak
      His way unto ane Merchand off the Toun,
      And sauld the woll that he bure on his bak;
      Syne bocht the breid, and to the Doig couth mak   1255
      Reddie payment, as it commandit was;
      Naikit and bair syne to the feild couth pas.

      MORALITAS°

180   This selie Scheip may present the figure
      Of pure commounis, that daylie ar opprest
      Be Tirrane men, quhilkis settis all thair cure   1260
      Be fals meinis to mak ane wrang conquest,
      In hope this present lyfe suld ever lest;
      Bot all begylit, thay will in schort tyme end,
      And efter deith to lestand panis wend.

181   This Wolf I likkin to ane Schiref stout,   1265
      Quhilk byis ane forfalt at the Kingis hand,
      And hes with him ane cursit Assyis about,
      And dytis all the pure men up on land.
      Fra the Crownar half laid on him his wand,

under the authority of the Coroner he shall be
slain, unless he make an agreement with the Judge.

182   This Raven I liken to a false Coroner who has a
list of indicted offenders and who goes before the
Justices in Eyre to bring all misdoers to judgment;
but judge for yourself if he be of true mind, to
scratch out John and write in Will or Walt, and
take a bribe from both the parties involved.

183   Of the significance and nature of this false Fox, of
whom I have spoken before, and of this Kite, at
the present time I will say no more; but I shall
tell on about this Sheep and of his woeful moan;
for passing close by where he lay, I happened to
look down, and I heard him make this heavy
lamentation.

184   'Alas' (said he) 'this accursed Consistory is held
now in the midst of Winter, when Boreas with
his blasts and harsh frosts bitterly shrivels up the
flowers; on the bare banks I can make my home
no longer.' And saying that, he crept off to a
hollow, for protection from the hoary weather
and the frosts.

185   Shivering from the cold, lamenting sorely all the
while, he cast his eyes up to the heights of heaven
and said: 'Lord God, why sleep You so long?
Awake, and pass judgment on my cause, which is
founded on truth; see how I by fraud, corruption,
and deception, am stripped full bare'; and so is
many a one in this world now, plagued in the extreme.

186   See how this cursed sin of covetousness has done
away with love, loyalty, and Law. Nowadays few
or none will administer Justice, through which
fault the poor man is destroyed. But even if the
Judges know the truth, they are so blinded by
prejudice and without fear, that for a bribe they
allow the just cause to perish.

187   Lord, do you not see this world is thrown into
chaos, just as if someone were to change pure gold

Thocht he wer trew as ever wes sanct Johne,   1270
Slain sall he be, or with the Juge compone.

182   This Ravin I likkin to ane fals Crownair,
       Quhilk hes ane porteous of the Inditement,
       And passis furth befoir the Justice Air,°
       All misdoaris to bring to Jugement;   1275
       Bot luke gif he be of trew Intent,
       To scraip out Johne, and wryte in Will or Wat,
       And swa ane bud at boith the parteis skat.°

183   Of this fals Tod, of quhilk I spak befoir,
       And of this Gled, quhat thay micht signify,   1280
       Of thair nature, as now I speik no moir;
       Bot of this Scheip, and of his cairfull cry
       I sall reheirs; for as I passit by
       Quhair that he lay, on cais I lukit doun,
       And hard him mak sair lamentatioun.   1285

184   'Allace' (quod he), 'this cursit Consistorie
       In middis of the winter now is maid,
       Quhen Boreas° with blastis bitterlie
       And frawart froistes thir flouris doun can faid;
       On bankis bair now may I mak na baid.'   1290
       And with that word in to ane coif he crap,
       Fra hair wedder and froistis him to hap.

185   Quaikand for cauld, sair murnand ay amang,
       Kest up his Ee unto the hevinnis hicht
       And said, 'Lord God, quhy sleipis thow sa lang?°   1295
       Walk, and discerne my cause, groundit on richt;
       Se how I am, be fraud, maistrie, and slicht,
       Peillit full bair';° and so is mony one
       Now in this warld, richt wonder, wo begone!

186   Se how this cursit syn of covetice   1300
       Exylit hes baith lufe, lawtie, and Law.
       Now few or nane will execute Justice,
       In falt of quhome the pure man is overthraw.
       The veritie, suppois the Jugis knaw,
       That ar so blindit with affectioun,   1305
       But dreid, for meid, thay thoill the richt go doun.

187   Seis thow not (Lord) this warld overturnit is,
       As quha wald change gude gold in leid or tyn;

into lead or tin; the poor man is stripped bare,
but the great man can do no wrong; and Simony
is considered no sin. Now he considers himself
happy who can win the greatest profit by extortion;
kindness is slain, and pity is a thing of the past.
Alas (good Lord), why do you suffer it so to be?

188   You suffer this even for our great offense; you
send us troubles and sore plagues, as hunger,
dearth, great war, and pestilence; and yet this
causes few to mend their way of living. We poor
people, as of now, may do no more than pray to
Thee. Since on this earth we are so oppressed, in
heaven may God grant us rest.

The Tale of the Lion and the Mouse

189   In mid-June, that sweet and lovely season, when
fair Phoebus with his bright sunbeams has dried
the dew from dale and down, and all the land
made luminous with his rays of light, one morning, between the night and the middle of the day,
I rose and put all sloth and sleep aside, and to the
wood I went alone, without a guide.

190   Sweet was the smell of flowers, white and red, the
sound of birds most delightful, the broad boughs
blooming above my head, the ground growing
thick with lovely grass; the place abounded with
every kind of pleasure, with odors sweet and the
harmony of birds, that morning mild. My joy was
all the more for these.

191   The red roses adorned the thickets and the
brushwood, as did the primrose and the purple
violet; such merriness the Thrush and Blackbird
made, to hear it was a hint of Paradise. The
pretty blossoms bloomed on bank and hillside;
the smell of herbs and the cry of birds both contending which should have the victory.

The pure is peillit, the Lord may do na mis;
And Simonie° is haldin for na syn.   1310
Now is he blyith with okker maist may wyn;
Gentrice is slane, and pietie is ago;
Allace (gude Lord) quhy thoilis thow it so?

188   Thow tholis this evin for our grit offence,
Thow sendis us troubill and plaigis soir,   1315
As hunger, derth, grit weir, or Pestilence;
Bot few amendis now thair lyfe thairfoir.
We pure pepill as now may do no moir
Bot pray to the, sen that we ar opprest
In to this eirth, grant us in hevin gude rest.   1320

The Taill of the Lyoun & the Mous

189   In middis of June, that joly sweit seasoun,
Quhen that fair Phebus with his bemis bricht
Had dryit up the dew ffra daill and doun,
And all the land maid with his lemis licht,
In ane mornyng betwix mid day and nicht   1325
I rais and put all sleuth and sleip asyde,
And to ane wod I went allone but gyde.

190   Sweit wes the smell off flouris, quhyte and reid,°
The noyes off birdis richt delitious,
The bewis braid blomit abone my heid,   1330
The ground growand with gresis gratious;
Off all plesance that place wes plenteous,
With sweit odouris and birdis harmony,
The Morning Myld; my mirth wes mair for thy.

191   The Roisis reid arrayit on Rone and Ryce,   1335
The Prymeros and the purpour viola;
To heir it wes ane poynt off Paradice,
Sic Mirth the Mavis and the Merle couth ma.
The blossummis blythe brak up on band and bra;
The smell off Herbis and the fowlis cry,   1340
Contending wha suld have the victory.

192   Then, to protect me from the heat of the sun,
       under the shadow of a green Hawthorn I lay
       down among the sweet flowers, then made the
       sign of the cross and closed both my eyes. I fell
       asleep among these pleasant trees, and in my
       dream I envisioned coming through the wood the
       fairest man that I had ever seen.

193   His gown was of a cloth as white as milk; his robe
       was of wool and silk, a purple-brown; his hood
       was made of scarlet, bordered well with silk, of
       the fringed style, and it hung down to his belt;
       his cap was round and in the ancient fashion; his
       beard was white; his eyes were large and grey; his
       hair was curled and spread over his shoulders.

194   He bore a roll of paper in his hand, a swan's-quill
       pen behind his ear; at his belt he carried an ink-
       horn, an attractive gold writing case, and a bag of
       silk; thus was he favorably furnished in his attire.
       Of large stature and with an awe-inspiring face,
       he came at a vigorous pace to the spot where I
       lay.

195   And said, 'God speed, my son'; and I was glad to
       hear that agreeable phrase and to have his com-
       pany. With reverence I greeted him in turn, 'Wel-
       come, Father'; and he took a seat by me. 'Please
       do not take offense, my good Master, if I ask of you
       your birth, your profession, and your name, why
       you are come here, or where you make your home?'

196   'My son' (said he), 'I am of gentle blood; my
       native land is Rome, to be certain; and it was in
       that town that first I went to school and studied
       the Civil Law full many a day; but now my dwell-
       ing is in Heaven for eternity. Aesop I am called;
       my writing and my work is known and studied by
       many a knowledgeable scholar.'

197   'O Master Aesop, Poet Lauriate, God knows I am
       delighted to meet you. Are you not he that has
       written all those Fables, which in their effect,
       although they be ficticious, are full of prudence
       and morality?' 'Fair son' (said he), 'I am the very

192   Me to conserve than ffra the sonis heit,
       Under the schaddow off ane Hawthorne grene
       I lenit doun amang the flouris sweit,
       Syne maid a cors° and closit baith my Ene.   1345
       On sleip I fell° amang thir bewis bene,
       And in my dreme me thocht come throw the schaw
       The fairest man that ever befoir I saw.°

193   His gowne wes off ane claith als quhyte as milk;
       His chymmeris wes off Chambelate Purpour Broun;   1350
       His hude off Scarlet,° bordourit weill with silk,
       On hekillit wyis, untill his girdill doun;
       His Bonat round and off the auld fassoun;
       His beird wes quhyte; his Ene wes grit and gray,
       With lokker hair, quhilk over his schulderis lay.   1355

194   Ane Roll off paper in his hand he bair;
       Ane swannis pen stikand under his eir;
       Ane Inkhorne, with ane prettie gilt Pennair,
       Ane bag off silk, all at his belt can beir;
       Thus wes he gudelie grathit in his geir.   1360
       Off stature large and with ane feirfull face,
       Evin quhair I lay he come ane sturdie pace,

195   And said, 'God speid, my sone'; and I wes fane
       Off that couth word, and off his cumpany;
       With reverence I salusit him agane: 1365
       'Welcome, Father';° and he sat doun me by.
       'Displeis you not, my gude maister, thocht I
       Demand your birth, your facultye, and name;
       Quhy ye come heir, or quhair ye dwell at hame?'

196   'My sone' (said he), 'I am off gentill blude;   1370
       My native land is Rome° withoutin nay,
       And in that Towne first to the Sculis I yude,
       In Civile Law studyit full mony ane day;
       And now my winning is in Hevin ffor ay;
       Esope I hecht; my writing and my werk   1375
       Is couth and kend to mony cunning Clerk.'°

197   'O Maister Esope, Poet Lawriate,°
       God wait ye ar full deir welcum to me;
       Ar ye not he that all thir Fabillis wrate,
       Quhilk in effect, suppois thay fenyeit be,   1380
       Ar full off prudence° and moralitie?'

man.' The Lord knows how happy my heart was
then.

198   I said, 'Aesop, my venerable Master, heartily I
beg you for charity's sake to relate, if you would,
a pleasant fable, concluding with a good morality.' Shaking his head he said, 'My son, let that
be; for of what worth is it to tell a ficticious tale,
when holy preaching has no good effect?

199   'Now in this world, it seems to me, very few or
none have reverence for the word of God. The
ear is deaf, the heart is hard as stone; now open
sin exists without correction, and the heart sinks
ever downwards towards the earth. So corrupted
is the world with a black disease that now my
tales may afford but little aid.'

200   'Yet, gentle Sir' (said I), 'at my request, not intending to appear disrespectful, I pray that you
would deign to tell a moral fable, using brute
beasts allegorically. Who know but that I may
learn from it and take away with me something
that may be of use hereafter.' 'I am willing' (he
said), and thus he began his tale.

The End of the Prologue and the Beginning of the Tale

201   A Lion, exhausted from chasing his prey, lay
down under a tree in the pleasant forest, to re-
store the vigor to his legs and to rest, warming his
belly and his breast in the sun. Then out from
their nest came a troop of Mice, playful and nim-
ble, dancing in a round, and over the Lion they
lept twice or thrice.

202   He lay so still that the Mice were not afraid, but
over him they ran their course to and fro; some
tugged at the whiskers of his beard, and others
did not fear to claw him on the face. Merry and
gay they danced like this for a while, until at last
the noble Lion awoke, and with his paw he captured their leader.

203   She gave a cry, and all the rest, amazed, left off
their dancing and quickly hid themselves else-

'Fair sone' (said he), 'I am the samin man.'
God wait gif that my hert wes merie than.

198   I said, 'Esope, my maister venerabill,
I yow beseik hartlie, ffor cheritie,   1385
Ye wald dedene to tell ane prettie Fabill,
Concludand with ane gude Moralitie.'
Schaikand his heid, he said, 'my sone lat be;
For quhat is it worth to tell ane fenyeit taill,
Quhen haly preching may na thing availl?   1390

199   'Now in this warld, me think, richt few or nane
To Goddis word that hes devotioun;
The eir is deif, the hart is hard as stane,
Now oppin sin without correctioun,
The hart inclynand to the eirth ay doun;   1395
Sa roustie is the warld with canker blak
That now my taillis may lytill succour mak.'

200   'Yis, gentill Schir' (said I), 'for my requeist,
Not to displeis your Fatherheid,° I pray,
Under the figure off ane brutall beist,   1400
Ane morall Fabill ye wald denye to say.
Quha wait nor I may leir and beir away
Sum thing thairby heirefter may availl?'
'I grant' (quod he), and thus begouth ane taill.

The end of the Prolog, & beginnis the Taill

201   Ane Lyoun, at his Pray wery foirrun,   1405
To recreat his limmis and to rest,
Beikand his breist and belly at the Sun,°
Under ane tre lay in the fair forest;
Swa come ane trip off Myis out off thair nest,
Richt tait and trig, all dansand in ane gyis,°   1410
And over the Lyoun lansit twyis or thryis.

202   He lay so still the Myis wes not effeird,
Bot to and fro out over him tuke thair trace;
Sum tirlit at the Campis off his beird,
Sum spairit not to claw him on the face;   1415
Merie and glad thus dansit thay ane space,
Till at the last the Nobill Lyoun woke,
And with his pow the maister Mous he tuke.

203   Scho gave ane cry, and all the laif agast
Thair dansing left and hid thame sone alquhair;   1420

where. The captive Mouse cried out and sorely
wept, and often said alas that she had ever come
there. 'Now am I taken a woeful prisoner, and for
my trespass I expect to suffer now a trial for my
very life.'

204   Then to that mournful Mouse the Lion spoke:
       'You miserable wretch and vile unworthy thing:
       You were malapert in the extreme and also pre-
       sumptuous to use me for a dancing ground. Knew
       you not well that I was both Lord and King of all
       the beasts?' 'Yes, I knew; but I failed to recognize
       you, you lay so low.

205   'Lord! I beseech your kingly Royalty, hear what I
       say and listen patiently: Consider first my simple
       poverty, and then your mighty, high magnifi-
       cence; think, moreover, that things which are
       done out of negligence, neither out of malice nor
       out of treason, sooner should be given grace and
       remission.

206   'We all were full, having had a great abundance
       of all kinds of things that we like best; the pleas-
       ant season provoked us into dancing and making
       mirth in the way that Nature has taught us. You
       lay so still and low upon the earth that, by my
       soul, we thought that you had died; otherwise we
       never would have danced upon your head.'

207   'Thy false excuse' (the Lion said in return) 'shall
       be of not the slightest help, I promise you. Con-
       sider the case: Say I had died or been killed, and
       my skin had then been stuffed full of straw;
       though you had found my body lying so, you still
       for fear should have fallen down on your knees, if
       only because it bore the imprint of my person.

208   'You can make no defense for your trespass, treat-
       ing my noble person with such contempt; you
       can find no way to excuse either your own negli-
       gence or that of your companions. Therefore, you
       shall suffer a shameful end, such as for treason
       is decreed, to be dragged to the gallows by
       the feet.'

Scho that wes tane cryit and weipit fast,
And said allace oftymes that scho come thair:
'Now am I tane ane wofull presonair,
And ffor my gilt traistis Incontinent
Off lyfe and deith to thoill the Jugement.   1425

204   Than spak the Lyoun to that cairfull Mous:
'Thow Cative wretche and vile unworthie thing,
Over malapart and eik presumpteous
Thou wes, to mak out over me thy tripping.
Knew thow not weill I wes baith Lord and King   1430
Off beistis all?' 'Yes' (quod the Mous), 'I knaw;
Bot I misknew, because ye lay so law.

205   'Lord! I beseik thy Kinglie Royaltie,
Heir quhat I say, and tak in patience;
Considder first my simple povertie,   1435
And syne thy mychtie hie Magnyfycence;
Se als how thingis done off Neglygence,
Nouther off malice nor of Prodissioun,
Erer suld have grace and Remissioun.

206   'We wer repleit and had grit aboundance   1440
Off alkin thingis, sic as to us effeird;
The sweit sesoun provokit us to dance,
And mak sic mirth as nature to us leird.
Ye lay so still and law upon the eird
That, be my sawll, we weind ye had bene deid,   1445
Elles wald we not have dancit ouer your heid.'

207   'Thy fals excuse,' the Lyoun said agane,
'Sall not availl ane myte, I underta;
I put the cace, I had bene deid or slane,
And syne my skyn bene stoppit full off stra,   1450
Thocht thow had found my figure lyand swa,
Because it bare the prent off my persoun,
Thow suld ffor ffeir on kneis have fallin doun.

208   'For thy trespas thow can mak na defence,
My Nobill persoun thus to vilipend;   1455
Off thy feiris, nor thy awin negligence,
For to excuse thow can na cause pretend;
Thairfoir thow suffer sall ane schamefull end,
And deith, sic as to tressoun is decreit,
Unto the Gallous harlit be the feit.'°   1460

209   'Ah! mercy, Lord; I invoke your generosity, as
       you are crowned King of all the beasts; lessen
       your anger and let it fade away, and allow your
       mind to be inclined to mercy. I admit that of-
       fense has been done to your station for which I
       deserve to suffer death, unless your kingly mercy
       grant me remission.

210   'In every Judge there should be mercy and com-
       passion, to act as colleagues and officers of the
       court. Without mercy, justice becomes cruelty, as
       it is stated in the Holy Laws: who may sustain the
       concept of Equity when Rigor sits in the tribunal?
       Precious few or none, unless Mercy intercedes.

211   'Also you know that the honor triumph brings to
       a victor depends upon the strength of those he
       conquers, those who defend themselves long and
       boldly in battle, through all the dangers of war.
       What honor or praise, when the battle is ended,
       is given to him that defeats a man who neither
       can nor may defend himself?

212   'It is little credit to the manhood of a strong Lion
       to kill and then devour a thousand Mice; full lit-
       tle commendation would you win for that deed,
       since our strength cannot be compared to yours.
       It will degrade somewhat your reputation to slay a
       Mouse that may make no defense, but rather is
       asking for mercy of your excellence.

213   'Moreover, it is unfitting for your Highness, who
       is accustomed to daily food that is delectable, to
       defile your teeth or lips with blood of mine,
       which will not be agreeable to your stomach. Un-
       wholesome is the meat of a single sorry Mouse,
       and especially so for a strong Lion, accustomed to
       be fed on noble venison.

214   'My life is worth little and my death less; and yet
       if I live on, I may by chance give aid to your
       Highness, should you ever be in distress. For
       often it is seen that a humble man has been able
       to rescue a Lord of great estate who was held cap-

209   'A, mercie, Lord, at thy gentrice I ase,
As thow art King off beistis Coronate,
Sober thy wraith and let it overpas,
And mak thy mynd to mercy Inclynate.
I grant offence is done to thyne estate,   1465
Quhairfoir I worthie am to suffer deid,
Bot gif thy Kinglie mercie reik remeid.

210   'In everie Juge mercy and reuth suld be,
As Assessouris and Collaterall.
Without mercie Justice is crueltie,   1470
As said is in the Lawis spirituall;
Quhen Rigour sittis in the Tribunall,
The equitie° of Law quha may sustene?
Richt few or nane, but mercie gang betwene.

211   'Alswa ye knaw the honour Triumphall   1475
Off all victour upon the strenth dependis
Off his conqueist, quhilk manlie in battell
Throw Jeopardie of weir lang defendis.
Quhat pryce or loving, quhen the battell endis,
Is said off him that overcummis ane man   1480
Him to defend quhilk nouther may nor can?

212   'Ane thowsand Myis to kill and eik devoir
Is lytill manheid to ane strang Lyoun;
Full lytill worschip have ye wyn thairfoir,
To quhais strenth is na comparisoun;   1485
It will degraid sum part off your renoun
To sla ane mous, quhilk may mak na defence,
Bot askand mercie at your excellence.

213   'Also it semis not your Celsitude,
Quhilk usis daylie meittis delitious,   1490
To fyle your teith or lippis with my blude,
Quhilk to your stomok is contagious;
Unhailsum meit is of ane sarie Mous,
And that namelie untill ane strang Lyoun,
Wont till be fed with gentill vennesoun.   1495

214   'My lyfe is lytill worth, my deith is les,
Yit and I leif, I may peradventure
Supple your hienes beand in distres;
For oft is sene ane man off small stature
Reskewit hes ane Lord off hie honour,   1500

tive, about to be overthrown through misfortune;
such a case may be your own.'

215   When this was said, the Lion reconsidered his
        words and tempered his thoughts with reason,
        and let mercy assuage his cruel anger; and he
        granted the Mouse remission. He opened his paw,
        and she fell down on her knees and raised both
        her hands to heaven, crying 'May almighty God
        requite you!'

216   When she was gone, the Lion went off to hunt,
        for he had nothing stored up, but lived on his
        prey; and he slew both tame and wild, as was his
        custom, and in the country created a great dis-
        turbance; until at last the people found the way
        they might capture this cruel Lion: of hempen
        cords they fashioned sturdy nets.

217   With strong ropes, tied from tree to tree, they bound
        off a path wherein he usually ran; then within the
        woods they spread themselves out in a row, with
        the sound of horns, calling the swift hunting dogs.
        The Lion fled, and running through the underbrush
        fell into the net and was entangled head and foot. For
        all his strength, he could do nothing about it.

218   He thrashed about with horrible roaring, now to,
        now fro, hoping help might come to him. But all
        was in vain: it helped him not at all. The more
        he tossed about, the tighter he was bound. The
        coarse ropes were so woven about him on every
        side that he saw no solution; so he lay still and,
        mourning, made his lament.

219   'O disabled Lion, lying here so low, where is the
        power of your magnificence, of which all earthly
        beasts used to stand in awe, and feared even to
        gaze upon your excellence? Without hope or
        help, without aid or defense, in sturdy bonds here
        must I lie (alas!) till I be slain; I see no other
        grace.

220   'There is no one who will avenge my harms, nor
        creature to do comfort to my crown. Who shall

Keipit that wes, in poynt to be overthrawin
Throw misfortoun; sic cace may be your awin.'

215   Quhen this wes said, the Lyoun his langage
Paissit, and thocht according to ressoun,
And gart mercie his cruell Ire asswage,   1505
And to the Mous grantit Remissioun;°
Oppinnit his pow, and scho on kneis fell doun,
And baith hir handis unto the hevin upheild,
Cryand: 'Almichty God mot yow fforyeild!'

216   Quhen Scho wes gone, the Lyoun held to hunt,   1510
For he had nocht, bot levit on his Pray,
And slew baith tayme and wyld, as he wes wont,
And in the cuntrie maid ane grit deray;
Till at the last the pepill fand the way
This cruell Lyoun how that thay mycht tak: 1515
Off Hempyn cordis strang Nettis couth thay mak.

217   And in ane Rod, quhair he wes wont to ryn,
With Raipis rude ffra tre to tre it band;
Syne kest ane Range on raw the wod within,
With hornis blast and Kennettis fast calland.   1520
The Lyoun fled, and throw the Ron rynnand
Fell in the Net, and hankit fute and heid;
For all his strenth he couth mak na remeid.

218   Welterand about with hiddeous rummissing,
Quhyle to, quhyle ffra, quhill he mycht succour get;   1525
Bot all in vane, it vailyeit him na thing;
The mair he flang, the faster wes he knet.
The Raipis rude wes sa about him plet,
On everilk syde, that succour saw he nane;
Bot styll lyand and murnand maid his mane.   1530

219   'O lamit Lyoun, liggand heir sa law,
Quhair is the mycht off thy Magnyfycence,
Off quhome all brutall beist in eird stude aw,
And dred to luke upon thy Excellence?
But hoip or help, but succour or defence,   1535
In bandis strang heir may I ly (allace!)
Till I be slane; I se nane uther grace.

220   'Thair is na wy that will my harmis wreik,
Nor creature do confort to my Croun.

help me? Who shall break my bonds? Who shall
deliver me from the pain of this prison?' But
when he had made this lamentation, just by
chance the little Mouse came near and heard the
piteous clamor of the Lion.

221   And suddenly the thought came to her mind that
this was the very Lion that had pardoned her; and
she said, 'Now I would be false and most unnatural
if I did not requite somewhat the gracious act you
once did for me'; and on her way she went to her
fellow Mice and quickly cried to them 'Come help!
Come help!', and all of them came running.

222   'Look' (said the Mouse), 'This is the very Lion that
granted grace to me when I was captured; and now
in prison here he is tightly bound, breaking his
heart with painful mourning and moaning. Unless we help him, he can expect no other aid. Come
help requite one good turn with another; go, free him
immediately'; and they said, 'Yes, good Sister.'

223   They took no knife; their teeth were sharp
enough. Truly, to see that sight it was a great
wonder, how they ran among the sturdy ropes;
before, behind, some went above, some below,
and sheared the ropes of the net asunder. The
they bade him rise; and he started up immediately
and thanked them; then on his way he went.

224   Now is the Lion safe from all danger, free, and
delivered to his liberty by little beasts of little
power, as you have heard, and all because he had
shown pity. 'Master' (I said), 'Is there a Morality
to this Fable?' 'Yes, son' (he replied), 'a very good
one.' 'I pray sir' (said I), 'that you end with it.'

MORALITAS

225   As I imagine, this mighty, handsome Lion may
stand for a Prince or Emperor, a Potentate, or yet
a King with crown, who should be the vigilant
guide and governor of his people, that takes no
pains at all to rule and direct the land and main-

Quha sall me bute? quha sall my bandis breik?   1540
Quha sall me put fra pane off this Presoun?'
Be he had maid this lamentatioun,
Throw aventure, the lytill Mous come neir,
And off the Lyoun hard the pietuous beir.

221   And suddanlie it come in till hir mynd   1545
And suddanlie it come in till hir mynd
That it suld be the Lyoun did hir grace,
And said, 'now wer I fals and rycht unkynd
Bot gif I quit sumpart thy gentilnes
Thow did to me;' and on this way scho gais
To hir fellowis, and on thame fast can cry,   1550
'Cum help, cum help!' and thay come all in hy.

222   'Lo' quod the Mous, 'this is the samin Lyoun
That grantit grace to me quhen I wes tane;
And now is fast heir bundin in Presoun,
Brekand his hart with sair murning and mane;   1555
Bot we him help, off succour wait he nane.
Cum help to quyte ane gude turne for ane uther,
Go, lous him sone;' and thay said, 'ye, gude brother.'°

223   Thay tuke na knyfe, thair teith wes sharpe anewch.
To se that sicht, forsuith it wes grit wounder,   1560
How that thay ran amang the rapis tewch;
Befoir, behind, sum yeid abone, sum under,
And schuir the raipis off the net in schunder;
Syne bad him ryse; and he start up anone,
And thankit thame; syne on his way is gone.   1565

224   Now is the Lyoun fre off all danger,
Lows and delyverit to his libertie
Be lytill beistis off ane small power,
As ye have hard, because he had pietie.
(Quod I) 'Maister, is thair ane Moralitie   1570
In this Fabill?' 'Yea, sone' (he said), 'richt gude.'
'I pray yow, Schir' (quod I), 'ye wald conclude.'

MORALITAS

225   As I suppois, this mychtie gay Lyoun
May signifie ane Prince or Empriour,
Ane Potestate, or yit ane King with Croun,   1575
Quhilk suld be walkrife gyde and Governour
Of his pepill, that takis na labour

tain justice, but lies still in pleasures, sloth, and
sleep.

226   The lovely forest, with leaves sheltered from the
wind, with the song of birds and the flowers wonderfully sweet, is but the World and its prosperity,
where false pleasures are mixed with pervading sorrow. Just as the rose fades with the frost and the
rain of Winter, so does the World, and it deceives
those who put most trust in their earthly pleasures.

227   These little Mice are but the Common folk, wanton, foolish, and without discipline. When they
see their Lords and Princes will not execute the
laws of Justice, they do not hesitate to make
rebellion and disobey, because they have no fear
of them, and that causes them to ignore their
sovereigns.

228   By means of this Fable you Lords of prudence may
consider the virtue of pity, and remit sometimes a
great offense, and mitigate cruelty with mercy.
Often it is seen that a man of low degree has re-
paid a debt for either good or ill, corresponding to
harsh or gracious treatment by his Lord.

229   Who knows how soon a Lord of great reknown,
wallowing in worldly lust and vain pleasure, may
be overthrown, destroyed, and overcome by false
Fortune, who is certain mistress of all uncertain-
ties and is leader of the dance for lawless men,
blinding them so completely that they cannot
provide beforehand for any peril.

230   These country men, who have stretched the net
in which the Lion suddenly was captured, are
waiting always to avenge themselves (for injured
men write their plaints in marble stone). And
now I will let this subject be; but King and Lord
may well know what I mean: examples like this
have oftentimes been seen.

231   Aesop said, when this was done: 'My fair child,
persuade the churchmen constantly to pray that

To reule and steir the land, and Justice keip,
Bot lyis still in lustis, sleuth, and sleip.

226   The fair Forest with levis lowne and le,   1580
       With foulis sang and flouris ferlie sweit,
       Is bot the warld and his prosperitie,
       As fals plesance myngit with cair repleit.
       Richt as the Rois with froist and wynter weit
       Faidis, swa dois the warld, and thame desavis   1585
       Quhilk in thair lustis maist confidence havis.

227   Thir lytill Myis ar bot the commountie,
       Wantoun, unwyse, without correctioun.
       Thair Lordis and Princis quhen that they se
       Of Justice mak nane executioun,   1590
       Thay dreid na thing to mak Rebellioun,
       And disobey, for quhy thay stand nane aw,
       That garris thame thair Soveranis misknaw.

228   Be this Fabill ye Lordis of Prudence
       May considder the vertew of Pietie;   1595
       And to remit sumtyme ane grit offence,
       And mitigate with mercy crueltie.
       Oftymis is sene ane man of small degre
       Hes quit ane commoun baith for gude and ill,
       As Lord hes done Rigour or grace him till.   1600

229   Quha wait how sone ane Lord of grit Renoun,
       Rolland in warldle lust and vane plesance,
       May be overthrawin, destroyit, and put doun
       Throw fals fortoun? quhilk of all variance
       Is haill maistres and leidar of the dance   1605
       Till Injust men, and blindis thame so soir
       That thay na perrell can provyde befoir.

230   Thir rurall men, that stentit hes the Net,
       In quhilk the Lyoun suddandlie wes tane,
       Waittit alway amendis for to get   1610
       (For hurt men wrytis in the Marbill Stane).
       Mair till expound as now I lett allane,
       Bot King and Lord may weill wit quhat I mene:
       Figure heirof oftymis hes bene sene.

231   Quhen this wes said (quod Esope): 'my fair child,   1615
       Perswaid the kirkmen ythandly to pray

treason be exiled from this country, that Justice
reign, and that Lords keep their faith to their
sovereign King, both night and day.' And with
that word he vanished, and I awoke; then
through the wood I took my journey home.

The Preaching of the Swallow

232   The great prudence and the marvellous works,
       the profound wisdom of God omnipotent are so
       perfect and so discerning, excelling by far the
       judgment of any mortal; because to Him all things
       are ever present, correct as they are or at any
       time shall be, before the face of His divinity.

233   Because our Soul is so fettered with sensuality
       within our body's prison, we may not clearly
       understand nor perceive God as he is, nor
       anything celestial. Our physical body, dark and
       sinful, blinds the working of the spirit, like a man
       who has been bound in prison.

234   In the *Metaphysics* Aristotle says that man's Soul
       is like the eye of a bat, which hides as long as
       there is light of day, but in the gloaming then
       comes forth to fly. Her eyes are weak; she may
       not see the sun. In just this way does fantasy op-
       press our Soul, hindering it from understanding
       the things which nature makes manifest.

235   For God is Infinite in His power, and the Soul of
       man is frail and overly small, weak and imperfect
       in its power to understand, unable to comprehend
       Him who embraces all. None should presume, by
       natural power of reason, to question the mysteries
       of the Trinity; but rather we should firmly be-
       lieve, and let reason alone.

That tressoun of this cuntrie be exyld,
And Justice Regne, and Lordis keip thair fay
Unto thair Soverane King, baith nycht and day.'
And with that word he vanist, and I woke;   1620
Syne throw the Schaw my Journey hamewart tuke.

The Preiching of the Swallow

232   The hie prudence and wirking mervelous,
       The profound wit off God omnipotent,
       Is sa perfyte and sa Ingenious,
       Excellent ffar all mannis Jugement;   1625
       For quhy to him all thing is ay present,
       Rycht as it is or ony tyme sall be,
       Befoir the sicht off his Divinitie.

233   Thairfoir our Saull with Sensualitie
       So fetterit is in presoun Corporall,   1630
       We may not cleirlie understand nor se
       God as he is, nor thingis Celestiall;
       Our mirk and deidlie corps Naturall
       Blindis the Spirituall operatioun,
       Lyke as ane man wer bundin in presoun.   1635

234   In Metaphisik Aristotell sayis
       That mannis Saull is lyke ane Bakkis Ee,
       Quhilk lurkis still als lang as licht off day is,
       And in the gloming cummis furth to fle;
       Hir Ene ar waik, the Sone scho may not se: 1640
       Sa is our Saull with fantasie opprest,
       To knaw the thingis in nature manifest.

235   For God is in his power Infinite,
       And mannis Saull is febill and over small,
       Off understanding waik and unperfite,   1645
       To comprehend him that contenis all.
       Nane suld presume, be ressoun naturall,
       To seirche the secreitis off the Trinitie,
       Bot trow fermelie and lat all ressoun be.

236 Yet nevertheless, through his creations we may
have certain knowledge concerning God al-
mighty, that He is good, just, knowing, and
benign. For example, take the lovely flowers, so
sweet in smell and pleasant of hue: some green,
some blue, some purple, white, and red, thus
varied by the gift of his Godly nature.

237 The firmament, painted with clear-shining stars,
rotating in a circle from east to west, and every
planet in its proper sphere, create harmony and
sound through their motions; the fire, the air, the
water, and the earth—it is enough to understand,
I know, that God has a purpose for each of His
works.

238 Consider well the fish that swim in the sea; consider the many kinds of beasts on earth; the
beautiful birds, so powerfully they fly, parting the
air with wings great and small; then look at man,
whom He made last of all, in His image and in
His likeness: by these we know that God is just
and good.

239 He fashioned all created things for the aid of man
and for his preservation on this earth, both under
and above, in number, weight, and due proportions; the differing lengths of days and the varia-
tions of the seasons, conforming to our needs, as
daily by experience we may see.

240 The Summer with his festive mantle green, with
fair flowers adorning every border, which Flora,
queen and goddess of the flowers, has sent the
Lord for use in his season, and which Phoebus,
with his gentle golden beams, has embroidered
and painted pleasantly, with heat and moisture
distilled from the sky.

241 Then warm Autumn, when that goddess Ceres
has stocked her barns with abundant crops; and
Bacchus, god of wine, has replenished the empty
casks in Italy and France with potent wines and
liquors that delight; and *Copia Temporis* comes to

236 Yit nevertheles we may haif knawlegeing   1650
   Off God almychtie, be his Creatouris,
   That he is gude, ffair, wyis and bening;
   Exempill takis be thir Jolie flouris,
   Rycht sweit off smell and plesant off colouris.
   Sum grene, sum blew, sum purpour, quhyte, and reid, 1655
   Thus distribute be gift off his Godheid.

237 The firmament payntit with sternis cleir,
   From eist to west rolland in cirkill round,
   And everilk Planet in his proper Spheir,
   In moving makand Harmonie and sound;°   1660
   The fyre, the Air, the watter, and the ground—°
   Till understand it is aneuch, I wis,
   That God in all his werkis wittie is.°

238 Luke weill the fische that swimmis in the se;
   Luke weill in eirth all kynd off bestiall;   1665
   The foulis ffair, sa forcelie thay fle,
   Scheddand the air with pennis grit and small;
   Syne luke to man, that he maid last off all,
   Lyke to his Image and his similitude:
   Be thir we knaw that God is ffair and gude.   1670

239 All Creature he maid ffor the behufe
   Off man, and to his supportatioun
   In to this eirth, baith under and abufe,
   In number, wecht, and dew proportioun;
   The difference off tyme and ilk seasoun,   1675
   Concorddand till our opurtunitie,
   As daylie by experience we may se.

240 The Somer° with his Jolie mantill grene,
   With flouris fair furrit on everilk fent,
   Quhilk Flora, Goddes off the flouris, Quene, 1680
   Hes to that Lord as ffor his seasoun sent,
   And Phebus with his goldin bemis gent
   Hes purfellit and payntit pleasandly,
   With heit and moysture stilland ffrom the sky.

241 Syne Harvest hait, quhen Ceres that Goddes 1685
   Hir barnis benit hes with abundance;
   And Bachus, God off wyne, renewit hes
   The tume Pyipis in Italie and France
   With wynis wicht and liquor off plesance;

fill her horn, which never could be full, of wheat
or other grain.

242   Then gloomy Winter, when severe Aeolus, god of
the winds, with Boreal blasts has rent and riven
into little pieces all the green garment of glorious
Summer. Then fair flowers faded by frost must
fall, and the happy birds near slain with snow and
sleet change their pleasant tune for a quiet
lament.

243   The dales are drowned in deep pools of water;
both hill and wood lie hidden under hoar-frost;
and goodly boughs are bereft of beauty by the
wicked winds of storm-ridden Winter. All wild
beasts then withdraw in fear from the barren
fields to their cavernous dens, cowering in caves
to protect themselves from the cold.

244   When Winter has departed, then comes Spring,
the Secretary of Summer with his seal, and the
Columbines, frightened before by the great frost,
peep their head up through the sod. The Thrushes
and the Blackbirds start to mate; the Lark on
high then comes out from hiding, along with
other birds over down and dale.

245   During that very season, one pleasant morning,
so happy that the bitter blasts were past, I walked
out towards the wood to see the flowers springing
up and hear the Thrushes sing, and other birds as
well; I walked out and looked all about to see the
soil ready for the season, fertile, prepared to nur-
ture all the seeds.

246   As I wandered thus, I was overjoyed to see the
industry of laborers: some were building a dyke,
some guiding the plough, some copiously sowing
seeds from place to place, the harrows hopping in
the sowers' tracks. Great joy it was for one who
loved the grain to see them labor both at evening
and at morn.

247   And as I rested on a beautiful bank, my heart
greatly rejoicing in that sight, to a hedge behind

And *Copia temporis*° to fil hir horne,   1690
That never wes full off quheit nor uther corne.

242   Syne Winter wan, quhen Austerne Eolus,°
God off the wynd, with blastis boreall,°
The grene garment off Somer glorious
Hes all to rent and revin in pecis small;   1695
Than flouris fair faidit with froist man fall,
And birdis blyith changeis thair noitis sweit
In styll murning, neir slane with snaw and sleit.

243   Thir dalis deip with dubbis drounit is,
Baith hill and holt heillit with frostis hair;   1700
And bewis bene ar bethit bair off blis
Be wickit windis off the winter wair.
All wyld beistis than ffrom the bentis bair
Drawis ffor dreid unto thair dennis deip,
coucheand ffor cauld in coifis thame to keip.   1705

244   Syne cummis Ver, quhen Winter is away,
The Secretar off Somer with his Sell,°
Quhen Colombie up keikis throw the clay,
Quhilk fleit wes befoir with froistes fell.
The Mavis and the Merle beginnis to mell;   1710
The Lark on loft, with uther birdis haill.
Than drawis furth ffra derne, over doun and daill.

245   That samin seasoun, in to ane soft morning,
Rycht blyth that bitter blastis wer ago,
Unto the wod to se the flouris spring   1715
And heir the Mavis sing and birdis mo
I passit ffurth, syne lukit to and ffro
To se the Soill that wes richt sessonabill,
Sappie, and to resave all seidis abill.

246   Moving thusgait, grit myrth I tuke in mynd,   1720
Off lauboraris to se the besines,°
Sum makand dyke,° and sum the pleuch can wynd,
Sum sawand seidis fast ffrome place to place,
The Harrowis° hoppand in the saweris trace;
It wes grit Joy to him that luifit corne   1725
To se thame labour, baith at evin and morne.

247   And as I baid under ane bank full bene,°
In hart gritlie rejosit off that sicht,

a green hawthorn there came a sudden flight of
little birds, who straightaway lighted down upon
the leaves on every side about me where I stood,
wonderful to see, a mighty multitude.

248   Among these birds a Swallow cried aloud, sitting
on the top of that tall hawthorn: 'O you birds on
these boughs here by me, well you shall know and
wisely understand: wherever there is danger or apparent peril, it is the better part of wisdom to provide beforehand in order to avoid it, fearing that
later it may hurt you more.'

249   'Sir Swallow' (said the Lark in reply, and laughed),
'What have you seen that causes you to fret?' 'Do
you see that Churl' (she said) 'behind that
plough, briskly sewing hemp—but look!—and seed
of flax? That flax will grow in little time indeed,
and from it will that Churl produce his nets;
within those nets he plans to capture us.

250   'Thus I suggest we go when he is gone, at even-
tide, and with our small sharp nails scrape that
seed out of the earth at once and eat it up; for if
it grows we shall have cause to weep hereafter,
one and all. Let us provide a remedy for it at
once, *nam leuius laedit quicquid praevidimus ante.*

251   'For scholars say that it is not sufficient to consider only what is before your eyes; but prudence
consists of an internal process of reasoning that
makes a man forsee and make provisions for
whatever good or evil is like to be, in everything
behold the final end, and thus be the better able
to defend himself against danger.

252   The Lark, laughing, showed his contempt for the
Swallow and said she fished long before she had a
net: 'The unborn child is easy to dress; not all that
is put in the ground will grow; it is soon enough
to bow your neck when the blow is about to de-
scend; death takes only him who is fated next to
die.' Thus they scorned the Swallow one and all.

Unto ane hedge, under ane Hawthorne grene,
Off small birdis thair come ane ferlie flicht,   1730
And doun belyif can on the leifis licht
On everilk syde about me quhair I stude,
Rycht mervellous, ane mekill multitude.

248   Amang the quhilks ane Swallow loud couth cry,
On that Hawthorne hie in the croip sittand: 1735
'O ye Birdis on bewis heir me by,
Ye sall weill knaw and wyislie understand:
Quhair danger is, or perrell appeirand,
It is grit wisedome to provyde befoir
It to deuoyd, ffor dreid it hurt yow moir.'   1740

249   'Schir Swallow' (quod the Lark agane, and leuch),
'Quhat haif ye sene that causis yow to dreid?'
'Se ye yone Churll' (quod scho) 'beyond yone pleuch
Fast sawand hemp—lo se!—and linget seid?
Yone lint will grow in lytill tyme in deid,   1745
And thairoff will yone Churll his Nettis mak,
Under the quhilk he thinkis us to tak.

250   'Thairfoir I reid we pas quhen he is gone,
At evin, and with our nailis scharp and small
Out off the eirth scraip we yone seid anone,   1750
And eit it up; ffor, giff it growis, we sall
Have cause to weip heirefter ane and all.
Se we remeid thairfoir ffurth with Instante,
Nam leuius laedit quicquid praevidimus ante.°

251   'For Clerkis sayis it is nocht sufficient   1755
To considder that is befoir thyne Ee;
Bot prudence is ane inwart Argument
That garris ane man prouyde befoir and se
Quhat gude, quhate evill, is liklie ffor to be,
Off everilk thing behald the fynall end   1760
And swa ffra perrell ethar him defend.'

252   The Lark, lauchand, the Swallow thus couth scorne,°
And said scho fischit lang befoir the Net;
'The barne is eith to busk that is unborne;
All growis nocht that in the ground is set;   1765
The nek to stoup, quhen it the straik sall get
Is sone aneuch; deith on the fayest fall.'—
Thus scornit thay the Swallow ane and all.

253 Dismissing thus her wholesome instruction, the
birds at once and suddenly took to flight; and
with a whirr some hurried off over the field, and
some returned to the green forest. Being left
alone in that country spot, I took my staff and
made my way back, wondering so, as if I had seen
a vision.

254 The time passed on till June, that pleasant season,
and the seeds that had been sown before were grown
so high that Hares might hide themselves, as well
as the Corn-crake, who was croaking in the fields
of grain. I ventured out between the morning
and midday to that hedge behind the green hawthorn where previously I had seen those birds.

255 And as I was standing there, just by chance and
good fortune, the same birds that I have told you
of before lighted down, I expect because it was
their usual haunt, a spot of great security and
seclusion. And when they all were settled, at
once the Swallow uttered a piteous cry and said,
'Woe is he who does not beware in time.

256 'O blind birds! So full of negligence, inattentive
to your own prosperity: Lift up your eyes and look
around you well. Look at the flax that grows in
yonder field: that, in truth, is the stuff that I ad-
vised we scratch from its earthen roots while still
it was seed. Now it is flax, and now the first
shoots are tall.

257 'Go now, while it is still tender and small, and
pull it up; let it grow no more. My flesh is trem-
bling; my body quakes all over; thinking about it
prevents me from sleeping in peace.' They all
cried out and bade the Swallow cease, and said,
'That flax will serve us well in times to come, for
its seeds provide food for little birds.

258 'When those pods of flax are ripe, we intend to
make a feast and eat our fill of that seed, despite
that Churl, and on it we will sing and peep.' 'Well'
(said the Swallow) 'so be it, friends, by all means.
Do as you will , but for sure I sorely fear that here-

253   Despysing thus hir helthsum document,
      The foullis ferlie tuke thair flicht anone;   1770
      Sum with ane bir thay braidit over the bent,
      And sum agane ar to the grene wod gone,
      Upon the land quhair I wes left allone
      I tuke my club and hamewart couth I carie,
      Swa ferliand as I had sene ane farie.   1775

254   Thus passit furth quhill June, that Jolie tyde,
      And seidis that wer sawin off beforne
      Wer growin hie, that Hairis mycht thame hyde,
      And als the Quailye craikand in the corne;
      I movit furth, betwix midday and morne,   1780
      Unto the hedge under the Hawthorne grene,
      Quhair I befoir the said birdis had sene.

255   And as I stude, be aventure and cace,
      The samin birdis as I haif said yow air,
      I hoip, because it wes thair hanting place,   1785
      Mair of succour, or yit mair solitair,
      Thay lychtit doun; and quhen thay lychtit wair,
      The Swallow swyth put furth ane pietuous pyme,
      Said, 'wo is him can not bewar in tyme.

256   'O blind birdis! and full of negligence,   1790
      Unmydfull of your awin prosperitie,
      Lift up your sicht and tak gude advertence;
      Luke to the Lint that growis on yon le;
      Yone is the thing I bad forsuith that we,
      Quhill it wes seid, suld rute furth off the eird;   1795
      Now is it Lint, now is it hie on breird.

257   'Go yit, quhill it is tender and small,
      And pull it up; let it na mair Incres;
      My flesche growis, my bodie quaikis all,
      Thinkand on it I may not sleip in peis.'   1800
      Thay cryit all, and bad the Swallow ceis'
      And said, 'yone Lint heirafter will do gude,
      For Linget is to lytill birdis fude.

258   'We think, quhen that yone Lint bollis ar ryip,
      To mak us Feist and fill us off the seid,   1805
      Magre yone Churll, and on it sing and pyip.'
      'Weill' (quod the Swallow), 'freindes hardilie beid;
      Do as ye will, bot certane sair I dreid,

after you will find it as sour as it now seems sweet,
when you are skewered on that Churl's roasting spit.

259   'The owner of that flax field is a Fowler, most
cunning and full of deception. Few are the times
he fails to get his prey, unless we birds take extreme precautions. He has caused the deaths of
many of our cousins and thought it but a sport to
spill their blood. God and the Holy Cross
preserve me from him.'

260   These little birds, who had but little care for the
danger that might befall them by chance, considered the Swallow's counsel worthless, and together
they took to flight and departed; some made their
way to the wood and some to the moor. I took
my staff, when this was said and done, and
walked on home, for it was drawing near noon.

261   The flax ripened, and the Churl pulled up the
stalks and bound them in sheaves, removing the
seeds from the pods, steeped it in the stream and
then dried it; and with a beetle he struck and pounded
it, then scutched it well and combed it in the house.
His wife spun it up and twined it into thread, out
of which the Fowler made his nets indeed.

262   The Winter came; the wicked wind blew; the
green woods were withered by the wetness; both
firth and fell were discolored by the frosts; the
dells and hollows were made slippery by the sleet.
The beautiful birds collapsed for lack of food. It
was no use to perch on boughs that were bare, so
they scurried into houses to hide themselves.

263   Some in the barn, some in the stacks of grain
took their lodging and made their residence. The
Fowler watched and swore to himself great oaths
that because of their pilfering they surely would
be captured. He set his nets about with great diligence, and in the snow he shovelled clear a space
and covered it over again with a layer of chaff.

264   These little birds were glad to see the chaff.
Thinking it was grain, they lighted down; but

Heirefter ye sall find als sour as sweit,
Quhen ye ar speldit on yone Carlis speit.   1810

259   'The awner off yone lint ane fouler is,
Richt cautelous and full off subteltie;
His pray full sendill tymis will he mis,
Bot giff we birdis all the warrer be;
Full mony off our kin he hes gart de,   1815
And thocht it bot ane sport to spill thair blude:
God keip me ffra him, and the halie Rude.

260   Thir small birdis haveand bot lytill thocht
Off perrell that micht fall be aventure,
The counsell off the Swallow set at nocht,   1820
Bot tuke thair flicht and furth togidder fure;
Sum to the wode, sum markit to the mure.
I tuke my staff, quhen this wes said and done,
And walkit hame, ffor it drew neir the none.

261   The Lint ryipit, the Carll pullit the Lyne,°   1825
Rippillit the bollis, and in beitis set,
It steipit in the burne, and dryit syne,
And with ane bittill knokkit it, and bet,
Syne swingillit it weill, and hekkillit in the flet;
His wyf it span, and twynit it in to threid,   1830
Of quhilk the Fowlar Nettis maid in deid.

262   The wynter come, the wickit wind can blaw,
The woddis grene were wallowit with the weit,
Baith firth and fell with froistys were maid faw,
Slonkis and slaik maid slidderie with the sleit;   1835
The foulis ffair ffor falt thay ffell off feit;
On bewis bair it wes na bute to byde,
Bot hyit unto housis thame to hyde.

263   Sum in the barn, sum in the stak off corne
Thair lugeing tuke and maid thair residence;   1840
The Fowlar saw, and grit aithis hes sworne,
Thay suld be tane trewlie ffor thair expence.
His Nettis hes he set with diligence,
And in the snaw he schulit hes ane plane,
And heillit it all over with calf agane.   1845

264   Thir small birdis seand the calff wes glaid;
Trowand it had bene corne, they lychtit doun;

they had no suspicion of the nets, nor of the
Fowler's false intentions; they prepared themselves to scrape up the food. The Swallow, on a
little branch near by, fearing a trick, cried to
them loudly:

265   'You may scrape in that chaff until your nails are
       bleeding, but there is no grain; your labor is all in
       vain. Do you think that Churl will feed you out
       of pity? No, no, he has laid it here for you as a
       trap. Be off, I tell you, or else you will be slain.
       He has stealthily set his nets, which are ready to
       be drawn around you; therefore take heed in time.'

266   Great fool is he that puts his life, his honor, in
       jeopardy for a worthless thing. Great fool is he
       that will not gladly listen to good counsel in time
       for it to serve him best. Great fool is he who can
       think of nothing but the present, and has no
       thought of what may happen afterwards, nor of
       the end.

267   These little birds, hungry near to starvation,
       preoccupied with scraping to seek their food,
       would not hear the counsel of the Swallow, even
       though their labor did them little good. And
       when she was assured that their attitude was
       foolish and most obstinate, she flew up to a tree;
       and then this Churl caught them in his nets.

268   Alas! it made the heart lament to see that bloody
       Butcher beating down those birds and to hear
       their woeful song and lamentation when they
       could tell they were about to die. Some he
       clubbed unconscious to the earth; he beat the
       head of some, he broke the neck of others, and
       some he stuffed into his bag half-dead.

269   And when the Swallow saw that they were dead,
       'Lo' she said, 'This happens many times to those
       that will not take the counsel or advice of pru-
       dent men or of scholars that are wise. I warned
       them of this peril more than thrice; now they are
       dead, and woe is me therefore!' She took her
       flight, and I saw no more of her.

Bot of the Nettis na presume thay had,
Nor of the Fowlaris fals Intentioun;
To scraip and seik thair meit thay maid thame boun.   1850
The Swallow on ane lytill branche neir by,
Dreiddand for gyle, thus loud on thame couth cry:

265   'In to the calf scraip quill your naillis bleid,
Thair is na corne, ye labour all in vane;
Trow ye yone Churll for pietie will yow feid?   1855
Na, na, he hes it heir layit for ane trane;
Remove, I reid, or ellis ye will be slane;
His Nettis he hes set full prively,
Reddie to draw; in tyme be war ffor thy.'

266   Grit fule is he that puttis in dangeir   1860
His lyfe, his honour, ffor ane thing off nocht;
Grit fule is he that will not glaidlie heir
Counsall in tyme, quhill it availl him mocht;
Grit fule is he that hes na thing in thocht
Bot thing present, and efter quhat may fall   1865
Nor off the end hes na memoriall.

267   Thir small birdis ffor hunger famischit neir,
Full besie scraipand ffor to seik thair fude,
The counsall off the Swallow wald not heir,
Suppois thair labour did thame lytill gude.   1870
Quhen scho thair fulische hartis understude
Sa Indurate, up in ane tre scho flew;
With that this Churll over thame his Nettis drew.

268   Allace! it wes grit hart sair for to se
That bludie Bowcheour beit thay birdis doun,   1875
And ffor till heir, quhen thay wist weill to de,
Thair cairfull sang and lamentatioun.
Sum with ane staf he straik to eirth on swoun;
Off sum the heid he straik, off sum he brak the crag,
Sum half on lyfe he stoppit in his bag.   1880

269   And quhen the Swallow saw that thay wer deid,
'Lo' (quod scho), 'thus it happinnis mony syis
On thame that will not tak counsall nor reid
Off Prudent men or Clerkis that ar wyis;
This grit perrell I tauld thame mair than thryis;   1885
Now ar thay deid, and wo is me thairfoir!'
Scho tuke hir flicht, bot I hir saw no moir.

MORALITAS

270   Lo, worthy folk, that noble scholar Aesop (a poet
worthy to be Laureate), while resting from more
serious work wrote the previous fable, along with
many others, which now appropriately may be
transformed into sound moral edification, possess-
ing a meaning in accordance with reason.

271   This Churl, a peasant lacking in true gentility,
sowing this chaff to slay these little birds—he is
the Fiend, who from the angelic state is exiled for
having deserted the true God; who day and night
never tires from going about, sowing his poison in
many a wicked thought in the Soul of man,
which Christ has bought full dear.

272   And when the Soul gives consent to fleshly
delight, the wicked thought, just like a seed in
earth, then begins to sprout in deadly sin, which
leads to damnation. Reason is blinded by selfish
interest, and carnal lust blossoms and grows
attractive, nurtured by habit practiced from day
to day.

273   Continuing to grow by daily use and habit, the
sin ripens, and all shame is set aside. The Devil
weaves his nets, severe and rough, and craftily
disguises them in pleasures. Then on the field he
spreads around the chaff, which is nothing but
the empty vanity of fleshly lust and vain
prosperity.

274   These hungry birds we may call wretched people,
scraping about among this world's vain pleasures,
greedy to gather up the goods of this life, which
like the chaff are void and without substance, of
little avail and impermanent, resembling the dust
which is whisked about in the face of the wind
and makes poor wretches blind.

275   This Swallow, which escaped the snare, well may
represent the holy Preacher, exhorting folk to
keep awake and constantly beware the nets of our
wicked enemy, who never sleeps but is ever prepared, when wretches go scraping after the chaff

MORALITAS

270   Lo, worthie folk, Esope, that Nobill clerk,
       Ane Poet worthie to be Lawreate,
       Quhen that he waikit from mair autentik werk,   1890
       With uther ma, this foirsaid Fabill wrate,
       Quhilk at this tyme may weill be applicate
       To guid morall edificatioun,
       Haifand ane sentence, according to ressoun.

271   This Carll and bond of gentrice spoliate,   1895
       Sawand this calf, thir small birdis to sla,
       It is the Feind, quhilk fra the Angelike state
       Exylit is, as fals Apostata,
       Quhilk day and nycht weryis not for to ga
       Sawand poysoun in mony wickit thocht   1900
       In mannis Saull, quhil Christ full deir hes bocht.

272   And quhen the Saull, as seid in to the eird,
       Gevis consent unto delectatioun,
       The wickit thocht beginnis for to breird
       In deidlie sin, quhilk is dampnatioun;   1905
       Ressoun is blindit with affectioun,
       And carnall lust grouis full grene and gay,
       Throw consuetude hantit from day to day.

273   Proceding furth be use and consuetude,
       The sin ryipis, and schame is set on syde;   1910
       The Feynd plettis his Nettis scharp and rude,
       And under plesance previlie dois hyde;
       Syne on the feild he sawis calf full wyde,
       Quhilk is bot tume and verray vanitie
       Of fleschlie lust and vaine prosperitie.   1915

274   Thir hungrie birdis wretchis we may call,
       As scraipand in this warldis vane plesance,
       Greddie to gadder gudis temporall,
       Quhilk as the calf ar tume without substance,
       Lytill of availl, and full of variance,   1920
       Lyke to the mow befoir the face of wind
       Quhiskis away and makis wretchis blind.

275   This Swallow, quhilk eschaipit is the snair,
       The halie Preichour° weill may signifie,
       Exhortand folk to walk and ay be wair   1925
       Fra Nettis of our wickit enemie,
       Quha sleipis not, bot ever is reddie,

of this world, to draw his net that they may not
escape.

276   Alas! What care, what weeping, and what woe
there is when Soul and Body go their separate
ways! The Body goes off to the worms' Kitchen,
and the Soul to the Fire, to everlasting pain. Of
what help then is this chaff, these worthless
goods, when you are stuffed into the bag of Lucifer
and brought to Hell and hanged up by the neck?

277   It is best to be most on guard when you are most
in prosperity, to see and comprehend these hidden nets and wisely understand how worthless is
this chaff, for nothing lasts forever in this world.
No man knows how long his state will endure,
how long his life will last, nor what shall be his
ending after death, nor whither he shall go.

278   Therefore let us pray, while still we inhabit this
world, for four things: The first, to be removed
from sin; the second, to end all war and strife; the
third, to maintain perfect charity and love; the
fourth, and most important for our needs, that in
bliss with Angels we be fellowed; and thus con-
cludes the preaching of the Swallow.

*The Tale of the Wolf that Got the Blow on the Neck
through the Tricks of the Fox that Beguiled the
Cadger*

279   A long time ago there dwelt in the wilderness (as
my author expressly has declared) a thieving Wolf
that lived on hunting livestock, which afforded
him a good living. There were none about him so
strong that he would spare them if he were
hungry, either for love or in fear, but in his fury
he killed them.

Quhen wretchis in this warldis calf dois scraip,
To draw his Net, that thay may not eschaip.

276   Allace! quhat cair, quhat weiping is and wo,   1930
      Quhen Saull and bodie departit ar in twane!
      The bodie to the wormis Keitching° go,
      The Saull to Frye, to everlestand pane.
      Quhat helpis than this calf, thir gudis vane,
      Quhen thow art put in Luceferis bag,   1935
      And brocht to hell, and hangit be the crag?

277   Thir hid Nettis for to persave and se,
      This sarie calf wyislie to understand,
      Best is bewar in maist prosperite,°
      For in this warld thair is na thing lestand;   1940
      Is na man wait how lang his stait will stand,
      His lyfe will lest, nor how that he sall end
      Efter his deith, nor quhidder he sall wend.

278   Pray we thairfoir, quhill we ar in this lyfe,
      For four thingis: the first, fra sin remufe;   1945
      The secund is to seis all weir and stryfe;
      The thrid is perfite cheritie and lufe;
      The feird thing is, and maist for oure behufe,
      That is in blis with Angellis to be fallow.
      And thus endis the preiching of the Swallow.   1950

*The Taill of the Wolff that Gat the Nekhering
throw the Wrinkis of the Foxe that Begylit the
Cadgear*

279   Quhylum thait wynnit in ane wildernes
      (As myne Authour expreslie can declair)
      Ane revand Wolff, that levit upon purches
      On bestiall, and maid him weill to ffair;
      Wes nane sa big about him he wald spair   1955
      And he war hungrie, outher ffor favour or feid,
      Bot in his breith he weryit thame to deid.

280   One day while he was going along, searching, he
       happened to meet a Fox in the middle of the
       road. The Fox saw him first and pretended to be
       overcome, and with a bow he bade the Wolf
       good-day. 'How good to see you, O Russel grey,'
       he said; then he knelt down and took him by the
       hand. 'Rise up, Lawrence; I give you leave to stand.

281   'Where have you been so long now from my sight?
       You shall hold an office and be my Steward, for you
       can strike down capons in the night, and crouching
       down low you can slaughter hens.' 'Sir' (said the
       Fox), 'that kind of post would not suit me; and I
       am afraid that if they see me from a distance, bird
       and beast will be scared away by my appearance.'

282   'No' (said the Wolf), 'You can creep in secret on
       your stomach and catch them by the head; and
       you can suddenly pounce upon a sheep, then with
       your teeth you can shake him till he is dead.' 'Sir'
       (said the Fox), 'You know my coat is red, and
       thus no beast will wait around for me, even if I
       were cunning enough to hide myself.'

283   'Yes' (said the Wolf), 'Through bushes and by hill-
       sides you can creep, low down, until you've reached
       your goal.' 'Sir' (said the Fox), 'You can tell what
       would happen; a long way off they would detect my
       scent, and then they would escape, even if it meant
       my ruin; and I would be ashamed to come up behind
       them in the field, even if I should find them sleeping.'

284   'No' (said the Wolf), 'for you can approach them
       upwind; for their every trick, in truth, you have
       another.' 'Sir' (said the Fox), 'You might as well
       call a beast blind that is not able to escape from
       me by a mile. How might I trick one of them that
       way? My pair of pointed ears and my two grey
       eyes cause me to be recognized in places where I
       have never been seen before.'

285   'Then, Lawrence' (said the Wolf), 'I think you
       are lying and fishing for problems to preserve your
       tricks for yourself. But all your excuses shall avail
       you naught, though constantly you beat about the
       bush; falsehood always fails when the tale is done.

280   Swa happinnit him in watching, as he went,
        To meit ane Foxe in middis off the way;
        He him foirsaw, and fenyeit to be schent,   1960
        And with ane bek he bad the Wolff gude day.
        'Welcum to me' (quod he) 'thow Russell° gray';
        Syne loutit doun and tuke him be the hand.
        'Ryse up, Lowrence, I leif the for to stand.

281   'Quhair hes thow bene this sesoun ffra my sicht?   1965
        Thow sall beir office, and my Stewart be,
        For thow can knap doun Caponis on the nicht,
        And lourand law thow can gar hennis de.'
        'Schir' (said the Foxe), 'that ganis not for me;
        And I am rad, gif thay me se on far,   1970
        That at my figure, beist and bird wil skar.'

282   'Na' (quod the Wolff), 'thow can in covert creip
        Upon thy wame and hint thame be the heid;
        And mak ane suddand schow upon ane scheip,
        Syne with thy wappinnis wirrie him to deid.'   1975
        'Schir' (said the Foxe), 'ye knaw my Roib is reid,
        And thairfoir thair will na beist abyde me,
        Thocht I wald be sa fals as ffor to hyde me.'

283   'Yis' (quod the Wolff), 'throw buskis and throw brais
        Law can thow lour to cum to thy Intent.'   1980
        'Schir' (said the Foxe), 'ye wait weill how it gais;
        Ane lang space ffra thame they will feill my sent,
        Then will thay eschaip, suppois I suld be schent;
        And I am schamefull ffor to cum behind thame
        In to the feild thocht I suld sleipand find thame.'   1985

284   'Na' (quod the Wolff). 'thow can cum on the wind;
        Foe everie wrink, forsuith, thow hes ane wyle.'
        'Schir' (said the Foxe) 'that beist ye mycht call blind
        That micht not eschaip than ffra me ane myle.
        How micht I ane off thame that wyis begyle?   1990
        My typpit twa eiris and my twa gray Ene
        Garris me be kend quhair I wes never sene.

285   'Than' (said the Wolff) 'Lowrence I heir the le,
        And castys ffor perrellis thy ginnes to defend;
        Bot all thy senyes sall not availl the,   1995
        About the busk with wayis thocht thow wend;
        Falset will failye ay at the latter end;

Thus I give you the best advice I can: bend when commanded, and do not wait until you burst.'

286   'Sir' (said the Fox), 'It is Lent now, as you see; I cannot fish, for fear of wetting my feet, to take a Stickleback; though we both should starve to death, I have no other means of getting my food. But were it Easter, when men can once more eat poultry, as Kids or Lambs or Capons in good condition, I would willingly accept the post.'

287   'Now' (said the Wolf, in anger), 'do you think to baffle me with tricks and many quibbles? Have no doubt—is it an old Dog you are trying to fool; you think to draw the straw before the Cat!' 'Sir' (said the Fox), 'God knows that is not my intention; were I to do such a thing, you would have good reason to hang me from a tree with a hangman's rope.

288   'But now I see he is a perfect fool who would fall into an argument with his master. I did but try to see what you would see; God knows, my mind was on another thing. I shall do your bidding in all things, whatever you order me, by night or day,' 'Well' (said the Wolf), 'I hear clearly what you say.

289   'But still I would like you to swear an oath to be true to me above all living beings.' 'Sir' said the Fox, 'that request distresses me, for now I see you have your doubts about me. Yet I shall swear, although there is no need: "By Jupiter, and on pain of losing my head, I shall be true to you until I am dead." '

290   Just then a Cadger with horse and saddlebaskets appeared, singing away; then Lawrence caught sight of him. The Fox recognized the smell of fresh herring, and secretively he whispered the smell of fresh herring, and secretively he whispered to the Wolf: 'Sir, those are herrings the Cadger carries by; and therefore I suggest we search for a plan to get some fish as provisions for these days of fasting.

291   'Since I am the Steward, I care that we should have some supplies; and you are out of money, I

To bow at bidding and byde not quhill thow brest,
Thairfoir I giff the counsall ffor the best.'

287 'Schir' said the Foxe, 'it is Lentring, ye se; 2000
I can nocht fische, ffor weiting off my feit,
To tak ane Banestikill; thocht we baith suld de;
I have nane uther craft to win my meit.
Bot wer it Pasche, that men suld pultrie eit,
As Kiddis, Lambis, or Caponis in to ply, 2005
To beir your office than wald I not set by.'

287 'Than' said the Wolff in wraith, 'wenis thow with wylis
And with mony mowis me to mat?
It is ane auld Dog, doutles, that thow begylis;
Thow wenis to draw the stra befoir the cat!' 2010
'Schir' (said the Foxe), 'God wait, I mene not that;
For and I did, it wer weill worth that ye
In ane reid Raip had tyit me till ane tre.

288 'Bot now I se he is ane fule perfay
That with his maister fallis in ressoning; 2015
I did bot till assay quhat ye wald say;
God wait, my mynd wes on ane uther thing;
I sall fulfill in all thing your bidding,
Quhat ever ye charge, on nichtis or on dayis.'
'Weill' (quod the Wolff), 'I heir weill quhat thow sayis. 2020

289 'Bot yit I will thow mak to me ane aith,
For to be leill attour all levand leid.'
'Schir' said the Foxe, 'that ane word make me wraith,
For now I se ye haif me at ane dreid;
Yit sall I sweir, suppois it be not neid: 2025
Be Juppiter, and on pane off my heid,
I sall be trew to you, quhill I be deid.'

290 With that ane Cadgear,° with capill and with creillis,
Come carpand ffurth; then Lawrence culd him spy.
The Foxe the flewer off the fresche hering feillis, 2030
And to the Wolff he roundis prively:
'Schir, yone ar hering the Cadgear caryis by;
Thairfoir I reid that we se ffor sum wayis
To get sum fische aganis thir fasting dayis.

291 'Sen I am Stewart, I wald we had sum stuff, 2035
And ye ar silver seik, I wait richt weill;

am quite sure. Were we to beg, that truly churlish
Clown would not give us a single herring from
his creels, even if we knelt before him on our
knees. But yet I trust that you will soon see if I
can manage to blear that fellow's eye.

292 'One thing more, Sir: for us to get some of that
merchandise, you must do some work and lend a
hand; for he that will not labor and help himself
in times like these is not worth a fly. I also plan
to work as busily as a bee; and you shall follow a
little ways behind and gather the herring; for that
will be your job.'

293 With that he made a detour far around and lay
himself down in the middle of the road; and he
pretended to be dead, without any question; and
there he lay stretched out, no pretty sight. The
whites of both his eyes were turned up; his tongue
hung out of his mouth a hand's breadth; and he
lay still, as stiff as if he were dead.

294 The Cadger found the Fox and was overjoyed;
and softly to himself he said, 'When next we
stop, in faith, you shall be flayed, and from your
skin I shall make a pair of mittens.' He leapt
about him lightly where he lay, and danced about
on his toes all over the road; he carried on as if
he heard a piper play.

295 'Here' (he said) 'lies the Devil, dead in a ditch. I
have not seen such a marvel these seven years. I
imagine you have been tussling about with some
dog, who has caused you to lie so still without
stirring. Sir Fox, in faith, you are dearly welcome
here; I imagine it must be some wife's curse for
stealing poultry that has descended on you now.

296 'No pedlar shall weedle this skin of yours from me
in exchange for a purse nor gloves nor even laces.
With it I shall make mittens for my hands, to
warm them up wherever I may be. Never shall it
sail the sea to Flanders.' With that, he swiftly
grabbed him by the heels, and with a heave he
swung him up onto the creels.

Thocht we wald thig, yone verray Churlische chuff,
He will not giff ane hering off his Creill,
Befoir yone Churle on kneis thocht we wald kneill;
Bot yit I trou alsone that ye sall se, 2040
Giff I can craft to bleir yone Carllis Ee.

292 'Schir, ane thing is, and we get off yone pelff,
Ye man tak travell and mak us sum supple;
For he that will not laubour and help him selff,
In to thir dayis he is not worth ane fle;° 2045
I think to work als besie as ane Be.
And ye sall follow ane lytill efterwart
And gadder hering, ffor that sall be your part.'

293 With that he kest ane cumpass ffar about,
And straucht him doun in middis off the way; 2050
As he wer deid he fenyeit him, but dout,
And than upon lenth unliklie lay;
The quhyte he turnit up off his Ene tway;
His toung out hang ane handbreid off his heid,
And still he lay, als straucht as he wer deid.° 2055

294 The Cadgear fand the Foxe, and he was fane,
And till him self thus softlie can he say:
'At the nixt bait, in Faith, ye sall be flane,
And off your skyn I sall mak mittennis tway.'
He lap full lichtlie about him quhair he lay, 2060
And all the trace he trippit on his tais;
As he had hard ane pyper play, he gais.

295 'Heir lyis the Devyll' (quod he), 'deid in ane dyke.°
Sic ane selcouth saw I not this sevin yeir;
I trow ye have bene tussillit with sum tyke, 2065
That garris you ly sa still withouttin steir;
Schir Foxe, in Faith, ye ar deir welcum heir;
It is sum wyfis malisone, I trow,
For pultrie pyking, that lychtit hes on yow.

296 'Thair sall na Pedder, for purs, nor yit for gluifis, 2070
Nor yit ffor poyntis pyke your pellet ffra me;
I sall of it mak mittennis to my lufis,
Till hald my handis hait quhair ever I be;
Till Flanderis° sall it never saill the se.'
With that in hy, he hint him be the heillis, 2075
And with ane swak he swang him on the creillis.°

297   Then briskly he led the horse by the head. The de-
        ceitful Fox noticed the Cadger's attention was oc-
        cupied; and with his teeth he tugged on the stop-
        per until he had succeeded in pulling it out; and
        then one by one he heaved the herring out of the
        creels and threw a great many down. The Wolf
        was ready and quickly gathered them in; from
        above the Cadger sang, 'The hunt is up, is up!'

298   But at a stream the Cadger looked around; at that
        the Fox jumped clear away from the baskets. The
        Cadger would have given the Fox a blow, but all
        in vain; the Fox made it home that day. Then
        with a shout the Cadger said: 'Stay awhile, and
        you shall have a Nekhering that is worth my
        horse, my creels, and all the rest.'

299   'Now curses on me' (said the Fox) 'if we meet
        again. I heard what you promised to do with my
        skin. Your hands will never warm themselves
        in those mittens; would you were hanged, Churl,
        and all your kin! Go look to your trading—for
        you'll make no profit by me—and sell the herring
        you have at the highest price, or else you'll
        make no profit from your merchandise.'

300   The Cadger trembled for anger on the spot where
        he stood: 'It serves me right' (he said) 'that this
        mongrel got away, for I had nothing useful close
        at hand as a staff or pole to hit the beggar with.'
        At that he deftly leapt up over the ditch and cut
        himself a staff that was stout and taken from a
        green Holly, for he was angry.

301   With that the Fox returned again to the Wolf
        and found him lying down next to the herring.
        'Sir' (he then said), 'Did I not defend myself well?
        A strong man never wants if he is wise; and a
        hardy heart is hard to surprise.' (Then said the
        Wolf), 'You are a very bold fellow, and wise when
        you wish to be, if the truth be told.

302   'But what was that the Churl cried out so loudly,
        shaking his fist?' he asked; 'Do you know?' 'Sir'

297   Syne be the heid the hors in hy hes hint;
      The fraudfull Foxe thairto gude tent hes tane,
      And with his teith the stoppell, or he stint,
      Pullit out, and syne the hering ane and ane   2080
      Out of the creillis he swakkit doun gude wane.
      The Wolff wes war and gadderit spedilie;
      The Cadgear sang, 'Huntis up, up'° upon hie.

298   Yit at ane burne the Cadgear luikit about;
      With that the Foxe lap quyte the creillis ffray;   2085
      The Cadgear wald haif raucht the Foxe ane rout,
      Bo all ffor nocht, he wan his hoill that day.
      Than with ane schout thus can the Cadgear say:
      'Abyde, and thou ane Nekhering° sall haif,
      Is worth my Capill, Creillis, and all the laif.'   2090

299   'Now' (quod the Foxe), 'I schrew me and we meit!
      I hard quhat thow hecht to do with my skyn.
      Thy handis sall never in thay mittinnis tak heit,
      And thow wer hangit, Carll, and all thy kyn!
      Do furth thy mercat; at me thou sall nocht wyn;   2095
      And sell thy hering thow hes thair till hie price,
      Ellis thow sall wyn nocht on thy merchandice.'

300   The Cadgear trimillit for teyne quhair that he stude;
      'It is weill worthie' (quod he) 'I want yone tyke,
      That had nocht in my hand sa mekill gude   2100
      As staff or sting yone truker ffor to stryke.'
      With that lychtlie he lap out over ane dyke
      And hakkit doun ane staff, ffor he wes tene,
      That hevie wes and off the Holyne grene.

301   With that the Foxe unto the Wolff could wend,   2105
      And fand him be the hering, quhair he lyis;
      'Schir' (said he than), 'maid I not fair defend?
      Ane wicht man wantit never, and he wer wyis:
      Ane hardie hart is hard for to suppryis.'
      (Than said the Wolff): 'thow art ane Berne full bald,   2110
      And wyse at will, in gude tyme be it tald.

302   'Bot quhat wes yone the Carll cryit on hie,
      And schuke his hand,' quod he, 'hes thou no feill?'

(said the Fox), 'that I can tell you truly; he said the
Nekhering was still in the basket.' 'Do you know
of that herring?' 'Yes, Sir, I know it well, and at
the edge of the creel I had it three times for sure;
but the sheer weight of it nearly tore out my teeth.

303   'Now truly, Sir, if we could capture that herring,
       it would be fish enough for all these forty days.'
       (Then said the Wolf), 'Now God let me be hanged,
       but just to be there I would give all my clothes, to see
       if my teeth are strong enough to lift it.' 'Sir' (said
       the Fox), 'God knows I wished for you often
       when I did not have the strength to pull it out.

304   'It is a side of Salmon, or very like, and fresh as
       could be, wet and glossy as a Partridge's eye. It is
       well worth all the herring you have there; indeed,
       if we had it for sure, it is worth three of these.'
       'Then' (said the Wolf), 'what counsel do you give
       me?' 'Sir' (the Fox replied), 'act according to my
       plans and you shall have it, if you come to no harm.

305   'First you must make a detour far around, then
       stretch yourself out in the middle of the road; both
       head and feet and tail you must stretch out; let your
       tongue hang out, and tightly close both your eyes.
       Then see you lay your head down on a hard spot; and
       be not afraid of any danger that may appear, but keep
       yourself completely still when the Churl comes near.

306   'And even should you see a club, have no fear,
       but keep wonderfully still on that spot; and see
       your eyes be closed as if they were out, and look
       you twitch neither foot nor head. Then will this
       churlish Cadger believe you are dead, and then at
       once he will grab you by the heels, as he did me,
       and heave you up onto his creels.'

307   'Now' (said the Wolf), 'I swear to you by my luck,
       I believe that Carl will not be able to lift me.'
       'Sir' (said the Fox), 'He will lift you way up onto
       his baskets, and it will cause him little trouble.
       But one thing I can swear to you in truth: If you
       can get that herring safely to some place, you will
       not have to go fishing again until Easter.

'Schir' (said the Foxe), 'that I can tell trewlie;
He said the Nekhering wes in till the creill.'   2115
'Kennis thow that hering?' 'Ye, Schir, I kin it weill,
And at the creill mouth I had it thryis but doubt;
The wecht off it neir tit my tuskis out.

303   'Now, suithlie, Schir, micht we that hering fang,
It wald be fische to us thir fourtie dayis,'°   2120
Than (said the Wolff), 'Now God nor that I hang,
Bot to be thair, I wald gif all my clays,
To se gif that my wappinnis mycht it rais.'
'Schir' (said the Foxe), 'God wait, I wischit you oft,
Quhen that my pith micht not beir it on loft.   2125

304   'It is ane syde off Salmond, as it wair,
And callour, pypand lyke ane Pertrik Ee;
It is worth all the hering ye have thair,
Ye, and we had it swa, is it worth sic thre.'
'Than' (said the Wolff) 'quhat counsell gevis thou me?'   2130
'Schir' (said the Foxe), wirk efter my devyis
And ye sall have it, and tak you na suppryis.

305   'First, ye man cast ane cumpas far about,
Syne straucht you doun in middis of the way;
Baith heid and feit and taill ye man streik out,   2135
Hing furth your toung, and clois weill your Ene tway;
Syne se your heid on ane hard place ye lay;
And dout not for na perrell may appeir,
Bot hald you clois, quhen that the Carll cummis neir.

306   'And thocht ye se ane staf, have ye na dout,   2140
Bot hald you wonder still in to that steid;
And luke your Ene be clois, as thay wer out,
And se that ye schrink nouther fute nor heid;
Than will the Cadgear Carll trow ye be deid,
And in till haist will hint you be the heillis   2145
As he did me, and swak you on his creillis.

307   'Now' (quod the Wolff), 'I sweir the be my thrift,
I trow yone Cadgear Carll dow not me beir.'
'Schir' (said the Foxe), 'on loft he will you lift,
Upon his Creillis, and do him lytill deir.   2150
Bot ane thing dar I suithlie to you sweir:
Get ye that hering sicker in sum place,
Ye sall not fair in fisching mair quhill Pasche.

308   'I will say the *In Principio* on you and cross your
body from head to toe. Go whenever you will, I
dare to guarantee that you shall die no sudden
death this day.' With that the Wolf prepared
himself and went and made a large detour about
the Cadger; then he stretched himself out in the
road, before the Carl approached.

309   Firmly he laid the side of his head securely on the
ground, stretched his four feet from him and his
head, and hung his tongue out as the Fox would
have him. He lay as still as if he truly were dead,
without a care for the Cadger's favor or anger,
but he was thinking ever on the Nekhering and
quite forgot the Fox and all his tricks.

309   Then the Cadger, as angry as the wind, came
riding on his catch, for it was light, thinking ever
on the Fox that was behind, and upon the ways
he might best avenge himself. And finally he
caught sight of the Wolf, where he lay all stretched
out in the road; but if he lighted down or not,
God knows!

311   Under his breath he said, 'Once I was tricked; if I
be tricked again, then curses on us both. The evil
that shall light upon your bones should have
come to the one that did me harm.' He raised his
club on high, for he was angry, and hit him on
the head with such force that the Wolf near
swooned and died right then and there.

312   Three blows he took before he could get to his
feet, but yet the Wolf was strong and managed to
escape. He could not see, he was so thoroughly
blinded, nor tell easily if it was night or day. The
Fox observed this happen from where he lay and
laughed aloud when he saw the Wolf, both deaf
and dazed, fall swooning to his knees.

313   He that cannot be content with a reasonable amount
but covets all deserves to forfeit all. When he saw
the Wolf had been undone, the Fox said to himself, 'These herring shall be mine.' I would be
lying if I did not say he was most cunning who

308   'I sall say In *principio*° upon yow,
       And crose your corps from the top to tay;   2155
       Wend quhen you will, I dar be warrand now
       That ye sall de na suddan deith this day.'
       With that the Wolff gird up sone and to gay,
       And caist ane cumpas about the Cadgear far;
       Syne raucht him in the gait, or he come nar.   2160

309   He laid his halfheid sicker hard and sad,
       Syne straucht his four feit ffra him, and his heid,
       And hang his toung furth as the Foxe him bad;
       Als styll he lay, as he war verray deid,
       Rakkand na thing off the Carlis ffavour nor feid,   2165
       Bot ever upon the Nekhering he thinkis,
       And quhyte forgettis the Foxe and all his wrinkis.

310   With that the Cadgear, als wraith as ony wind,
       Come rydand on the laid, for it wes licht,°
       Thinkand ay on the Foxe that wes behind,   2170
       Upon quhat wyse revenge him best he micht;
       And at the last of the Wolff gat ane sicht,
       Quhair he in lenth lay streikit in the gait;
       Bot giff he lichtit doun or nocht, God wait!

311   Softlie he said, 'I wes begylit anis;   2175
       Be I begylit twyis, I schrew us baith,
       That evill bot it sall licht upon thy banis,
       He suld have had that hes done me the skaith.'
       On hicht he hovit the staf, ffor he wes wraith,
       And hit him with sic will upon the heid,   2180
       Quhill neir he swonit and swelt in to that steid.

312   Thre battis he bure, or he his feit micht find,
       Bot yit the Wolff wes wicht, and wan away.
       He mycht not se, he wes sa verray blind,°
       Nor wit reddilie quhether it was nicht or day.   2185
       The Foxe beheld that service quhair he lay,
       And leuch on loft, quhen he the Wolff sa seis,
       Baith deif and dosinnit, fall swonand on his kneis.

313   He that of ressoun can not be content,
       Bot covetis all, is abill all to tyne.   2190
       The Foxe, quhen that he saw the Wolf wes schent,
       Said to him self, 'thir hering sall be myne;'
       I le, or ellis he wes efterwart fyne

found such ways to bring his master to grief. With
all the fish, thus Lawrence took his leave.

314   The Wolf was nearly beaten to death, so that he
barely got away with his life, for his skull was
cracked by the club. Then hastily the Fox returned to his den, having betrayed both his
master and the man: the latter lacked the herring
from his creels, and the former's blood was running down to his heels.

MORALITAS

315   This tale is blended with morality, as I shall show
in part before I cease. The Fox may be likened to
the World, this thieving Wolf assuredly to a
Man, and the Carl to Death, against whom all
must struggle. Whoever was born must in the
course of nature die, both men and beast and fish
that live in the sea.

316   The world, you know, is Steward to the man, and
causes him to have no awareness of death, but
rather turns all his ingenuity towards earthly gain.
The herring I compare to shining gold, which
made the Wolf expose his head to danger; in just
this way gold causes lands and cities to be wasted
with war, as men can daily see.

317   And as the Fox with dissembling and guile caused
the Wolf to believe he would be true forever, just
so this world with vain glory flatters folk into
thinking for awhile that they will never fail; yet
often men will see it suddenly vanish. For those
who think they can often fill the sack, Death
comes from behind and nips them by the neck.

318   The might of gold makes many men so blind,
who set all their happiness on the hope of possessions, that they forget the Cadger is coming from
behind to strike them, no matter of what estate
they be. What is more dark than blind prosperity?
Wherefore I counsel mighty men to think of the
Nekhering, interpreted in this way.

That fand sic wayis his Maister for to greif;
With all the fische thus Lowrence tuke his leif.   2195

314   The Wolff wes neir weill dungin to the deid,
That uneith with his lyfe away he wan,
For with the Bastoun weill brokin wes his heid.
The Foxe in to his den sone drew him than,
That had betraisit his Maister and the man: 2200
The ane wantit the hering off his creillis,
The utheris blude wes rynnand over his heillis.

MORALITAS

315   This Taill is myngit with Moralitie,
As I sall schaw sumquhat, or that I ceis;
The Foxe unto the warld may likkinit be;   2205
The revand Wolf unto ane man but leis;
The Cadgear Deith, quhome under all men preis—
That ever tuke lyfe throw cours of kynd man dee,
As men, and beist, and fische in to the see.

316   The warld, ye wait, is Stewart to the man,   2210
Quhilk makis man to haif na mynd of Deid,
Bot settis for winning all the craftis thay can;
The Hering I likkin unto the gold sa reid,°
Quhilk gart the Wolf in perrell put his heid;
Richt swa the gold garris Landis and Cieteis   2215
With weir be waistit, daylie as men seis.

317   And as the Foxe with dissimulance and gyle
Gart the Wolff wene to haif worschip for ever,
Richt swa this warld with vane glore for ane quhyle
Flatteris with folk, as thay suld failye never;   2220
Yit suddandlie men seis it oft dissever;
With thame that trowis oft to fill the sek,
Deith cummis behind and nippis thame be the nek.

318   The micht of gold makis mony men sa blind,
That settis on Avarice thair felicitie,   2225
That thay forget the Cadgear cummis behind
To stryke thame, of quhat stait sa ever thay be.
Quhat is mair dirk than blind prosperitie?
Quhairfoir I counsell mychtie men to haif mynd
Of the Nekhering, Interpreit in this kynd.   2230

The Tale of the Fox that Beguiled the Wolf
by the Reflection of the Moon

319 In the days of our elders, as Aesop has told us,
there was a Farmer who had a plough which he
worked. His custom was ever to rise early in the
morning; and thus it happened that at the beginning of the ploughing season, early in the morning, he followed the path he had marked to his
plough, accompanied only by his Goadsman. He
put his young Oxen to work with '*Benedicite.*'

320 The Teamster shouted loudly: 'Ho there! March on!
Pull straight, my hearties!' Then he prodded them
with vigor. The Oxen were inexperienced, young and
light-hearted, and in their high spirits they ruined
the furrow. This made the Farmer angry as a hare;
he shouted, and threw his pattle and large rocks at
them, saying 'The Wolf can have the whole lot of you.'

321 But the Wolf was nearer than he thought, for in a
bush he lay, together with Lawrence, in a thorny
thicket that was at the furrow's end, and they heard
the oath. Then Lawrence gave a quick laugh and
said, 'To take that gift would be no harm.' 'Well'
(said the Wolf), 'I swear to you by my hand: that
fellow's word will stand as if he were King.'

322 At last the Oxen behaved in a more orderly
fashion. Eventually they unyoked them, since it
was getting late; the Farmer started homeward
with his cattle. Then the Wolf came limping (as
is his wont) in front of the Oxen and prepared to
cause some trouble. The Farmer saw him and was
somewhat stunned and would have retreated with
his animals, had he been able.

323 The Wolf said, 'Where are you taking these
stolen animals? I lay claim to them, for none of
them is yours.' This threw the man into a deadly
fright, and solemnly he then replied to the Wolf:
'Sir, by my soul, these Oxen belong to me; and
therefore I wonder why it is you stop me, since
truly I have never done you injury.'

319   In elderis dayis, as Esope can declair,
        Thair wes ane Husband quhilk had ane pleuch to steir.°
        His use wes ay in morning to ryse air;
        Sa happinnit him in streiking tyme of yeir
        Airlie in the morning to follow ffurth his feir   2235
        Unto the pleuch,° bot his gadman° and he;
        His stottis he straucht with 'Benedicite.'°

320   The Caller° cryit: 'How! Haik!' upon hicht,
        'Hald draucht, my dowis'; syne broddit thame ffull sair.
        The Oxin wes unusit, young, and licht,   2240
        And ffor fersnes they couth the fur fforfair.
        The Husband than woxe angrie as ane hair,
        Syne cryit, and caist his Patill° and grit stanis:
        'The Wolff' (quod he) 'mot have yow all at anis.'

321   Bot yit the Wolff wes neirar nor he wend,   2245
        For in ane busk he lay, and Lowrence baith,
        In ane Rouch Rone, wes at the furris end,
        And hard the hecht; than Lowrence leuch full raith:
        'To tak yone bud' (quod he) 'it wer na skaith.'
        'Weill' (quod the Wolff), 'I hecht the be my hand;   2250
        Yone Carllis word, as he wer King, sall stand.'

322   The Oxin waxit mair reullie at the last;
        Syne efter thay lousit ffra that it worthit weill lait;
        The Husband hamewart with his cattell past.
        Than sone the Wolff come hirpilland in his gait   2255
        Befoir the Oxin, and schupe to mak debait.
        The Husband saw him and worthit sumdeill agast,
        And bakwart with his beistis wald haif past.

323   The Wolff said, 'quhether dryvis thou this Pray?
        I chalenge it, ffor nane off thame ar thyne.'   2260
        The man thairoff wes in ane felloun fray,
        And soberlie to the Wolff answerit syne:
        'Schir, be my Saull, thir Oxin ar all myne;
        Thairfoir I studdie quhy ye suld stop me,
        Sen that I faltit never to you, trewlie.'   2265

324   The Wolf said, 'Carl, did you not give this team
       to me earlier, when you were ploughing on that
       bank? And tell me, is there anything freer than
       gift? This stalling will deprive you of your thanks;
       far better it is freely to give a pittance than to be
       compelled to hand over a fattened ox. Fie on
       generosity that comes not from the heart!'

325   'Sir' (said the Farmer), 'A man may say something
       in anger and then change his mind when he has
       thought it over. If I make an oath to steal, am I
       therefore a thief? God forbid, Sir, all promises
       should be held as binding! Did I give my hand or
       make my bond?' (he asked): 'or have you a
       witness, or something in writing to show? Sir, do
       not rob me, but go seek redress by the Law!'

326   'Carl' (said the Wolf), 'A Lord, if he is honest
       and shrinks from shameful things and fears re-
       proval, his word is ever as reliable as his seal. Fie
       on that man that is not honest and praiseworthy!
       Your argument is false, and also contrived, for it
       is said in *Proverbs*: "Without loyalty, all other vir-
       tues are not worth a fly." '

327   'Sir' (said the Farmer), 'Remember this one thing:
       a true man is not taken in by half a story. I may
       say something and then retract it; I am no king.
       Where is your witness that heard me promise them
       all?' The Wolf replied, 'My claim will not fail for
       that; Lawrence' (he said), 'Come out of that
       thicket, and tell us only what you heard and saw.'

328   Lawrence came creeping, for he never loved the
       light, and soon appeared before them. The Farmer
       had no cause to laugh when he saw that sight. The
       Wolf said, 'Lawrence, you must tell what you know,
       from which we shall easily demonstrate the truth. I
       call on you to bear witness to the truth; what promise
       did you hear this man make to me a while ago?'

329   'Sir' (said the Fox), 'I cannot give you, with undue
       haste, at this very moment, a final judgment; but
       if you would both submit yourselves here to me,
       and agree to abide by my decision without appeal,
       I shall try to please you both, if it can be done.'

324   The Wolff said, 'Carle, gaif thou not me this drift°
       Airlie, quhen thou wes eirrand on yone bank?
       And is thair oucht (sayis thou) frear than gift?'
       This tarying wyll tyne the all thy thank;
       Far better is frelie ffor to giff ane plank   2270
       Nor be compellit on force to giff ane mart.
       Fy on the fredome that cummis not with hart!'

325   'Schir' (quod the Husband), 'ane man may say in
              greif,
       And syne ganesay, fra he advise and se.
       I hecht to steill, am I thairfoir ane theif?°   2275
       God forbid, Schir, all hechtis suld haldin be!
       Gaif I my hand or oblissing' (quod he),
       'Or have ye witnes or writ ffor to schaw?
       Schir, reif me not, but go and seik the law!'

326   'Carll' (quod the Wolff), 'ane Lord, and he be leill,   2280
       That schrinkis for schame, or doutis to be repruvit,
       His saw is ay als sickker as his Seill.
       Fy on the Leid that is not leill and lufit!
       Thy argument is fals and eik contrufit,
       For it is said in Proverb:° "But lawte   2285
       All uther vertewis ar nocht worth ane fle." '

327   'Schir' said the husband, 'remember of this thing:
       Ane leill man is not tane at halff ane tail.
       I may say, and ganesay; I am na King:°
       Quhair is your witnes that hard I hecht thame haill?'   2290
       Than said the Wolff, 'thairfoir it sall nocht faill;
       Lowrence' (quod he), 'cum hidder of that Schaw,
       And say na thing bot as thow hard and saw.'°

328   Lowrence come lourand, for he lufit never licht,°
       And sone appeirit befoir thame in that place: 2295
       The man leuch na thing quhen he saw that sicht.
       'Lowrence' (quod the Wolff), 'thow man declair this cace,
       Quhairof we sall schaw the suith in schort space;
       I callit on the leill witnes for to beir:
       Quhat hard thow that this man hecht me lang eir?'   2300

329   'Schir' (said the Tod), 'I can not hastelie
       Swa sone as now gif sentence finall;°
       Bot wald ye baith submit yow heir to me,
       To stand at my decreit perpetuall,
       To pleis baith I suld preif, gif it may fall.'   2305

'Well' (said the Wolf), 'for my part I am content.'
The man said, 'So am I, whatever the outcome.'

330   Then they both submitted their cases frankly, and
       both set forth their pleas to him in full. Lawrence
       said, 'Now I am a judge agreed to by both: You
       shall be sworn to stand by my decree, whether
       hereafter you think it bitter or sweet.' The Wolf
       stretched forth his foot, the man his hand, and
       on the Fox's tail they swore compliance.

331   Then Lawrence took the man off to one side and
       said to him, 'Friend, you have committed a
       blunder. The Wolf will not remit a single oxhide.
       I myself would like to help you if I might; but I
       am loath to go against my conscience. Do not
       lose your claim by defending it yourself; this will
       not be settled without great cost and expense.

332   'Do you not see how bribes can help a man through,
       and how gifts can help make crooked matters
       straight? Sometimes a hen secures for a man his
       cow. Not all who raise their hands to heaven are
       holy.' 'Sir' (said the man), 'You shall have six or
       seven of the very fattest hens of all the flock; I care
       not for the rest, if you but leave me the cock.'

333   'I am really a Judge' (said Lawrence then, and
       laughed). 'No bribe should distract me from the path
       of righteousness; I may take the hens and capons
       well enough because God has gone to sleep; as for
       the doings of this night, small things such as
       these do not come to His attention. These hens'
       (he said) 'shall secure your case for you, for with
       empty hand no man should lure the hawk.'

334   This having been settled, Lawrence then took
       leave and went straightaway to the Wolf. Then
       privately he plucked him by the sleeve: 'Are you
       serious in pursuing this claim?' (he asked); 'No, by
       my soul, I believe you must be joking.' Then the
       Wolf said, 'Lawrence, who do you say this? You
       heard for yourself the promise that he made.'

335   'The oath' (said he) 'this man made while he was
       ploughing—is that the basis on which you claim

'Weill' (quod the Wolff), 'I am content for me.'
The man said, 'swa am I, how ever it be.'

330   Than schew thay furth thair allegeance but fabill,
And baith proponit thair pley to him compleit.
(Quod Lowrence): 'now I am ane Juge amycabill.°   2310
Ye sall be sworne to stand at my decreit,
Quhether heirefter ye think it soure or sweit.'
The Wolff braid furth his fute, the man his hand,
And on the Toddis Taill sworne thay ar to stand.

331   Than tuke the Tod the man furth till ane syde,   2315
And said him, 'friend, thow° art in blunder brocht;
The Wolff will not forgif the ane Oxe hyde,
Yit wald my self fane help the, and I mocht;
Bot I am laith to hurt my conscience ocht.
Tyne nocht thy querrell in thy awin defence;   2320
This will not throw but grit coist and expence.

332   'Seis thow not Buddis beiris Bernis throw,
And giftis garris crukit materis hald ffull evin?
Suntymis ane hen haldis ane man in ane Kow.
All ar not halie that heifis thair handis to hevin.'   2325
'Schir' (said the man), 'ye sall have sex or sevin
Richt off the fattest hennis off all the floik;
I compt not all the laif, leif me the Coik.'

333   'I am ane Juge'° (quod Lowrence than, and leuch);
'Thair is na Buddis suld beir me by the rycht;   2330
I may tak hennis and caponis weill aneuch,
For God is gane to sleip;° as ffor this nycht,
Sic small thingis ar not sene in to his sicht;
Thir hennis' (quod he) 'sall mak thy querrell sure;
With emptie hand na man suld Halkis lure.'   2335

334   Concordit thus, than Lowrence tuke his leiff,
And to the Wolff he went in to ane ling;
Syne prevelie he plukkit him be the sleiff:
'Is this in ernist' (quod he) 'ye ask sic thing?
Na, be my Saull, I trow it be in heithing.'   2340
Than said the Wolff, 'Lowrence, quhy sayis thow sa?
Thow hard the hecht thy selff that he couth ma.'

335   'The hecht' (quod he) 'yone man maid at the pleuch,
Is that the cause quhy ye the cattell craif?'

these cattle?' In a jesting tone then Lawrence continued, and laughed: 'Sir, by the Rood, you really are
ranting and raving. By the Devil, for all your trouble
you won't win even an oxtail. How could I take it upon
my conscience to do offense to such a poor man as that?

336   'Yet I have communicated with the Carl,' (he said);
'we have agreed to the following arrangement:
Quit all your claims, and if you make him free, he
shall give you in return a great Cheese, the like of
which shall not be found in all this land, for it is
Summer Cheese, both fresh and fair. He says it
weighs a stone, and somewhat more.'

337   'Is that what you advise I do,' (asked the Wolf),
'that I should let this Carl go free for a great Cheese?'
'Yes, by my soul, and if I had sworn you an oath, no
other counsel would you have had from me. For
should you take this case to its furthest extreme, it
would not win for you the value of a withered turnip.
Don't you know, Sir, that I have a soul to protect?'

338   'Well' (said the Wolf), 'It is not to my liking that
this fellow should go free for a great Cheese.' 'Sir'
(said the Fox), 'you must not take this badly, for
by my soul you yourself had all the blame.'
'Then' (the Wolf replied), 'I will no longer argue;
but I would see this Cheese of such great value.'
'Sir' (said the Fox), 'he told me where it lies.'

339   Then hand in hand they went up to a hill. The
Farmer was making his way back home, which he
was eager to do; he had escaped their evil, and on
his feet he stood guard at the door until dawn.
Now we will turn back to the other two. Through
wild woods these creatures went on foot, from
bush to bush, till midnight came and went.

340   Lawrence was ever concocting tricks and
stratagems whereby he could fool the Wolf. He
was starting to regret that he had promised the
Cheese, but finally he was able to devise a hoax;
and then he smiled to himself with pleasure. The
Wolf said, 'Lawrence, you're playing Blind-man's-
bluff; we search all night, but nothing do we find.'

Halff in to heithing (said Lowrence than), and leuch: 2345
'Schir, be the Rude, unroikit now ye raif;
The Devill ane stirk taill thairfoir sall ye haif;
Wald I tak it upon my conscience
To do sa pure ane man as yone offence?

336   'Yit haif I communit with the Carll' (quod he);   2350
'We ar concordit upon this cunnand:
Quyte off all clamis, swa ye will mak him fre,
Ye sall ane Cabok have in to your hand
That sic ane sall not be in all this land;
For it is Somer Cheis,° baith fresche and ffair;   2355
He sayis it weyis ane stane,° and sumdeill mair.'

337   'Is that thy counsell' (quod the Wolff) 'I do,
That yone Carll ffor ane Cabok suld be fre?'
'Ye, be my Saull, and I wer sworne yow to,
Ye suld nane uther counsell have for me;   2360
For gang ye to the maist extremitie,
It will not wyn yow worth ane widderit neip;
Schir, trow ye not, I have ane Saull to keip?'

338   'Weill' (quod the Wolff), 'it is aganis my will
That yone Carll for ane Cabok suld ga quyte.'   2365
'Schir' (quod the Tod), 'ye tak it in nane evill,
For, be my Saull, your self had all the wyte.'
'Than' (said the Wolf) 'I bid na mair to flyte;
Bot I wald se yone Cabok off sic pryis.'
'Schir' (said the Tod), 'he tauld me quhair it lyis.'   2370

339   Than hand in hand thay held unto ane hill;
The Husband till his hous hes tane the way,
For he wes fane; he schaipit ffrom thair ill,
And on his feit woke the dure quhill day.
Now will we turne vnto the uther tway.   2375
Throw woddis waist thir Freikis on fute can fair,
Fra busk to busk, quhill neir midnycht and mair.

340   Lowrence wes ever remembring upon wrinkis
And subtelteis the Wolff for to begyle;
That he had hecht ane Caboik, he forthinkis,   2380
Yit at the last he findis furth ane wyle,
Than at him selff softlie couth he smyle.
The Wolff sayis, 'Lowrence, thow playis bellie blind;
We seik all nycht, bot na thing can we find.'

341   'Sir' (said the Fox), 'We are almost there; keep
calm a while longer and you shall see it soon.'
Shortly they came to a manor house; the night
was bright, the moon full and round as a penny.
Then without delay these fine fellows went to a
well, where two buckets were hanging side by
side; as one came up, the other would go down.

342   The reflection of the moon shone in the well.
'Sir' (said Lawrence), 'for once you shall find me
true. Now do you not clearly see the Cheese for
yourself, white as a turnip and round as a seal? He
lowered it down there so no one could steal it.
Sir, believe it: that Cheese you see down there
could be a gift for any Lord or King.'

343   'Ah' (said the Wolf), 'If I could have that Cheese
up on dry land as I see it down there, I would free
the Carl from paying all the rest. I consider his
puny Oxen not worth a fly; that Cheese is more
fitting for such a man as I. Lawrence,' (he said),
'jump quickly into this bucket, and I shall hold
onto the other until you have finished.'

344   Lawrence leapt in quickly and with skill; the
other remained above and held the crank.
'It is so large' (said Lawrence) 'it has the better of
me. On all my toes it has not left a claw. You
must help me pull it up. Quickly, jump in the
other bucket and come right down here to give
me a hand.'

345   Then deftly the silly fellow leapt into the bucket. Without a doubt, his weight made the other bucket rise
up; the Fox was being drawn up as the Wolf descended.
Then angrily the Wolf cried out at him: 'When I am
coming down like this, why are you going upwards?'
'Sir' (replied the Fox), 'that is how it goes with Fortune: as one comes up, she wheels another down!'

346   The Wolf reached bottom in no time at all; the
Fox leapt to the land, as merry as a bell, and left
the Wolf in water up to his waist. I have no idea
who hauled him out of the well. Here ends the
Text; there is no more to tell. Yet men may find

341   'Schir' (said the Tod), 'we ar at it almaist;   2385
    Soft yow ane lytill, and ye sall se it sone.'
    Than to ane Manure place thay hyit in haist;
    The nicht wes lycht, and pennyfull the Mone.
    Than till ane draw well thir Senyeours past but hone,
    Quhair that twa bukkettis severall suithlie hang;   2390
    As ane come up, ane uther doun wald gang.

342   The schadow of the Mone schone in the well.
    'Schir' (said Lowrence), 'anis ye sall find me leill;
    Now se ye not the Caboik weill your sell,
    Quhyte as ane Neip and round als as ane seill?   2395
    He hang it yonder, that na man suld it steill.
    Schir, traist ye weill, yone Caboik ye se hing
    Micht be an present to ony Lord or King.'

343   'Aa' (quod the Wolff) 'mycht I yone Caboik haif
    On the dry land, as I it yonder se,   2400
    I wald quitclame the Carll of all the laif;
    His dart Oxin I compt thame not ane fle;
    Yone wer mair meit for sic ane man as me.
    Lowrence' (quod he), 'leip in the bukket sone,
    And I sall hald the ane, quhill thow have done.'   2405

344   Lowrence gird doun baith sone and subtellie;
    The uther baid abufe and held the flaill.
    'It is sa mekill' (quod Lowrence) 'it maisteris me;
    On all my tais it hes not left ane naill;
    Ye man mak help upwart, and it haill   2410
    Leip in the uther bukket haistelie
    And cum sone doun and mak me sum supple.'

345   Than lychtlie in the bukket lap the loun;
    His wecht but weir the uther end gart ryis;
    The Tod come hailland up, the Wolf yeid doun;   2415
    Than angerlie the Wolff upon him cryis:
    'I cummand thus dounwart, quhy thow upwart hyis?'
    'Schir' (quod the Foxe), 'thus fairis it off Fortoun:
    As ane cummis up, scho quheillis ane uther doun!'°

346   Than to the ground sone yeid the Wolff in haist;   2420
    The Tod lap on land, als blyith as ony bell,
    And left the Wolff in watter to the waist.
    Quha haillit him out, I wait not, off the well.
    Heir endis the Text; thair is na mair to tell.

a good morality in this work, though it be only a
Fable.

MORALITAS

347   This Wolf I liken to a wicked man, one who op-
        presses the poor in every place and with them
        picks all the quarrels that he can, by harshness,
        theft, and other wickedness. This Fox I call the
        Devil, in this case, inducing each man to run an
        unrighteous course, planning thereby to lock him
        in his chains.

348   The Farmer may be called a godly Man, with whom
        the Fiend finds fault (as scholars tell us), eager to
        tempt him in any way he can. The hens are works
        that from firm faith proceed; where such sprouts
        spread, the Devil there will not thrive, but re-
        turns again unto the wicked man. He is greatly
        disappointed that all his pains are for naught.

349   The wild woods, wherein the Wolf was tricked,
        are wicked riches, which all men strive to attain.
        Whoever trusts in such trumpery is often beguiled;
        for riches may be called the Devil's Net, which
        Satan has set for all who are sinful. Whoever,
        proud in pleasure, sets his trust therein, cannot
        easily recover without the aid of special grace.

350   The great Cheese may be called Covetice, which
        abundantly grows in the eye of many a man. Ac-
        cursed be the well of that wicked vice! For it is
        naught but fraud and fantasy, driving each man
        to leap into the buttery that draws him downward
        to the pains of Hell.—Christ keep all Christians
        from that wicked well!

Yit men may find ane gude moralitie 2425
In this sentence, thocht it ane Fabill be.

MORALITAS

347 This Wolff I likkin to ane wickit man,
Quhilk dois the pure oppres in everie place
And pykis at thame all querrellis that he can,
Be Rigour, reif, and uther wickitnes. 2430
The Foxe the Feind I call in to this cais,
Arctand ilk man to ryn unrychteous rinkis,
Thinkand thairthrow to lok him in his linkis.

348 The Husband may be callit ane godlie man°
With quhome the Feynd falt findes (as Clerkis reids), 2435
Besie to tempt him with all wayis that he can.
The hennis ar warkis that fra ferme faith proceidis:
Quhair sic sproutis spreidis, the evill spreit thair not speids,
Bot wendis vnto the wickit man agane;
That he hes tint his travell is full unfane. 2440

349 The wodds waist, quhairin wes the Wolff wyld,
Ar wickit riches, quhilk all men gaipis to get;
Quha traistis in sic Trusterie ar oft begyld;
For Mammon° may be callit the Devillis Net,
Quhilk Sathanas for all sinfull hes set. 2445
With proud plesour quha settis his traist thairin,
But speciall grace, lychtlie can not outwin.

350 The Cabok may be callit Covetyce,
Quhilk blomis braid in mony mannis Ee;
Wa worth the well of that wickit vyce! 2450
For it is all bot fraud and fantasie,
Dryvand ilk man to leip in the buttrie
That dounwart drawis unto the pane of hell.—
Christ keip all Christianis from that wickit well!

351   Aesop tells us that once long ago there was Shepherd dwelling near a forest who had a Hound that
was of great comfort to him. This Dog watched
over the fold at night so alertly and fearlessly that
no Wolf nor Wildcat dared to appear, nor Fox
from the field, nor any other beast, because the
Hound would slay them, or at least give chase.

352   It so happened (for life must end for every beast)
that this Hound died of a sudden sickness; and
then (God knows) the keeper of the flock, out of
true grief, grew thinner than the withered grass.
'Alas' (said he), 'now I see no way to save the
defenseless beasts I keep, for all my Sheep will be
killed by the Wolf.'

353   It would have made a man's heart sad to hear the
poor Shepherd's lamentation: 'Now is my darling
dead, alas' (he said); 'Now I must be prepared to
beg for my bread, and with pikestaff and pack to
leave the farmhouse; for all the beasts that before
were subdued now will attack my Sheep with
wrath and rage.'

354   Just then a Wether walked up to him with confidence. 'Master' (he said). 'Be merry and of good cheer;
to crack your heart will not cure your hurt; don't
waste any worry over a Dog that is dead. Go fetch
him hither, and straightaway flay off his skin; then
sew it on me; and see that it be properly measured,
both head and neck, body, tail, and feet.

355   'Then the Wolf will believe that I am he; for I
shall track him tenaciously, wherever he may travel.
I will assume entirely the care of guarding your
sheep at midday, morn, and eve. And if the Wolf
pursues a Sheep, by God, I shall not hesitate to
follow him as fast as did your Dog, so that, I guarantee, you shall not lose even the youngest Lamb.'

356   'Now this plan' said the Shepherd, 'comes from a
sensible mind; your advice is both loyal, sure, and

351   Qwhylum thair wes (as Esope can Report)   2455
       Ane scheipheird dwelland be ane Forrest neir,
       Quhilk had ane Hound that did him grit comfort;
       Full war he wes to walk his Fauld but weir,
       That nouther Wolff nor Wildcat durst appeir,
       Nor Foxe on feild, nor yit no uther beist,   2460
       Bot he thame slew or chaissit at the leist.

352   Sa happinnit it (as euerilk beist man de),
       The Hound off suddand seiknes to be deid;
       Bot than (God wait) the keipar off the fe
       For verray wo woxe wanner nor the weid.   2465
       'Allace' (quod he), 'now se I na remeid
       To saif the selie beistis that I keip,
       For with the Wolff weryit beis all my scheip.

353   It wald have maid ane mannis hart sair to se
       The selie scheiphirdis lamentatioun: 2470
       'Now is my Darling deid, allace,' (quod he);
       'For now to beg my breid I may be boun,
       With pyikstaff and with scrip to fair off toun;
       For all the beistis befoir that bandonit bene
       Will schute upon my beistis with Ire and tene.'   2475

354   With that ane Wedder° wichtlie wan on fute:
       'Maister' (quod he), 'mak merie and be blyith;
       To brek your hart ffor baill it is na bute;
       For ane deid Dogge ye na cair on yow kyith.
       Ga ffeche him hither and fla his skyn off swyth;   2480
       Syne sew it on me; and luke that it be meit,
       Baith heid and crag, bodie, taill, and feit.

355   'Than will the Wolff trow that I am he;
       For I sall follow him fast quhar ever he fair.
       All haill the cure I tak it upon me,   2485
       Your scheip to keip at midday, lait and air.
       And he persew, be God, I sall not spair
       To follow him as fast as did your Doig,
       Swa that, I warrand, ye sall not want ane hoig.'

356   'Than' said the scheipheird, 'this come of ane gude wit;   2490
       Thy counsall is baith sicker, leill, and trew;

true; whoever says all Sheep are stupid, he lies.'
With that he quickly stripped the skin from off
the Dog and sewed it on the Sheep with care.
This pelt produced some pride in the Wether:
'Now of the Wolf' he said 'I have no fear.'

357   He imitated the Dog in every way: he stood
watch all night long and took no sleep; thus, for a
long while not a Lamb was missing. So alert was
he and vigilant in guarding them that Lawrence
dared not even look upon a Sheep; for when he
did, the Wether chased him so fast that he made
him fear for his life.

358   There was neither Wolf nor Wildcat nor even Fox
that dared come anywhere within those bounds, but
he would chase them over ground both rough and
smooth. These woeful beasts feared greatly for their
lives because he was large and seemed to be stout; and
each and every beast dreaded him like death, so that
none would dare show his face within that wood.

359   And yet one day a hungry Wolf happened to creep
in among the Sheep as they lay in a field; 'I shall have
one' (he said), 'no matter what the danger, even
though I be killed, for otherwise I shall die of hunger.'
Saying that, he grabbed a Lamb with his claws.
The rest gave a start, so shocked were they all; but,
God knows, the Wether was quick to pursue him.

360   Never went a Hound more lively when loosed,
when running most recklessly after a Roe, than
went this Wether over bog and steam, stopping at
neither bank, bush, nor brae; but ever he followed fiercely on his foe with such a dash, while
dust and dirt enveloped him, and he made a vow
to God that he would capture him.

361   At that the Wolf ran so fast that his tail unfurled,
for he was weak from hunger and evening was
drawing near; and he forced himself to run with
all his might, for he saw the Wether catching up
to him. He feared for his life, should he be over-
taken; therefore he heeded neither bush nor bog,
for he was well aware of the fierceness of the Dog.

Quha sayis ane scheip is daft, thay lieit of it.'
With that in hy the Doggis skyn off he flew,
And on the scheip rycht softlie couth it sew.
Than worth the Wedder wantoun off his weid: 2495
'Now off the Wolff' (quod he) 'I have na dreid.'

357   In all thingis he counterfait the Dog;
       For all the nycht he stude, and tuke na sleip
       Swa that weill lang thair wantit not ane Hog.
       Swa war he wes and walkryfe thame to keip,   2500
       That Lowrence durst not luke upon ane scheip;
       For and he did, he followit him sa fast
       That off his lyfe he maid him all agast.

358   Was nowther Wolff, Wildcat, nor yit Tod
       Durst cum within thay boundis all about,   2505
       Bot he wald chase thame baith throw rouch and snod.
       Thay bailfull beistis had of thair lyvis sic dout,
       For he wes mekill and semit to be stout,
       That everilk beist thay dred him as the deid,
       Within that woid, that nane durst hald thair heid.   2510

359   Yit happinnit thair ane hungrie Wolff to slyde
       Out throw his Scheip, quhair thay lay on ane le;
       'I sall have ane' (quod he), 'quhat ever betyde,
       Thocht I be werryit, for hunger or I de.'
       With that ane Lamb in till his cluke hint he.   2515
       The laif start up, ffor thay wer all agast;
       Bot (God wait) gif the Wedder followit fast.

360   Went never Hound mair haistelie fra the hand,
       Quhen he wes rynnand maist raklie at the Ra,
       Nor went this Wedder baith over Mois and strand,   2520
       And stoppit nouther at bank, busk, nor bra;
       Bot followit ay sa ferslie on his fa
       With sic ane drift, quhill dust and dirt over draif him,
       And maid ane Vow to God that he suld have him.

361   With that the Wolff let out his Taill on lenth,   2525
       For he wes hungrie and it drew neir the ene,
       And schupe him for to ryn with all his strenth,
       Fra he the Wedder sa neir cummand had sene.
       He dred his lyfe, and he overtane had bene;
       Thairfoir he spairit nowther busk nor boig,   2530
       For weill he kennit the kenenes off the Doig.

362   To make himself lighter he discarded the Lamb; then
over the field he leapt, plunging through puddles and
mire. 'No' (said the Wether), 'in faith, we shall not
part like this; it is not the Lamb but you that I desire; I
shall overtake you, for now I see you tire.' The Wolf
kept running until he passed a stream, but the Wether
continued to narrow the distance between them.

363   Soon after that the Wether approached so near
that the Wolf, out of fright, defiled the field;
than he left the road and ran through bush and
briar, hoping to hide himself in the woods. He
ran without stopping, for he knew of no safe
place. The Wether followed him in and out, until
the briars of a bush abruptly tore off his disguise.

364   Being alert, the Wolf glanced behind him and saw
the Wether come twisting through the briar; then
he spied the dog's skin hanging from the Wether's
rear. 'Ah' (said the Wolf), 'is it only you that is so
close?—but a moment ago a Hound, now as white as
a Friar. I fled further than I needed, had I known
the facts. I vow to God that you shall rue this race.

365   'What could have caused you to give me such a chase?'
At that, he quickly grabbed the Wether by the horn.
'For all your clever tricks, this time you have met your
match, even though you have laughed me to scorn
all this year. For what reason did you wear the skin
of this Dog? 'Master' (he replied), 'only to have a game
with you; I hope you do not think it was anything else.'

366   'Is your jesting then in earnest?' (said the Wolf),
'for in truth I have been frightened and much up-
set; come back with me and I shall show you.'
Then he brought him to where the road was defiled. 'Is this what you call fair play, or not?—to
throw your better into so great a fright that for
fear he befouled the way?

367   'Three times (by my Soul) you made me shit; the
evidence can be seen on my haunches; for fear I
frequently defiled the wind. Now do I find it is
only you?—not much of a Hound, I think. Your
teeth seem much too short to be so sharp. Blessed

362   To mak him lycht, he kest the Lamb him fra,
     Syne lap ouer leis and draif throw dub and myre.
     'Na' (quod the Wedder), 'in Faith we part not swa:
     It is not the Lamb, bot the, that I desyre;   2535
     I sall cum neir, ffor now I se the tyre.'
     The Wolff ran still quhill ane strand stude behind him,
     Bot ay the neirar the Wedder he couth bind him.

363   Sone efter that he followit him sa neir,
     Quhill that the Wolff ffor fleidnes fylit the feild;   2540
     Syne left the gait and ran throw busk and breir,
     And schupe him ffra the schawis ffor to scheild.
     He ran restles, for he wist off na beild.
     The Wedder followit him baith out and in,
     Quhill that ane breir busk raif rudelie off the skyn.   2545

364   The Wolff wes wer, and blenkit him behind,
     And saw the Wedder come thrawand throw the breir;
     Syne saw the Doggis skyn hingand on his lind.
     'Na' (quod he), 'is this ye that is sa neir?
     Richt now ane Hound, and now quhte as ane Frier;°   2550
     I fled over fer, and I had kennit the cais:
     To God I vow that ye sall rew this rais.°

365   'Quhat wes the cause ye gaif me sic ane katche?'
     With that in hy he hint him be the horne.
     'For all your mowis ye met anis with your matche,   2555
     Suppois ye leuch me all this yeir to scorne.
     For quhat enchessoun this Doggis skyn have ye borne?'
     'Maister' (quod he), 'bot to have playit with yow;
     I yow requyre that ye nane uther trow.'

366   'Is this your bourding in ernist than?'° (quod he),   2560
     'For I am verray effeirit, and on flocht;
     Cum bak agane and I sall let yow se.'
     Than quhar the gait wes grimmit he him brocht.
     'Quhether call ye this fair play, or nocht?
     To set your Maister in sa fell effray,   2565
     Quhill he ffor feiritnes hes fylit up the way.

367   'Thryis (be my Saull) ye gart me schute behind;
     Upon my hoichis the senyeis may be sene;
     For feirtnes full oft I ffylit the wind.
     Now is this ye? na, bot ane Hound, I wene;   2570
     Me think your teith over schort to be sa kene.

be the bush that stripped off your disguise, else I
would have burst myself in fleeing today.'

368   'Sir' (said the Wether), 'although I ran so quickly,
I never intended your person any harm; he who
flees usually attract a pursuer, either in play or in
earnest—test it for yourself. Since I but played
with you, be gracious unto me, and I shall have
my friends bless your bones; even the best servant
will cross his master once.'

369   'Often have I been thrown into great fear, but (by
the Rood) never yet so terrified as you have made
me with your precious playing. I was so scared
that I shit when you were catching up to me; but
surely from now on we shall never be apart.'
Then roughly he grabbed him by the neck, and,
before he finished, he had shaken it to pieces.

MORALITAS

370   Aesop, the poet who originated this fable, wrote
this allegory, which is a fitting one. Because the
message was meaningful and suitable for furnish-
ing a wise example of morality, whose enigmatic
applications are truly excellent, and by virtue
of the aptness of its allegory, it still gives a lesson
to its readers to this day.

371   Here you may see that fine clothing will cause poor
men to be presumptuous; they think they have no
superiors if only they are dressed well enough;
and thus they imitate a Lord in every particular.
From their own station they climb so high in
pride that nowhere do they show respect for their
betters, until some man turns them head over heels.

372   Indeed, there are some servants who can outdo their
masters, and who, if they have success, wealth, and
encouragement, will disparage Lords by their deeds
and consider neither their blood nor their heritage; but yet none knows how long that rule will
last. He was wise who bade his son consider: Be
wary in times of wealth, for hall benches are slippery.

373   Therefore, I counsel men of every station to
know themselves, and know to whom they should

Blissit be the busk that reft yow your array,
Ellis, fleand, bursin had I bene this day.'

368 'Schir' (quod the Wedder), 'suppois I ran in hy,
My mynd wes never to do your persoun ill;   2575
Ane flear gettis ane follower commounly,
In play or ernist, preif quha sa ever will.
Sen I bot playit, be gracious me till,
And I sall gar my freindis blis your banis;
Ane full gude servand will crab his Maister anis.'   2580

369 'I have bene oftymis set in grit effray,
Bot (be the Rude) sa rad yit wes I never,
As thow hes maid me with thy prettie play.
I schot behind quhen thow overtuke me ever;
Bot sickkerlie now sall we not dissever.'   2585
Than be crag bane smertlie he him tuke,
Or ever he ceissit, and it in schunder schuke.

MORALITAS

370 Esope, that poete, first Father of this Fabill,
Wrait this Parabole, quhilk is convenient.
Because the sentence wes fructuous and agreabill,   2590
In Moralitie exemplative prudent,
Quhais problemes bene verray excellent,
Throw similitude of figuris, to this day,
Gevis doctrine to the Redaris of it ay.

371 Heir may thow se that riches of array   2595
Will cause pure men presumpteous for to be;
Thay think thay hald of nane, be thay als gay,
Bot counterfute ane Lord in all degre.
Out of thair cais in pryde thay clym sa hie
That thay forbeir thair better in na steid,   2600
Quhill sum man tit thair heillis over thair heid.

372 Richt swa in service uther sum exceidis,
And thay haif withgang, welth, and cherising,
That thay will lychtlie Lordis in thair deidis,
And lukis not to thair blude, nor thair offspring: 2605
Bot yit nane wait how lang that reull will ring;
Bot he was wyse that bade his Sone considder:
Bewar in welth, for Hall benkis ar rycht slidder.°

373 Thairfoir I counsell men of everlik stait
To knaw thame self, and quhome thay suld forbeir,   2610

yield, and not to fall into debate with their betters. Even should he wear magnificent clothing, it
is not fitting for a servant to perpetuate strife, nor
to climb so high that he falls off the ladder: Just
remember the Wolf, and remember the Wether.

The Tale of the Wolf and the Lamb

374   A long while ago, a cruel Wolf, vicious and very
ravenous, went to a river which descended from a
cliff unto a pool; he drank of the clear water to
quench his thirst. It happened that an innocent
Lamb came by, knowing nothing of his enemy
the Wolf, and drank of the stream to cool his
thirst.

375   Thus they both drank, but not with one intent:
the Wolf's thought was ever on wickedness; the
spotless Lamb was meek and innocent: and from
the river at another place, downstream from the
Wolf, he drank a little while till he thought it enough,
presuming there to be no harm in it. The
Wolf saw the Lamb and, rearing up, approached him.

376   With teeth all bared and an awesome, angry look,
he said to the Lamb: 'You miserable, wretched thing,
how dare you be so bold as to defile this brook, in
which I should drink, with your unsavory slobber-
ing? It would be a charitable act to draw and hang
you, who dares to presume with your foul, vile lips
to muddy my drink and defile this pleasant stream.'

377   The innocent Lamb, actually quaking for fear,
fell on his knees and said. 'Sir, by your leave,
although I dare not suggest that you have lied
about this, yet by my Soul I know you cannot
prove that I did anything to bring you grief. You
know also that your accusation is far from the
truth and is contrary to reason.

And fall not with thair better in debait;
Suppois thay be als galland in thair geir,
It settis na servand for to uphald weir,
Nor clym so hie quhill he fall of the ledder;
Bot think upon the Wolf and on the Wedder.   2615

The Taill of the Wolf and the Lamb

374   Ane cruell Wolff, richt ravenous and fell,
       Upon ane tyme past to an Reveir
       Descending from ane Rotche unto ane well;
       To slaik his thirst, drank of the watter cleir.
       Swa upon cace ane selie Lamb° come neir,   2620
       Bot of his fa, the Wolff, na thing he wist,
       And in the streme laipit to cule his thirst.

375   Thus drank thay baith, but not of ane Intent;
       The Wolfis thocht wes all on wickitnes;
       The selie Lamb wes meik and Innocent: 2625
       Upon the Rever, in ane uther place,
       Beneth the Wolff, he drank ane lytill space,
       Quhill he thocht gude, presomyng thair nane ill;
       The Wolff him saw, and Rampand° come him till.

376   With girnand teith and awfull angrie luke,   2630
       Said to the Lamb: 'Thow Cative wretchit thing,
       How durst thow be sa bald to fyle this bruke
       Quhar I suld drink with thy foull slavering?
       It wer Almous the ffor to draw and hing,
       That suld presume, with thy foull lippis wyle,   2635
       To glar my drink and this fair watter fyle.'

377   The selie Lamb, quaikand for verray dreid,
       On kneis fell and said, 'Schir, with your leif,
       Suppois I dar not say thairoff ye leid;
       Bot, be my Saull, I wait ye can nocht preif   2640
       That I did ony thing that suld yow grief;
       Ye wait alswa that your accusatioun
       Failyeis ffra treuth and contrair is to ressoun.

378   'Though I am unable, Nature and a true
        knowledge of the facts of the case will defend me.
        All heavy things must by themselves descend;
        unless something resists by force, the stream may
        in no way make ascent nor run backwards. I
        drank far downstream from you; *Ergo*, your water
        was never the worse for me.

379   'Also, since the day I was born, my lips have
        touched no infectious things, but only have sucked
        the milk from the paps of my dam, completely
        natural, sweet, and also delicious.' 'Well' (said
        the Wolf), 'You have inherited your legalistic lan-
        guage from your father before you; he was always
        disputing, both with menace and threat.

380   'He made me angry; and then I gave him warning
        that within a year, if I had the use of my head, I
        should be revenged on him, or on his child, for
        his perverse and exorbitant argument. Without a
        doubt you shall die for his misdeeds.' 'Sir, it is
        wrong than an innocent son should suffer punish-
        ment or harm for a father's guilt.

381   'Have you not heard what the Holy Scripture
        says, dictated from the mouth of God Almighty?
        For his own deeds each man shall bear the conse-
        quences, such as punishment for sin and reward
        for righteous works. Why should my son be-
        shamed for my misdeed? Whoever trespassed, let
        him suffer the penalty.' 'Oh!' (said the Wolf);
        'Are you at your quibbling again?

382   'I will have you know that when the father
        offends me, I will not spare anyone of his succes-
        sion; and of his descendents I may well make my
        amends, even unto the twentieth generation.
        Your father intended to make a potent poison,
        and with his mouth to spew it into my water.'
        'Sir' (said the Lamb), 'neither of these charges is true.

383   'The Law says, if you will understand it, that no
        man, for a misdeed or act of violence, should
        punish his adversary by his own hand, without
        due process of Law and due hearing. He should
        have leave to make a lawful defense and in that

378   'Thocht I can nocht, Nature will me defend,
       And off the deid perfyte experience;   2645
       All hevie thing man off the selff discend;
       Bot giff sum thing on force mak resistence,
       Than may the streme on na way mak ascence,
       Nor ryn bakwart: I drank beneth yow far;
       Ergo,° ffor me your Bruke wes never the war.   2650

379   'Alswa my lippis, sen that I wes ane Lam,
       Tuitchit na thing that wes contagious,
       Bot sowkit milk ffrom Pappis off my dam,
       Richt Naturall, sweit, and als delitious.'
       'Weill' (quod the Wolff), 'thy language Rigorous   2655
       Cummis the off kynd; swa thy Father before
       Held me at bait, baith with boist and schore.

380   'He wraithit me, and than I culd him warne°
       Within ane yeir, and I brukit my heid,
       I suld be wrokkin on him or on his barne,   2660
       For his exorbetant and frawart pleid;
       Thow sall doutles ffor his deidis be deid.'
       'Schir, it is wrang that ffor the ffatheris gilt
       The saikles sone suld punist be or spilt.

381   'Haiff ye not hard quhat halie Scripture sayis,   2665
       Endytit with the mouth of God Almycht?
       Off his awin deidis ilk man sall beir the pais,
       As pyne ffor sin, reward ffor werkis rycht;
       For my trespas quhy suld my sone have plycht?
       Quha did the mis lat him sustene the pane.'   2670
       'Yaa' (quod the Wolff), 'yit pleyis thow agane?°

382   'I let the wit, quhen that the ffather offendis,
       I will refuse nane off his Successioun;
       And off his barnis I may weill tak amendis
       Unto the twentie degre descending doun.   2675
       Thy ffather thocht to mak ane strang poysoun,
       And with his mouth in to my watter spew.'
       'Schir' (quod the Lamb), 'thay twa ar nouther trew.

383   'The Law sayis, and ye will vnderstand,
       Thair suld na man, ffor wrang nor violence,   2680
       His adversar punis at his awin hand,
       Without proces off Law and audience;
       Quhilk suld have leif to mak lawfull defence,

matter be summoned peremptorily in order to
plead his case, contradict, or rebut.

384 'Set me a lawful court; I shall appear before the
Lion, Lord and honest Justice, and by this hand I
give my word here and now that I shall wait for
an impartial Assize. This is the Law, the legal
custom at present. You should therefore bring an
action; make a summons for a specific day to
plead your case and hear mine.'

385 'Ha' (said the Wolff), 'you would be inserting
reason where villainy and ill-doing should rightly
rule. You make an example and instance of false
treason, to try to make compassion abide with
cruelty. By God's wounds, lying traitor, you shall
die for your misdeed, and for your father's too.'
That said, he swiftly grabbed him by the neck.

386 The innocent Lamb could do nothing but bleat;
quickly he was beheaded. The Wolf would grant him
no grace, but proceeded to drink of his blood and
eat of his flesh until he was full, then went on his
way apace. Of his murder, alas, what shall we say? Was
this not a shame, was this not great pity, that this innocent, guiltless Lamb was made to die in this way?

MORALITAS

387 This Lamb may symbolize the poor people, such
as tenant farmers, merchants, and all laborers, for
whom life is half a Purgatory, as they try to secure
by honest means a suitable living. The Wolf betokens false extortioners and oppressors of the
poor, succeeding, as commonly we see, by violence or cunning misuse of their abilities.

388 Three kinds of Wolves now dominate this world:
The first is the false perverter of the Laws, who
veils his falsehoods under polished terms, imply-
ing that everything he alleges is Gospel; but for a
bribe he ruins the poor man, suppressing the right
and causing the wrong to advance. For such
Wolves, the fires of Hell shall be their reward.

389 O man of Law! Forsake your devious ways, with
subtle tricks and complicated frauds, and consider

And thairupon Summond Peremptourly,
For to propone, contrairie, or reply.   2685

384   'Set me ane lauchfull Court, I sall compeir
Befoir the Lyoun, Lord and leill Justice,
And, be my hand, I oblis me rycht heir
That I sall byde ane unsuspect Assyis.
This is the Law, this is the Instant wyis;   2690
Ye suld pretend thairfoir; ane Summondis mak
Aganis that day, to gif ressoun and tak.

385   'Ha' (quod the Wolff), 'thow wald Intruse ressoun
Quhair wrang and reif suld dwell in propertie.
That is ane poynt and part of fals tressoun,   2695
For to gar reuth remane with crueltie.
By Goddis woundis, fals tratour, thow sall de
For thy trespas, and for thy Fatheris als.'
With that anone he hint him be the hals.

386   The selie Lamb culd do na thing bot bleit;   2700
Sone wes he hedit; the Wolff wald do na grace,
Syne drank his blude and off his flesche can eit,°
Quhill he wes full, syne went his way on pace.
Of his murther quhat sall we say, allace?
Wes not this reuth, wes not this grit pietie,   2705
To gar this selie Lamb but gilt thus de?

MORALITAS°

387   The pure pepill this Lamb may signifie,
As Maill men, Merchandis, and all lauboureris,
Of quhome the lyfe is half ane Purgatorie,
To wyn with lautie leving as efferis.   2710
The Wolf betakinnis fals extortioneris
And oppressouris of pure men, as we se,
Be violence, or craft in facultie.

388   Thre kynd of Wolfis in this warld now Rings:
The first as fals perverteris of the Lawis,   2715
Quhilk under poleit termis falset mingis,
Lettand that all wer Gospell that he schawis;
Bot for ane bud the pure man he overthrawis,
Smoirand the richt, garrand the wrang proceid:
Of sic Wolfis hellis fyre sall be thair meid.   2720

389   O man of Law! let be thy subteltie,
With nice gimpis and fraudis Intricait,

well that God in his Divinity knows the right and
wrong of all your deeds. Take care not to defend
a fraudulent claim, for prayer nor price, for high
estate nor low. Support the right, and do not
harm your conscience.

390   Another kind of ravenous Wolf are the mighty
men, who have great store of plenty but are so
greedy and so covetous they will not suffer the
poor to live in peace. Should both the poor man
and his household die from lack of food, the
mighty ones give no heed, but dispossess him of
his property by offering for it a higher price.

391   O man without mercy, what are the thoughts that
fill your head?—worse than those of a wolf, if you
could but understand. You have enough; but the
lowly farmer has nothing but crops and a hovel
and a little piece of land. For the fear of God,
how can you dare to take it upon you—and you
with your barn and byre so large and well supplied—
to throw him off his land and make him beg?

392   The third sort of Wolf is the man of inheritance,
like the lords that have their land as a loan from
God, who lease the cottars land to till and inhabit,
and set the Gressom for a limited term to be paid
and collected. Then they vex him, ere half his term
is gone, with fabricated quarrels, to make him eager
to leave or force him to pay his Gressom over again.

393   His horse, his mare, he must lend to the Master
to draw and drag a cart in carrying things. He and
his servant are forced to work and sweat, without
food or compensation. This is his situation in
labor and bondage: that scarcely can he contrive
by working his land to live upon dry bread and
cabbage soup.

394   Have you no pity, that you make your tenants sweat
to do your work, with faint and hungry stomach,
and with little good to drink or eat with his
family when he returns home in the evening? You
should fear incurring the wrath of the righteous
God; for to make a poor man work without food
or pay cries for vengeance to the heavens above.

And think that God in his Divinitie
The wrang, the richt, of all thy werkis wait.
For prayer, price, for hie nor law estait, 2725
Of fals querrellis se thow mak na defence;
Hald with the richt, hurt not thy conscience.

390 Ane uther kynd of Wolfis Ravenous
Ar mychtie men, haifand aneuch plentie,
Quhilkis ar sa gredie and sa covetous 2730
Thay will not thoill the pure in pece to be;
Suppois he and his houshald baith suld de
For falt of fude, thairof thay gif na rak,
Bot over his heid his mailling will thay tak.°

391 O man but mercie, quhat is in thy thocht? 2735
War than ane Wolf, and thow culd understand!
Thow hes aneuch; the pure husband richt nocht
Bot croip and crufe upon ane clout of land.
For Goddis aw, how durst thow tak on hand,
And thow in Barn and Byre° sa bene and big, 2740
To put him fra his tak and gar him thig?

392 The thrid Wolf ar men of heritage,
As Lordis that hes land be Goddis lane,
And settis to the Mailleris ane Village,
And for ane tyme Gressome° payit and tane; 2745
Syne vexis him, or half his terme be gane,
With pykit querrellis for to mak him fane
To flit, or pay his Gressome new agane.

393 His Hors, his Meir, he man len to the Laird,
To drug and draw in Cairt and Cariage; 2750
His servand or his self may not be spaird
To swing and sweit, withoutin Meit or wage.°
Thus how he standis in labour and bondage,
That scantlie may he purches by his maill
To leve upon dry breid and watter caill.° 2755

394 Hes thow not reuth to gar thy tennentis sweit
In to thy laubour with faynt and hungrie wame,
And syne hes lytill gude to drink or eit,
With his menye at evin quhen he cummis hame?
Thow suld be rad for rychteous Goddis blame; 2760
For it cryis ane vengeance unto the hevinnis hie
To gar ane pure man wirk but Meit or fe.

395   O thou great Lord, who has both riches and
rents, be not a Wolf, devouring thus the poor.
Consider that nothing cruel or violent may endure in this world perpetually. This shall you
believe and know with confidence: that you shall
suffer penalities for your own oppression as great
as if you had slain the poor with your own hand.

396   God keep the Lamb, who is the Innocent one,
from the bite of these Wolves and fierce extortioners; God grant that evil men of false intent be
exposed and punished as is suitable; and God, as
You hear all righteous prayers, please save our
King, and give him the desire and power to
banish all such Wolves from the land.

The Tale of the Paddock and the Mouse

397   Once a long while ago (Aesop tells us) a little
Mouse came to a river's bank. She could not
wade across, her legs were so short; she could not
swim; she had no horse to ride. By sheer necessity
she was compelled to remain there; and back and
forth beside that deep river she ran, crying with
many a piteous peep.

398   'Help me over, help!' this poor Mouse cried; 'For
God's love somebody help me over the water.' At
that, a Paddock in the water nearby, who was able
by nature to dive and swim strongly, raised her
head and climbed up on the bank. With a voice
most hoarse she spoke in the following way: 'Good
morning, Dame Mouse; what is your errand here?'

399   She replied 'Do you see that lovely field of grain,
of ripened oats, of barley, peas and wheat? I am
hungry, and much would like to be there, but I
am prevented by this great expanse of water; and
on this side I can get naught to eat but hard nuts,
which I must break with my teeth. Were I
yonder, my dinner would be greatly improved.

<blockquote>

395   O thow grit Lord, that riches hes and rent,
        Be nocht ane Wolf, thus to devoir the pure;
        Think that na thing cruell nor violent   2765
        May in this warld perpetuallie Indure.
        This sall thow trow and sikkerlie assure:
        For till oppres thow sall haif als greit pane
        As thow the pure had with thy awin hand slane.

396   God keip the Lamb, quhilk is the Innocent,   2770
        From Wolfis byit and fell extortioneris;
        God grant that wrangous men of fals Intent
        Be manifest, and punischit as effeiris;
        And God, as thow all rychteous prayer heiris,
        Mot saif our King, and gif him hart and hand   2775
        All sic Wolfis to banes of the land.

</blockquote>

The Taill of the Paddok & the Mous

<blockquote>

397   Upon ane tyme (as Esope culd Report)
        Ane lytill Mous come till ane Rever syde:
        Scho micht not waid, hir schankis were sa schort;
        Scho culd not swym; scho had na hors to ryde.   2780
        Of verray force behovit hir to byde,
        And to and ffra besyde that Revir deip
        Scho ran, cryand with mony pietuous peip.

398   'Help over, help over,' this sillie Mous can cry,
        'For Goddis lufe, sum bodie over the brym.'   2785
        With that ane Paddok,° in the watter by,
        Put up hir heid and on the bank can clym,
        Quhilk be nature culd douk and gaylie swim;
        With voce full rauk, scho said on this maneir:
        'Gude morne (schir Mous),° quhat is your erand heir?' 2790

399   'Seis thow' (quod scho) 'off corne yone Jolie flat,
        Off ryip Aitis, off Barlie, Peis, and Quheit?
        I am hungrie, and fane wald be thair at,
        Bot I am stoppit be this watter greit;
        And on this syde I get na thing till eit   2795
        Bot hard Nuttis, quhilkis with my teith I bore.°
        Wer I beyond, my feist wer fer the more.

</blockquote>

400   'I have no boat; here is no mariner; and even if
      there were, I do not have the price of passage.'
      The Paddock said, 'Sister, put aside your gloomy
      mood; heed my advice and I shall find the way
      without horse, brig, boat, or even galley, to bring
      you safely over—be not afraid!—and even the
      whiskers of your beard shall not get wet.'

401   'I wonder greatly,' said the little Mouse, 'how you
      contrive to swim without feather or fin. The river
      is so deep and dangerous, it seems to me you
      would drown if you waded in it. Tell me, there-
      fore, what skills or craft you have to bring your-
      self over this dark water.' To answer her the
      Paddock began as follows.

402   She said, 'With my two feet, webbed and broad,
      in place of oars, I cross the stream most quietly;
      and though the deep be perilous to wade in, I
      swim wherever I wish, both there and back. I
      cannot drown because my open gill continually
      voids the water I take in; therefore, I truly have
      no fear of drowning.'

403   The Mouse looked on her wrinkled face, her
      sagging cheeks, and her wide lips, her drooping
      brows, and her voice so hoarse, her loosely hang-
      ing legs, and her rugged skin. She started back
      and cried out to the Paddock, 'If I have any
      knowledge of Physiognomy, you have in you
      some falsehood and malice.

404   'For scholars say the inclination of man's thought
      tends most often toward good or evil as suits his
      nature, and that is reflected in his bodily ap-
      pearance. If ill the will, then ill the physiognomy.
      The old proverb is witness to this conclusion:
      Distortum vultum sequitur distortio morum.'

405   'No' said the Paddock, 'that proverb is not true;
      for fair things are often found to be deceitful. The
      bilberries, though they may be dull in color, are
      gathered up when the primrose is forsaken. The
      face may fail to be a token of the heart. Thus I

400 'I have no Boit; heir is no Maryner;°
     And thocht thair war, I have no fraucht to pay.'
     Quod scho, 'sister, lat be your hevie cheir;   2800
     Do my counsall, and I sall find the way
     Withoutin Hors, Brig, Boit, or yit Galay,°
     To bring yow over saiflie,—be not afeird!—
     And not wetand the campis off your beird.'

401 'I haif grit wounder,' quod the lytill Mous,   2805
     'How can thow fleit without fedder or fyn.
     This Rever is sa deip and dangerous,
     Me think that thow suld droun to wed thairin.
     Tell me, thairfoir, quhat facultie or gin
     Thow hes to bring the over this watter wan?'   2810
     That to declair the Paddok thus began.

402 'With my twa feit' (quod scho), 'lukkin and braid,
     In steid off Airis, I row the streme full styll;
     And thocht the brym be perrillous to waid,
     Baith to and ffra I swyme at my awin will.   2815
     I may not droun, ffor quhy my oppin Gill°
     Devoidis ay the watter I resaiff:
     Thairfoir to droun forsuith na dreid I haif.'

403 The Mous beheld unto hir fronsit face,
     Hir runkillit cheikis, and hir lippis syde,   2820
     Hir hingand browis, and hir voce sa hace,
     Hir loggerand leggis, and hir harsky hyde.
     Scho ran abak, and on the Paddok cryde:
     'Giff I can ony skill of Phisnomy,
     Thow hes sumpart off falset and Invy.   2825

404 'For Clerkis sayis the Inclinatioun
     Of mannis thocht proceidis commounly
     Efter the Corporall complexioun
     To gude or evill, as Nature will apply:
     Ane thrawart will, ane thrawin Phisnomy.   2830
     The auld Proverb is witnes off this *Lorum*:°
     Distortum vultum sequitur distortio morum.'°

405 'Na' (quod the Taid), 'that Proverb is not trew;
     For fair thingis oftymis ar fundin faikin.
     The Blaberyis° thocht thay be sad of hew,   2835
     Ar gadderit up quhen Primeros is forsakin.
     The face may faill to be the hartis takin.

find this motto everywhere: Thou shouldst not
judge a man because of his face.

406   'Though I may be distressing to look upon, I can-
      not see why I should be reproached; were I as fair
      as handsome Absolom, I still would not have
      been the cause of that great beauty. The differ-
      ence between the form and quality almighty God
      has caused Dame Nature to imprint and establish
      on each and every creature.

407   'Some people may have a well endowed face, to-
      gether with a silken tongue and a most loving aspect;
      but at the same time their mind may be incon-
      stant, false, and variable, full of deceit and of
      cunning tricks.' 'Cease your preaching' (said the
      hungry Mouse), 'and help me understand by what
      device you would convey me to that distant shore.'

408   'You know' (she said), 'a person that has need to
      help herself should seek out many ways; there-
      fore, go take a double thread of twine and bind
      your leg to mine with sturdy knots. I'll teach you
      how to swim—be not afraid—as well as I.' 'As
      you?' (then said the Mouse); 'To chance that ex-
      periment would be most risky.

409   'Should I become bound and fast where I had been
      free, merely to be in hope of receiving help? Nay,
      then I would curse us both, for I might lose life
      and liberty. If that came to pass, then who would
      pay the damages for my injury?—unless of course
      you swear to me the murder-oath, without deceit
      or guile, to bring me across this river without
      hurt or harm.' 'In faith' (said she), 'I do swear it.'

410   She looked to the heavens in seeming innocence
      and cried: 'Ho, Jupiter, God and King of Nature,
      to thee I truly make an oath that I shall bring this
      little Mouse over the water.' This oath was fin-
      ished. The Mouse, without perceiving the false
      designs of this foul, chattering Paddock, took
      thread and bound her leg, as she had bidden her.

411   Then foot for foot they both leapt into the water;
      but their intentions could not have differed more:

Thairfoir I find this Scripture in all place:
Thow suld not Juge ane man efter his face.

406   'Thocht I unhailsum be to luke upon,   2840
I have no cause quhy I suld lakkit be;
Wer I als fair as Jolie Absolon,°
I am no causer off that grit beutie.
This difference in forme and qualitie
Almychtie God hes causit dame Nature   2845
To prent and set in everilk creature.°

407   'Off sum the face may be full flurischand
Off silkin toung and cheir rycht amorous,
With mynd Inconstant, fals, and wariand,
Full of desait and menis Cautelous.'   2850
'Let ne thy preiching' (quod the hungrie Mous),
'And be quhat craft thow gar me understand
That thow wald gyde me to yone yonder land?'

408   'Thow wait' (quod scho), 'ane bodie that hes neid
To help thame self suld mony wayis cast;   2855
Thairfoir ga tak ane doubill twynit threid,
And bind thy leg to myne with knottis fast.
I sall the leir to swym—be not agast!—
Als weill as I.' 'As thow?' (than quod the Mous).
'To preif that play it war richt perrillous.   2860

409   'Suld I be bund and fast quhar I am fre,
In hoip off help? Na than I schrew us baith,
For I mycht lois baith lyfe and libertie.
Gif it wer swa, quha suld amend the skaith?
Bot gif thow sweir to me the murthour aith,°   2865
But fraud or gyle to bring me over this flude,
But hurt or harme.' 'In faith' (quod scho), 'I dude.'

410   Scho goikit up, and to the hevin can cry
'How, Juppiter, off Nature God and King,
I mak ane aith trewlie to the, that I   2870
This lytill Mous sall over this watter bring.'
This aith wes maid. The Mous, but persaving
The fals Ingyne of this foull carpand Pad,
Tuke threid and band hir leg, as scho hir bad.

411   Then fute for fute° thay lap baith in the brym;   2875
Bot in thair myndis thay wer rycht different:

the Mouse thought of nothing else but swimming,
while the Paddock's only interest was to drown her.
When they reached the middle of the stream,
with all her might the Paddock struggled downwards, intending without mercy to drown the Mouse.

412   Perceiving this, the Mouse cried out at her:
'Traitor to God, and perjured unto me, you swore
the murder-oath just now, that I without hurt or
harm should be ferried, free of charge.' And when
she saw that it was but do or die, with all her
might she forced herself to swim and struggled to
climb up on the Paddock's back.

413   The fear of death gave her extra strength and the power
to defend herself with might and main. The Mouse
strove upwards, the Paddock downward; sometimes
to, sometimes fro, sometimes diving, sometimes up
again. The poor Mouse, so overwhelmed with
great distress, struggled as long as breath was in
her body, till at last she cried out for a Priest.

414   While they struggled thus, the Kite, perched on a
branch, was paying close attention to this wretched
battle; and with one swoop, before either of them no-
ticed, he clutched the thread that bound them with
his claw. Then to land he swiftly flew with them,
happy with his hunt, piping out many a 'pew.' Then
he loosed them and slew them both without pity.

415   Then that Butcher disembowelled them with his beak
and deftly flayed them in one quick, thorough motion; but all their flesh, with guts and all, would scarce
be half a meal for such a greedy Kite. Thus their debate was brought to an end, so I have heard; and he
took his flight and flew out over the fields. If you want
to know whether this is true, ask someone who saw it.

MORALITAS

416   My brother, if this Fable can awaken your interest,
you may perceive and understand that a wicked
mind, coupled with words both fair and sly, by far
surpasses any kind of pestilence. Be wary, therefore, whom you keep for company. Better for you
to push a cart of stones, to dig for all your days

The Mous thocht off na thing bot ffor to swym,
The Paddok ffor to droun set hir Intent.
Quhen thay in midwart off the streme wer went,
With all hir force the Paddok preissit doun,   2880
And thocht the Mous without mercie to droun.

412   Persavand this, the Mous on hir can cry:
       'Tratour to God, and manesworne unto me,
       Thow swore the murthour aith richt now, that I
       But hurt or harme suld ferryit be and fre;'   2885
       And quhen scho saw thair wes but do or de,
       With all hir mycht scho forsit hir to swym,
       And preissit upon the Taiddis bak to clym.

413   The dreid of deith hir strenthis gart Incres,
       And forcit hir defend with mycht and mane.   2890
       The Mous upwart, the Paddok doun° can pres;
       Quhyle to, quhyle ffra,° quhyle doukit up agane.
       The selie Mous, this plungit in grit pane,
       Gan fecht als lang als breith wes in hir briest,
       Till at the last scho cryit ffor ane Preist.   2895

414   Fechtand thusgait, the Gled sat on ane twist,
       And to this wretchit battell tuke gude heid;
       And with ane wisk, or owthir off thame wist,
       He claucht his cluke betuix thame in the threid;
       Syne to the land he flew with thame gude speid,   2900
       Fane off that fang, pyipand with mony pew;
       Syne lowsit thame, and baith but pietie slew.

415   Syne bowellit thame, that Boucheour with his bill,
       And belliflaucht full fettillie thame flaid;°
       Bot all thair flesche wald scant be half ane fill,°   2905
       And guttis als, unto that gredie gled.
       Off thair debait, thus quhen I hard outred,
       He tuke his flicht, and over the feildis flaw:
       Giff this be trew, speir ye at thame that saw.

       MORALITAS

416   My Brother, gif thow will tak advertence°   2910
       Be this Fabill, thow may persave and se
       It passis far all kynd of Pestilence
       Ane wickit mynd with wordis fair and sle.
       Be war theirfore with quhome thow fallowis the;
       To the wer better beir the stane barrow,   2915

while you can endure it, than to be mated with a
false companion.

417   A false design under a fair pretense has caused
the death of many an innocent one; it is great
folly to believe too quickly everyone who speaks
pleasantly to you; a silken tongue, a heart of
cruelty, stings more than any arrow-shot. Brother,
if you would be wise, I advise you to avoid
associating with a crooked, crafty companion.

418   I warn thee also, it is great negligence to bind yourself
fast where before you were completely free; from
the moment you are bound, you may make no defense to save your life, nor even your liberty.
Brother, take this simple advice from me, and see
you do not delay in committing it to memory: it
is better to live alone in quiet without strife than
to be matched with a wicked companion.

419   Remember this well; I shall tell you a good deal
more of how these beasts may be considered allegorical: The Paddock, used to dwelling in the river, is
the Body of man, swimming early and late in this
world, with complicated cares; now high, now
low, sometimes struggling up, sometimes down,
ever in peril and on the point of drowning;

420   Now full of grief, now blithe as a bird on a briar;
now in freedom, now imprisoned in distress; now
hale and hearty, now dead and brought to the funeral
bier; now poor as Job, now rolling in riches; now
in gay gowns, now in tattered clothes, carefully
tended; now full as a fish, now hungry as a hound;
now on top of the wheel, now dashed to the ground.

421   This little Mouse, here bound in this way by the
leg, may indeed betoken the Soul of man—lashed
to and inseparable from the Body, until cruel
death comes to break the thread of life. It stands
ever in dread of being drowned by the temptations of carnal lust, which always entices the Soul
and drags it down.

For all thy dayis to delf quhill thow may dre,
Than to be machit with ane wickit marrow.

417   Ane fals Intent under ane fair pretence
       Hes causit mony Innocent for to de;
       Grit folie is to gif over sone credence   2920
       To all that speikis fairlie unto the;
       Ane silkin toung, ane hart of crueltie,
       Smytis more sore than ony schot of arrow.°
       Brother, gif thow be wyse, I reid the fle,
       To matche the with ane thrawart, fenyeit marrow.   2925

418   I warne the als, it is grit nekligence
       To bind the fast quhair thow wes frank and fre;
       Fra thow be bund, thow may mak na defence
       To saif thy lyfe, nor yit thy libertie.
       This simpill counsall, brother, tak of me,   2930
       And it to cun perqueir se thow not tarrow:
       Better but stryfe to leif allane in le
       Than to be matchit with ane wickit marrow.

419   This hald in mynde; riycht more I sall the tell
       Quhair by thir beistis may be figurate: 2935
       The Paddok, usand in the flude to duell,
       Is mannis bodie, swymand air and lait
       In to this warld, with cairis Implicate;
       Now hie, now law, quhylis plungit up, quhylis doun,
       Ay in perrell and reddie for to droun;   2940

420   Now dolorus, now blyth as bird on breir;
       Now in fredome, now wardit in distres;
       Now haill and sound, now deid and brocht on beir;
       Now pure as Job, now rowand in riches;
       Now gouins gay, now brats laid in pres;   2945
       Now full as fische, now hungrie as ane hound;
       Now on the quheill, now wappit to the ground.

421   This lytill Mous, heir knit thus be the schyn,
       The Saull of man betakin may in deid;
       Bundin, an fra the bodie may not twyn,   2950
       Quhill cruell deith cum brek of lyfe the threid;
       The quhilk to droun suld ever stand in dreid
       Of carnall lust be the Suggestioun
       Quhilk drawis ay the Saull and druggis doun.

422   The water is the World, ever turbulent, with
many waves of tribulation, in which the Soul and
Body were travelling, each maintaining an op-
posite objective: upward strives the Soul, downward the Body; the Soul strongly wishes to be
transported, I know, out of this world into the
bliss of Heaven.

423   The Kite is Death, that appears suddenly, as does
a thief, and soon cuts short the battle; be
vigilant, therefore, and ever ready, for the life of
man is brittle and ever mortal. Therefore, my
friend, build for yourself a strong fortress of good
deeds, for Death will find you out you know not
when—evening, morning, or mid-day.

424   Adieu, my friend; and if any should ask you about
this Fable (and shortly now I will conclude), you
can say I left the remainder to the Friars, to use
in their examples and interpretations. Now
Christ, who perished for us on the cross, as You
are Savior of our soul and life, grant that we
might die happily and with blessings.

422   The watter is the warld, ay welterand   2955
       With mony wall of tribulatioun,
       In quhilk the saull and body wer steirrand,
       Standand distinyt in thair opinioun:
       The Saull upwart, the body precis doun;
       The Saul rycht fane wald be brocht over, I wis,   2960
       Out of this warld into the hevinnis blis.

423   The Gled is Deith, that cummis suddandlie
       As dois ane theif, and cuttis sone the battall;
       Be vigilant, thairfoir, and ay reddie,
       For mannis lyfe is brukill and ay mortall.   2965
       My freind, thairfoir, mak the ane strang Castell
       Of gude deidis, for deith will the assay,
       Thow wait not quhen—evin, morrow, or midday.

424   Adew, my freind; and gif that ony speiris
       Of this Fabill, sa schortlie I conclude,   2970
       Say thow, I left the laif unto the Freiris,°
       To mak a sample or similitude.
       Now Christ for us that deit on the Rude,
       Of saull and lyfe as thow art Salviour,
       Grant us til pas in till ane blissit hour.   2975

NOTES TO THE TEXT

The Prologue

1.2   **grunded upon truth**: Cf. the opening of Barbour's long nationalistic poem, *The Bruce*, which insists that no fiction can equal the worth of historical writing.

1.3   **polite termes**: 'Polished diction': Caxton explains the expression when he remarks that Skelton translated 'not in rude and olde langage, but in polysshed and ornate termes craftely, as he that hath read Vyrgyle, Ovyde, Tullye, and all the other noble poetes and oratours.'

1.7   **be figure of ane uther thing:** See Introduction, pp. 7-8.

4.28   **Dulcius arrident seria picta iocis**: 'People are pleased more sweetly with light matters than with serious ones.' Lines 19-28 are a standard Medieval justification for poetry.

5.32   **ane maner of Translatioun**: Henryson apologizes for using the vernacular because Latin was the language most often used for writing of serious import. His 'Translatioun' is actually an adaptation rather than a translation. See Introduction, p. 7.

5.34   **be requeist and precept of ane Lord**: Henryson may well have had no particular lord in mind, this disclaimer being the conventional 'humility *topos*,' through which writers appear to direct attention away from themselves and to the work. Cf. Stanzas 6 and 17.

7.44   **beistis spak . . . eik conclude:** See Introduction, p. 8.

8.53   **appetyte:** The sin Henryson attacks most frequently. Animals are expected to concern themselves only with self-gratification, but humans, endowed with the power of reason, are expected to restrain themselves.

The Cock and the Jasper

10.69   **Jasp**: 'The name among the ancients for any bright-colored chalcedony except carnelian, the most esteemed being of a green color' [OED]. It was used in the Middle Ages as a generic term for some of the varieties of non-crystalline quartz.

13.86   **Thy grit vertew**: Precious stones were considered to have several kinds of powers (to heal, to protect, to bring good luck, etc.). Cf. Stanza 18.

14.94   **small wormis or snaillis**: Considered highly repulsive in the Middle Ages.

18.120   **properteis sevin**: The number seven connoted, among other things, perfection. For the magical powers of the Jasper, see Albertus Magnus, *Book of Minerals*.

19ff.   **Moralitas**: Through the *Moralitas* to each fable, Henryson suggests ways for the reader to view the action and draw moral conclusions. See Introduction, pp. 24-30.

20.137   **Science**: See Introduction, p. 8.

21.146-7   As dois ane Sow . . . stanis: Matt. 7:6, 'Neither cast ye your pearls before swine . . .'

23.161   This fable often appears first in fable collections because of its applicability to the reader, who is thereby warned not to overlook the wisdom in the fables that follow.

The Country Mouse and the City Mouse

24.164   **ane Borous toun**: A town organized as a municipal corporation, often having special powers of trade granted by the crown.

24.166   quhyle . . . quhyle . . : Perhaps with a pun on the 'Wheel' of Fortune. (Cf. Stanza 413.)

25.172   Gild brothers: A member of the merchant guild (which would have controlled the town and its craftsmen). **fre Burges**: a citizen who enjoyed full rights and privileges.

25.173   custom mair or les: The Great Custom (*magna custuma*) was levied on imports and exports; the Little Custom (*parva custuma*) was levied on goods sent to the market.

27.189   be verray kynd: See Introduction, p. 8.

32.222-24   Cf. 11. 15-6.

36.251   na fall, na trap: These two traps were of different construction and stratagem. Mice were a great and general concern at the time, and the problem of building a better mouse trap was an intriguing one. See Gosta Berg, 'Medieval Mouse Traps,' *Studia Ethnographica Upsaliensia* 26, *Varia* 2 (1966), 1-13.

39.268   thay wesche: Not for religious reasons, but in imitation of the nobility. No mention is made of washing before their meal in the country.

41.281   ane subcharge: A small additional course served between two regular courses; an 'entremess.'

46.321   watter caill: A cabbage broth made without meat; a meagre fare.

47.326   Gib: A common name for a cat at that time.

47.327   And bad God speid: Cf. 1. 262.

48.331-33   Cf. 1. 116 and note.

48.336   Betwix ane burde and the wall: The mouse finds a hole in the baseboard of a partition wall and climbs to safety. Scottish homes of this period were commonly one large room divided into areas by partition walls. The text is somewhat unclear, though, and may refer to the Mouse climbing a tapestry.

49.338   Gilbert: Gib, the name of the cat, is also an abbreviation of 'Gilbert,' thus producing a humorous backformation here, much as 'tabby' produced 'Tabitha.'

52.360   baith but and ben: The inner and outer rooms of a small, one-door dwelling. The first room (or room division), normally the kitchen, was the *but*, and the furthest, normally the parlor, was the *ben*. To go from kitchen to parlor was to '*go ben*' and to return was to '*go but*'.

53-56   The **Moralitas** is written in eight-lines stanzas instead of the Rhyme Royal stanza of the rest of the *Morall Fabillis*. The only other exception is the first three stanzas of the last *Moralitas*. No reasonable justification for these exceptions has been suggested to date.

56.391   Solomon sayis: Not found in any of the books attributed to Solomon, but perhaps a blending of Eccl. 3:12, 3:22, 5:18, and 8:15.

Sir Chanticlere and the Fox

58   This Stanza is another example of the modesty *topos* (Cf. Stanzas 5, 6, and 17), this time developed into a jest by the suggestion that the story happened *this ather yeir*. This story was clearly adapted from Chaucer's *Nun's Priest's Tale*, written a century earlier.

59.417   Devydit nicht: Literary tradition notwithstanding, cocks crow at other times than at dawn. Chanticlere seems to have enjoyed the midnight hour. The term '*devydit nicht*' may come from the Latin, referring to the sounding of trumpets dividing the night into separate watches.

61.428   Werie for nicht: Suggestive of the various duties he was called upon to perform during the night. Cf. Stanzas 59, 75, and 76.

62.434   Chanticlere: A common name for a cock, found in the *Roman de Renart* and in Chaucer's tale; it means 'one who sings clearly.'

64.449   the Dirigie: Referring to the service of Matins in the Office for the dead, being the first words of the antiphon *Dirige, Domine, Deus meus, in conspectu tuo viam meam* (Psalm 5:8). Cf. modern 'dirge.'

69.483   Pertok, Sprutok, and Toppok: Names used elsewhere in literature for hens. Pertok is related both to Pertelote in Chaucer and Pinte in the *Roman de Renart*; Sprutok may come from the word meaning 'speckled'; and Toppok may come from 'tuft' or 'top.'

72   A parody of the formal lament for the dead, even to the 'who shall' formula.

73.511   Sanct Johne to borrow: A commonplace in Scottish literature, having the form of an expletive.

73.515   'wes never wedow sa gay!': Presumably a popular song, no longer identifiable.

74.519   off Nature cauld and dry: A preponderance of cold and dry elements in one's psychological makeup was supposed to cause impotence.

75.529   claw oure breik: '*breik*' sometimes has the meaning 'breeches' in Middle Scots, but here seems to mean 'rump.' '*Claw*' applies well enough to a rooster but also was used in Middle Scots as a term for human sexual caresses.

76.533   ma than sevin: Seven also connoted 'a large quantity'; 'more than seven' might then indicate innumerability. For the irony of the usage here, Cf. I. 120 and note.

78.546-47   Berrie . . . Nutticlyde: It is almost a proverb that the less money a farmer has, the more dogs the farmer owns. The names of the Widow's dogs are all quite common ones: 'Berrie' means 'shaggy'; 'Bawsie Brown' suggests 'tawny'; 'Curtes' resembles 'Curtois,' the name of the dog in the Reynardian tales. **Rype schaw** and **Rin well** might be names of yet other dogs, rather than commands from the Widow.

78.550   Or ellis to me se ye cum never agane: This Spartan command-ment indicates the importance of the Cock to the financial and the emotional well-being of the entire household. The Widow was so poor that she could ill

afford to lose any of her possessions; but if the dogs could not retrieve Chanticlere, ruin would be so certain that the loss of the dogs would make no difference.

80.563   ffor ane yeir: The phrase suggests 'for a long time to come,' but
it was also language commonly used in employment contracts.

83.585   Lewer: 'A domed turret-like erection on the roof of the hall or
other apartment in a Medieval building with the lateral openings for the passage
of smoke or the admission of light' [OED].

The Confession of the Fox

90.631   thair moving in the Spheir: The spheres were once imagined as
hollow, transparent, concentric globes revolving around the earth and bearing
the heavenly bodies.

90.634   as Lowrence leirnit me: It is unclear why the narrator claims the
Fox as his instructor. This recurs in Stanza 126.

91   Five of the six deities named here are in the signs that they rule, indicating that whatever happens will happen in the extreme: (1) Saturn in Capricorn—self-reliance; pressure towards honesty and intelligent ordering of affairs;
tendency to hurry through experiences; (2) Jupiter in Saggitarius—self-sufficiency;
enthusiasm; sense of free-living; (3) Mars in Aries—inclination to act with simple
assurance, meeting the needs of the moment, ignoring more long-term consequences; violence; (4) Venus in Cancer—concerned with own desires; attempts
to insulate self from negative experiences; (5) Mercury in Virgo—worry; intense
self-analysis and self-criticism; (6) Sun in Leo—self-reliance; complacency; high
degree of imagination. Since the Sun is in Leo, the month must be July or August.

94.661   Widdinek: A rogue hanged by the neck by a withe or withy, a
halter of willow twigs (as opposed to a hempen rope).

95.667   Waitskaith: 'one who lies in wait to do hurt ('skaith').'

96.671   with hude in to his nek: In pretended humility, as a sign of respect
for the station of Friar Wolf.

97.679   Russet: A coarse, home-spun cloth; not a color.

99.693   Benedicitie: 'God's blessing on you,' a prayer recited in preface
to confession.

102.714   the thrid part of penitence: The Sacrament of Penance consists
of three parts: (1) *Contritio*; (2) *Confessio*; and (3) *Satisfactio* (to repent of the
deed; to confess the deed, promising never to do it again; and to make amends
through some form of action).

111.776   without contritioun: Variants of this line in other manuscripts
and prints, as well as variants of lines 778, 779, and 794 in this tale and of several
others throughout, show evidence of Protestant revision. For example, '*without
contritioun*' here is amended to '*without provisioun*' in three other witnesses. '*Gois
now to confessioun*' in l. 779 is amended to '*now hes gude professioun*,' and so forth.

The Trial of the Fox

114.798   That to his airschip micht of law succeid: By law, illegitimate
children had none of the rights of inheritence enjoyed by legitimate offspring.

120.839   ane busteous Bugill blaw: The noise alluded to here and in the next stanza may be connected to the bellowing noise sometimes attributed to a Unicorn.

120.844   pursephant: A Pursuivant was an heraldic officer, attendant to a lord or king, who often had the power to serve and deliver legal documents.

121.848   Oyas! Oyas!: The traditional call to attention of an officer of the Court, still in use today (normally as 'Oyez').

122.855   The Nobil Lyoun: a conventional epithet from the Reynardian stories, used so commonly that 'Noble' became a proper name for the Lion.

123.862   Parliament: By the end of the thirteenth century, 'Parliament' in Scotland referred primarily to the council sitting in its capacity as the Supreme Court of Law.

125.873   Thre Leopardis: This might well be a heraldic jest. Three 'leopards' appear on the English coat of Arms; thus the Scottish lion here is being royally attended by the English leopards. (The 'leopards' are actually lions, but only the lion pictured in a rearing position was actually called 'lion.')

126.884   to me as Lowrence leird: see l. 634 and note.

127-131   Formal lists describing an assembly of beasts, based on the Bestiaries, were common in Middle English and Middle Scots literature. See especially Chaucer's *Parliament of Foules* (330 ff.) and King James's *The Kingis Quair* (St. 154-158).

127.887   The Minotaur, ane Monster mervelous: marvellous both because of its bodily make-up and its birth (from Pasiphae and a bull).

127.888   Bellerophont, that beist of Bastardie: Presumably a mistaken reference for the Chimaera slain by Bellerophon. Its multiform body, with heads of lion, goat, and dragon, justifies the label of 'Bastardy.'

127.889-90   the Pegase . . . sorcerie: Pegasus, the winged horse, was 'dangerous' to the Chimaera. Minerva (through 'sorcery') gave Pegasus a magic bit, through which aid he helped to kill the Chimaera.

127.892   the Dromedarie: In the Bestiaries, the dromedary was a species of camel, but smaller and swifter.

128.895   The Anteloip: Not our modern antelope, but a heraldic concoction with the body of a tiger.

The Sparth: not identified as the name of an animal. There are several editorial suggestions, none of which seem satisfying. Given its placement in the group of antelope, panther, and unicorn, we can assume that whatever it was, it must have been large, swift, and powerful.

128.897   The Rayndeir: In heraldry, represented by a stag with one set of horns branching upward and another branching downward.

129.906   The wylde Once: Probably a heraldic beast; something like the leopard, lynx, or wildcat.

130.910   the Glebard: Perhaps a member of the rodent family, given the animals that surround it in the description.

130.912   The Feitho: A fitchew or polecat.

130.914   The Bowranbane: Again nothing certain is known of this word.

Werewolf, badger, and white otter are some possibilities; one editor has suggested the word is really three words meaning 'the whole pack ran quickly.'

the Lerioun: Another mystery. Young rabbit, hare, grey dormouse, and small greyhound have all been suggested.

133-135   I lat yow wit . . . nor ryde: A familiar pronouncement by the Lion in medieval beast-fables, echoing the motto of the kings of Scotland: '*Parcere prostratis scit nobilis ira leonis.*'

134.940-41   **The Dromedarie . . . The grit Camel**: See note to l. 892.

135.943   **be twentie mylis**: A common proclamation used by courts when travelling from county to county. The slightest illegal action, if perpetrated near the court and during a session, was treated as an act in contempt of court and punished most harshly.

135.948   **to gar fence**: The opening of court proceedings by a formulaic proclamation forbidding interruption and obstruction.

139.975   **thy Phisnomie**: Cf. Stanzas 403, 404, and notes.

143.999   **rampand**: The heraldic pose for the Lion, as on the Scottish coat of arms. Cf. note to l.873.

143.1004   **Contumax**: 'in contempt of court.'

146.1025   **Lupus**: The Fox uses the Latin word for Wolf, perhaps in mockery of the Wolf's supposed classical education.

147.1033   **Felix . . . cautum**: 'Happy are they who learn from the misfortunes of others.'

149.1042   **Sydelingis abak**: Perhaps indicating the Fox's unwillingness to turn his back on the Wolf, even for a moment. In any event, his movement is anything but 'straightforward.'

150.1053   **With his reid cap**: As a sign of their academic status, holders of doctoral degrees were privileged to wear the *pileus*, a round and close-fitting red cap.

152.1064   **Clerkis**: The term was originally limited to the clergy but expanded to include all scholars, students, notaries, secretaries, accountants, and penmen.

155.1087   **Assyis**: A combination jury and grand jury, chosen from local residents.

155.1089   **pyking**: This word is redundant, coming after '*thift*,' but none of the other variants makes better sense.

156.1091   **To gif the dome**: This would be done by the dempster, an officer of the court directed to pronounce sentences.

159   Several of the textual witnesses show extensive Protestant revision in this stanza. E.g.: 'The Meir is men of gude conditioun,/ As Pilgrymes walkand in this wildernes,/ Approvand that for richt Religioun/ Thair God onlie to pleis in everilk place,/ Abrastractit from this warldis wretchitness,/ Fechtand with lust presumptioun and pryde,/ And fra this warld in mynd ar mortyfyde.'

161-162   The text of these two stanzas is uncertain at best. It is probable that none of the major witnesses has preserved the original text.

161.1130   **Salomonis saying**: Not Solomon's words, yet with a Solomonic ring to them. See Proverbs 28.5,14.

The Sheep and the Dog

164.1147   because that he wes pure: Secular matters could be brought before the ecclesiastical court only if the plaintiff was an ecclesiastic or someone in the care of the Church (the Dog, in this case, being one of the parish poor).

164.1148   the Consistorie: Scotland's ecclesiastical court. Henryson's descriptions appear quite accurate in detail.

165.1153-54   For by the use . . . Citatioun: A parodic example of legal jargon and style, especially in the multiplication of terms.

165.1156-67   off hie Suspensioun,/ Off grit Cursing, and interdictioun: The three major ecclesiastical penalties. (1) High Suspension deprives a cleric of his right to perform ecclesiastical functions; (2) Excommunication excludes the person in question from all sacraments and prayers of the Church; (3) Interdiction censures the person in question and excludes the person from the liturgy, sacraments, and holy burial.

166.1161   Quha pykit had fful mony Scheipis Ee: It is believed that a raven will dig out the eyeballs of a dead or dying sheep.

166.1162   letteris: Charges to pay or perform, issued in the name of the sovereign, are still called the 'King's letters.'

166.1164   Peremptourlie: A peremptory summons rendered the defendent in contempt of court for non-appearance (the state here called *contumax*). Normally it was issued only after two regular summonses had been ignored, but in extreme cases it could be the original issuance.

167.1169   Indorsat: The apparitor must endorse the summons in order to establish that he has served it.

167.1173   Hesperus: The evening star.

168.1175   at the bar: The barristers customarily stood at the bar, that is, at the railing in front of the judges' bench.

169.1183   worth fyve schilling or mair: The price of bread in fifteenth and sixteenth century Scotland ranged from halfpenny to four pence, varying with the date, and with the size and type of loaf. The Dog's claim, therefore, is inflated anywhere from 25 to 400 times.

169.1185   but Advocate, allone: The Court was supposed to supply free legal counsel for the poor, but it often failed to do so.

170.1189-90   The Law . . . Juge suspect: The very pleading of a case implied the plaintiff's having accepted the jurisdiction of the Judge. Were the Sheep to plead his case before objecting to the Judge's participation, he would lose his opportunity to do so.

171.1199   The place is fer: Under normal rules of procedure, defendants were not required to travel outside of their legal district to respond to a summons. **the tyme is feriate**: Courts were not allowed to convene within official legal vacations.

171.1201   Sa lait at evin: The ecclesiastical court was restricted to sitting during the hours of daylight.

172   The arbitrators were to decide only the question of the Judge's competence to sit on the case. However, given the one-side nature of the evidence, any decision by the arbitrators in favor of the Dog would bode ill for the Sheep's chances in the case proper.

174.1217   The Codes and Digests new and ald: Alluding to the accidental division of the Code of Justinian into *digestum vetus, infortiatum, et novum*, made by Bulgarus in the twelfth century. The entire Stanza is concerned with Roman Civil Law.

174.1221   the glose and Text of the Decreis: Probably a reference to the *corpus juris civilis* ('the decrees') with the marginal gloss of Accursius, which supplanted all other glosses and was held by the courts to have the force of law.

175.1228   ffra thair sentence couth he not appeill: Canon Law dictated that both parties to an arbitration are bound by the decision and have no right of appeal, because each had the right of veto in the selection of the arbitrators.

178.1249   the selie Innocent: 'Selie,' meaning 'poor, innocent' (cf. German *selig*, 'holy') is used by Henryson primarily for the Country Mouse, the Sheep, and the Lamb.

Moralitas   Henryson here switches his attention from the ecclesiastical Court to the Sheriff's Court, a notoriously corrupt forum, run by the controlling hand of a local politician. By switching courts for the *Moralitas*, Henryson may have been indicating that any corrupt court can represent any other. More unusual is the extention of the fable's satire into the stanzas of the *Moralitas*. The Sheep dominates five of these nine stanzas.

182.1274   the Justice Air: The Justices in Eyre were royal judges and sergeants-at-law who would travel about the country, bringing the law available in the centers of population to the outlying districts.

182.1277-78   To scraipe out . . . the partes skat: Presumably John would pay to get his name erased, and another party would pay to falsely involve Will or Walt.

184.1288   Boreas: The North wind.

185.1295   Lord God, quhy sleipis thow sa lang?: The 'sleep of God' was a common expression of the time describing a period of hardship, depression, and lawlessness. It has sources in Psalms, I Kings, and Matthew.

185.1298   Peillit full bair: In their editions, G. G. Smith, Wood, and Elliott end the Sheep's lament here (with the closing of the quote), giving the rest of the *Moralitas* to the narrator's voice. However, editors Laing, Murray, and Fox extend the Sheep's quotation to the end of the *Moralitas*. Either interpretation is possible, and both have distinct and striking effects.

187.1310   Simonie: 'The act or practice of buying or selling ecclesiastical preferments, benefices, or emoluments; traffic in sacred things' [*OED*].

The Lion and the Mouse

190.1328   flouris, quhyte and reid: The traditional colors of flowers in courtly allegory, usually referring either to lillies and roses or to the English daisy. White betokens chastity, purity, loyalty, etc.; red suggests courage, passion, youth, and the like.

192.1345   Syne maid a cors: Several witnesses show Protestant revision here to '*syne cled me heid*' ('then covered my head').

192.1346   On sleip I fell: This tale is told in the familiar Medieval form of the dream vision. See Introduction, p. 22.

192.1348   The fairest man that ever befoir I saw: In contrast to the more traditional portrayal of Aesop as a deformed and ugly slave. See Introduction, p. 6.

193.1351   Scarlet: A variety of cloth; not a color. Scarlet was so often produced in red that term eventually came to signify the familiar color instead of the material.

195.1366   Father: A term of respect.

196.1371   My native land is Rome: See Introduction, p. 6.

196.1376   kend to mony cunning Clerk: Aesopic fables were included on many Medieval reading lists for study as part of the Trivium. They had a reputation that rivalled that of Ovid's *Metamorphoses*.

197.1377   Poet Lawriate: Since the appointment in 1670 of John Dryden as the first English Poet Lauriate ('poet crowned with laurels'), the term has denoted an official of the royal household expected to write poetry in commemoration and celebration of important events. The position has been held both by the spinners of webs (Dryden, Wordsworth, Tennyson) and the boilers of pots (William Whitehead, Henry James Pye, etc.); in Henryson's time, however, the term was both the highest of compliments that could be paid a poet and a reference to the actual conferring of a 'degree' for poetry by a University. Outside of England the practice of Laureation had begun in the fourteenth century with Petrarch, who arranged to have himself so crowned.

197.1381   prudence: See Introduction, p. 8.

200.1399   Fatherheid: A term used especially in addressing ecclesiastics of high rank.

201.1407   Beikand his breist and belly in the Sun: Cf. 11. 756-57. 'Beik' ('bask,' 'warm') suggests dangerous complacency and immersion in sensual pleasures.

201.1410   all dansand in ane gyis: In Medieval art, music and dancing often symbolized sinful frivolity.

208.1460   harlit be the feit: Criminals guilty of high treason were traditionally dragged to the gallows by the feet.

210.1473   equitie: Under English law, once a person had been convicted or found liable under the rigid procedures of the courts of Law, he or she could seek a further remedy in the court of Equity, which had the power to use general principles of justice to temper the harshness of some strictly legal decisions.

215.1503-06   The Mouse has presented an exhaustive argument. Admitting (in Stanza 204) that she has no case under Law, she gives the Lion eleven different reasons why she should be absolved under Equity. For the only time in all of the *Morall Fabillis*, reasonable argument, based on truth and the concept of mercy, succeeds in persuading a beast to act justly.

222.1558   brother: elsewhere the Mouse is referred to as female, except perhaps in l. 1418 ('*maister mous*').

The Preaching of the Swallow

237.1660   makand Harmonie and sound: The ancient belief that the orderly motions of the heavenly bodies produced a perfect music, inaudible to humans (with the possible exception of true lovers and great philosophers).

237.1661   The fyre, the Air, the watter, and the ground: the four elements from which everything in existence is composed, according to medieval science. They are listed here from the highest to the lowest, paralleling the movement of the passage from God to man.

237.1663   God in all his werkis wittie is: the argument that the order in the Universe presupposes a divine Creator to establish that order. Henryson mirrors the order of divine creation by giving his own literary creation an underlying order and structure that is not necessarily apparent to the reader. See Introduction, p. 18.

240.1678   The Somer . . . : Henryson describes the seasons in their cyclical order here from Summer to Spring and then continues into a second cycle within the tale proper, that time progressing from Spring to Winter.

241.1690   Copia temporis: Literally 'the season's plenty,' here personified. She fills her horn, the cornucopia.

242-43   Note that while one stanza is sufficient to describe the other seasons, Winter here requires two—a reasonable ratio for a poet writing in Scotland.

242.1693   blastis boreall: See l. 1288 and note.

244.1707   The Secretar off Somer with his Sell: The seal was the legal symbol necessary for making any formal agreement legitimate and binding. It would be entrusted only to one's closest and most trustworthy associate.

246.1720-21   grit myrth I tuke in mynd,/ Off laubouris to se the besines: Throughout the *Morall Fabillis* Henryson praises those who labor and attacks those who shrink from it. Cf. Stanzas 11 and 101.

246.1722   dyke: Either stone walls or drainage ditches.

246.1724   Harrowis: Machines which break and smooth out plowed land.

247   Cf. Stanza 192. See Introduction, p. 22.

250.1754   Nam leuius . . . ante: 'For he who provides beforehand will suffer less.' Note that the proverb does not suggest that prudent provision will cancel suffering altogether.

252   See Appendix A for Henryson's use of proverbs in argumentation.

261   This passage accurately summarizes the procedure for making flax in Henryson's time and up into the early twentieth century, essentially the same process used by the ancient Egyptians. *pullit*: The flax is pulled up, never cut. *Rippillit*: The seed-pods ('*bollis*') are removed by drawing the flax through a kind of comb (a '*ripple*'). Then it is put in sheaves ('*beitis*') and soaked ('*steipit*') in water so that it will ferment and allow the valuable fibers to separate from the woody tissues. Then it is dried, and the fibers are extracted by breaking up the woody tissues, in this case by a most primitive method. The flax is pounded with a mallet or beetle ('*bittill*'). Then it is beaten and scraped with a wooden blade ('*swingillit*') in order to clean it. Finally it is repeatedly drawn through a flax comb ('*hekkillit*'). [Denton Fox's description]

275.1924   The halie Preichour: Cf. ll. 1389-90.

276.1932   the wormis Keitching: Cf. l. 94 and note. The situation is reversed.

277.1939   Best is bewar in maist properitie: Cf. Stanzas 42, 68, 108, 152, and 202.

The Fox, the Wolf, and the Cadger

280.1962   Russell: 'reddish' or 'reddish-brown.' Russell became a proper name for the Wolf in beast fables; but it was on occasion given to the Fox (e.g. Chaucer's *Nun's Priest's Tale*).

290.2028   Cadgear: An itinerant dealer who travels with a horse and basket selling foodstuffs from town to town or to remote farms. This is the first recorded use of the word.

292.2045   he is not worth ane fle: A common comparison (see also l. 2286 and l. 2402), perhaps because flies were such a constant problem. Cf. the proverb 'The blind may eat many a fly' (Whiting B 348).

293.2055   als straucht as he wer deid: Cf. l. 2027.

295.2063   Heir lyis the Devyill . . . deid in ane dyke: An ironic reference to the proverb 'Seldom lies the Devil dead in a ditch' (Whiting D 202).

296.2074   Till Flanderis: Where the great trading in skins took place.

296.2076   creillis: The saddlebaskets in which he carried the fish.

297.2083   Huntis up:: 'The hunt is up' is an English air of uncertain date but of well-attested popularity. Any song intended to arouse a sleeper was called a 'Hunt's up.' Thus the Cadger's singing it here presents a double irony: (1) The hunt is literally 'up,' as the Fox throws the fish down to theWolf; and (2) the Cadger should 'awaken' to the situation.

298.2089   Nekhering: A stiff blow on the neck. No other English example of this term has been recorded.

303.2120   thir fourtie dayis: the forty days of Lent.

308.2154   In Principio: The first words of Genesis and of John. The term became part of the jargon of the friars because the verses were thought to have special powers.

310.2169   Come rydand on the laid, for it wes licht: When the horse had been carrying a full load, the Cadger had gone on foot so as not to overburden him (Cf. l. 2077).

312.2184   He mycht not se, he wes sa verray blind: This involuntary sightlessness, betokening a spiritual blindness, results directly from his having closed his eyes voluntarily. All the beasts who either look down (see l. 1021, l. 1792) or close their eyes (see l. 477, l. 1412) find themselves deceived or endangered. The ill timed temporary sightlessness betokens a chronic spiritual blindness.

316.2213   the gold sa reid: A customary epithet for gold, since it was often alloyed with copper, which gave it a reddish tinge.

The Fox, the Wolf, and the Farmer

319.2232   ane pleuch to steir: The farming methods described in this fable are remarkably similar to those employed in the Island of Lewis in the early nineteenth century. See Appendix B for the full text of James Hogg's letter to Sir Walter Scott describing those methods.

319.2235-36   to follow furth his feir/ Unto the pleuch: The Farmer leaves his plough in the field at night and marks a path to enable him to find it easily the next morning.

319.2236   his gadman: The farmhand who uses a sharp spike or goad to lead the oxen while ploughing.

319.2237   Benedicite: See l. 693 and note.

320.2238   The Caller: the driver of the team. Here the teamster and the goadsman seem to be the same person.

320.2243   Patill: The paddle-shapped tool used by the ploughman for scraping off the heavy earth sticking to his plough.

324.2266   gaif thou not me this drift: Modern contract law could be said to have been born in 1425 with the Writ of Assumpsit, which eventually led to the enforcement of a promise without a sealed writing; but by Henryson's time contract law had not developed to the point where such an offhand statement might seriously pose a legal problem. Had the statement been made under or with an oath, the promisor might have been in danger of damaging his soul but not of paying damages to the promisee.

325.2275   I hecht to steil, am I thairfoir ane theif?: One of the theoretical difficulties being faced at the time in the development of contract law.

326.2285   it is said in Proverb: It is not clear whether the reference is to the Bible or to proverbial lore in general. The phrase does not appear in Proverbs, but Henryson's animals often quote the Bible ad libitum. Cf. l. 391, l. 1130, and notes.

327.2289   I am na King: Cf. l. 2251.

327.2293   say na thing bot as thou hard and saw: Witnesses at trial, then as now, were restricted to testifying as to what they saw and heard first-hand.

328.2294   for he lufit never licht: Cf. l. 203.

329.2301-02   I can not hastelie/ Swa sone as now gif sentence finall: Lawyerly avoidance, featuring six modifiers of 'gif sentence.'

330.2310   now I am ane Juge amycabill: Besides the possibility of 'agreed to by both,' 'amycabill' may suggest (1) a 'friendly' Judge, willing to accept tokens of 'friendship' from either or both parties; and (2) a 'friend of the court' who presents an objective view of the point of law under examination; here the Fox gives each his 'objective view' (see OED, 'amicable,' 2).

331.2316   thow: The Wolf uses the familiar form of address, 'thou,' when speaking to both the Fox and the Farmer; the Farmer uses the respectful form of address, 'ye,' to both animals; the Fox uses the respectful 'ye' to the Wolf and the familiar 'thou' to the Farmer.

333.2329   I am ane juge: Perhaps an attack on judicial corruption, referring to the success of his extortion attempt.

333.2332   For God is gane to sleip: Cf. l. 1295 and note.

336.2355   Somer Cheis: Cheese made in Summer, when the milk is at its best.

336.2356   it wayis ane stane: Since 1618 the weight of one stone has been standardized at 17.39 pounds avoirdupois.

345.2419   scho quheillis ane uther doun: Fortune and her Wheel.

348-349   These two stanzas are suggestive of textual corruption throughout, given their mixed metaphors, ambiguous references, and awkward rhythms.

349.2444   Mammon: The demon associated with gold.

The Wolf and the Wether

354.2476   **Wedder**: A male sheep.

364.2550   **quhyte as ane Freir**: The Carmelites were known as the 'white Friars' because of their white habits.

364.2552   **ye sall rew this rais**: Witticism on the part of the Wolf: 'to rue a race' is idiomatic for 'to repent of the course one has taken' (*OED*, 'race' sb.1, 1b), but the Wether is also literally racing after the Wolf.

366.2560   **Is this your bourding in ernist than**: The Wolf is playing with the common rhetorical oppostion of 'earnest' and 'game.'

372.2608   **Hall benkis ar rycht slidder**: Refers to the benches at tables in the dining hall. Seating placements were assigned according to rank and favoritism; from one's place one would know one's place.

The Wolf and the Lamb

374.2620   **ane selie Lamb**: Cf. l. 1249 and note.

375.2629   **Rampand**: Cf. l. 873, l. 999, and notes.

378.2650   **Ergo**: Latin for 'therefore'; used to announce the conclusion of a logical argument.

380-382   In these stanzas the Lamb offers an argument from Ezekiel 18, that 'the son shall not bear the iniquity of the father.' The Wolf counters with Exodus 20:5: 'I am the Lord thy God, mighty, jealous, visiting the iniquity of the fathers upon the children, even unto the third and fourth generation of them that hate me.' The Wolf misuses the Exodus text, both by assuming the voice of God and by applying the concept to a matter of private revenge.

381.2671   **yit pietis thow agane?**: The Lamb has presented arguments drawn from physics, Natural Law, the Word of God, and the Common Law. The Wolf, seeing that he cannot refute these by reason, dismisses them all as legal 'quibbling' and relies on a 'principle' of physical force.

386.2702   **Syne drank his blude and off his flesche can eit**: a perversion of the sacrament of Communion.

Moralitas   Henryson has structured this long *Moralitas* symmetrically. The first stanza establishes a general allegory, and the last stanza makes a plea based on the general allegory. The middle eight stanzas are divided into three more specific allegories, each of which is followed by a plea of the same length: 388, Wolf stands for corrupt lawyers; 389, Plea to lawyers not to be corrupt; 390, Wolf stands for greedy rich men; 391, Pleas to greedy men to share; 392-3, Wolf stands for landowners, Lamb for Cottars; 394-5, Plea to landowner to treat Cottars better.

390.2734   **Bot over his heid his mailling will they tak**: A rich person could deprive a poor person of his land by offering to pay a rent for the land so high that the poor person could not counter the offer when it was time to renew the lease.

391.2740   **Byre**: Cattle house.

392.2745   **Gressome**: A fee paid by a tenant to the landholder for entering into or renewing a lease (and therefore distinct from the annual rent). Should the tenant default on the lease in any way, the contract would be broken, and he would have to pay the Gressom again in order to reestablish his legal standing.

393.2749-52   he man len to the Laird . . . withoutin Meit or wage: A lord could requisition the labor of both tenants and tenants' animals a certain percentage of the year as part of the leasing agreement. No wages were to be paid, but the lord was expected to furnish adequate food on the days the work was required. Tenant farmers were more or less without effective remedy if the lord abused this power, since often the only justice that was local and immediate was presided over by the same lord or that lord's immediate superior.

393.2755   watter caill: Cf. l. 321 and note.

The Paddock and the Mouse

398.2786   Paddok: A frog or toad.

398.2790   schir Mous: '*Schir*' was occasionally used for females. See *OED*, 'sir,' 7b, 9.

399.2796   Bot har nuttis, quhilkis with my teith I bore: Cf. ll. 15-6 and l. 223.

400.2798   heir is no Maryner: Pompous hyperbole. A ferryman can hardly be considered a mariner.

400.2802   or yit Galay: Perhaps a pompous response to the Mouse's pompous '*Maryner*.' A galley is an armed warship.

402.2816   my oppin Gill: Perhaps a bit of deception on the part of the Paddock, since adult frogs do not have open gills.

404.2831   Lorum: An abbreviated form of '*culorum*' from '*in secula seculorum*,' signifying 'conclusion.'

404.2832   Distortum vultum sequitur distortio morum: 'A distorted mien denotes a distorted morality.'

405.2835   Blaberyis: The blue-black fruit of the dwarf shrub *Vaccinium Myrtillas*; also called 'whortleberries.'

406.2842   Wer I als fair as Jolie Absolon: a stock medieval comparison for extreme good looks in a man, referring to David's handsome son. See 2 Samuel 14:25.

406.2845-46   Almychtie God . . . creature: Commonplace medieval perception of the relationship between God and Nature.

409.2865   the murthour aith: This term is recorded only in Henryson (see also l. 2884). Its meaning is not certain and can only be guessed from this context.

411.2875   Then fute for fute: Cf. l. 196.

413.2891   upwart . . . doun: Cf. l. 331 and l. 2419.

413.2892   Quhyle to, quhyle ffra: Cf. l. 1525 and l. 2782.

415.2904   And belliflaucht full fettillie thame flaid: referes to pulling the skin over the head in one piece and suggests a high degree of deliberation, thoroughness, and grotesque skill.

415.2905   Bot all thair flesch wald scant be half ane fill: Cf. l. 1493.

**416-418   Three eight-line stanzas, instead of the normal seven-line Rhyme Royal stanzas. See the *Moralitas* to the fable of the Two Mice for the sole other exception (stanzas 53-56 and note). Here the change in form also marks a change in focus for the *Moralitas*, from a generalized interpretation of the action to a specific explanation of the allegory. Henryson has built in a hinge between the two forms of stanzas, beginning the seven-liners with '*This hald in mynde; rycht more I sall the tell . . .*'

417.2923   Smytis more sore than ony schot of arrow: See ll. 765-74 and compare the harshness of that outcome with ll. 2903-06.

424.2971   I left the laif unto the Freiris: The Friars used a great many *exempla* in their sermons. Henryson here may be criticizing their tendency to overinterpret ('*the laif*' referring to interpretations other than those he has set forth here); alternatively, he may simply be making a present of '*the laif*,' all other fables, to the Friars.

TEXTUAL VARIANTS

Reference Key:

(A)   the Asloan MS
(B)   the Bannatyne MS
(Bs)   the Bassandyne print
(C)   the Charteris print
(H)   the Harleian MS
(Ht)   the Hart print
(Mk)   the Makculloch MS
(S)   the Smith print

The Prologue

4.22	For as we se (B); Forther mair (BsCH).
5.30	To (BMkHtS); in (BsCH).
6.40	Gif ye find ocht that (BMk); Gif that ye find it (BsCH).
7.45	And (BMkS); In (BsCH).
7.47	Putting (BMk); Put in (BsCH).
8.55	the mynd (BMk); thair myndis (BsCH).
8.56	he (BMk); thay (BsCH).
	beist (BMkHt); beistis (BsCH).
	is (Mk); ar (BsCHHt).

The Cock and the Jasper

14.98	(BMk); For les availl may me as now dispyis (BsCHHt).
15.102	that (BMk); [omitted] (BsCH).
	werk is (Mk); werkis ar (BsCH).
15.104	weill (BMk); [omitted] (BsCH).
17.118	fabill (BMk); [omitted] (BsCH).
18.120	hes (BMk); had (BsCH).
18.121	is (BMk); was (BsCH).
18.126	Of (BMkHt); or (BsCH).
19.131	ay (BMk); for (BsCH).
20.139	can treit (CHtS); can screit (BsH).
21.145	argumentis (BMkHt); argument (BsCH).

The Country Mouse and the City Mouse

27.185	(B); Scho ran cryand quhill scho came to a balk (BsCH).
27.186	sueit (BA); [omitted] (BsCH).

30.206   peis (BA); candill (BsCH).
31.216   syre, levand in (AB); leving into (BsCH).
35.239   this (BA); hir (BsCH).
36.251   na fall, na trap (B); nor fall trap (BsCH).
37.263   skugry ay (B); stubill array (BsCH)
         rankest (BA); [omitted] (BsCH).
40.278   bot (B); [omitted] (BsCHA).
41.285   And mane full (C); And manfully (BsS).
49.337   Syne (BA); And (BsCH).
         the (BAS); ane (BsCH).
49.339   And (BA); Syne (BsCH).
         clukis (B); cluke thair (BsCH).

Sir Chanticlere and the Fox

58.407   it excedis (B); is excludit (BsCH).
65.457   Yow for to serve (B); To mak yow blyith (BsCH).
67.472   'Quhat?' quo the cok (B); 'For' (quod the Tod) (BsCH).
68.477   walkit (B); wawland (BsCH).
69.486   reylok (B); hay (BsCH).
75.523   that (B); with (BsCH).
75.524   (B); 'In lust but lufe he set all his delyte . . . (BsCH). BsCH be-
         gins the quote at 524; others at 525.
76.533   (B); He had' (quod scho) 'kittokis ma than sevin (BsCH).
76.536   (B); For Adulterie, that will thame not repent (BsCH).
78.546   Bell (B); [omitted] (BsCH).
79.555   raches (B); Kennettis (BsCH).
81.570   unto a (B); out off the (BsCH).
83.581   coud nocht be still (B); to be sa still (BsCH).

The Confession of the Fox

88.618   miching (B); waitting (BsCH).
89.621   Thetes (B); [Omitted] (BsCH).
93.649   watt (B); ken (BsCH).
93.651   fait (B); men (BsCH).
93.652   bot (BHt); bot gif (BsCH).
93.653   Deid (B); It (BsCH).
93.653   and (B); ane (BsCH).
93.655   all (B); my (BsCH).
94.659   alyk ar (B); ar lyke (BsCH).
94.662   ar hangit (B); hangit up (BsCH).
95.665   thence (HBHtS); hence (BsC).
95.666   of (HBHt); in (BsC).
95.668   cum (BHt); cummit (BsCH).
97.680   and (B); [omitted] (BsCH).

98.684	A (B); Na (BsCH).
99.697	mele (B); kneill (BsH).
104.729	I falt of (C); I fall no (BsHtS).
	in to (CB); unto (BsHtS).
105.736	walternad (B); water and (BsCH).
105.737	All stonist (B); Astonist all (BsCH).
106.741	For (B); and (BsCH).
	net nor; nor net (BsCH).
110.772	The hird him hynt (B); He harlit him (BsCH).
111.776	contritioun (B); provision (BsCH).
111.777	mend (HB); amend (BsC).
111.778	conclusioun (B); confusioun (BsCH).
111.779	gois now to confessioun (B); now hes gude professioun (BsCH).
	Can not repent (B); yit not repentis (BsCH).
113.791	hartis noit (CBHtS); hartis be noit (BsH).
113.794	Do wilfull pennance here (B); Obey unto your God (BsCH).

The Trial of the Fox

114.798	(B); Till airschip be Law that micht succeid (BsCH).
115.806	wrang (B); fals (BsCH).
116.812	is (B); hes (BsCH).
119.836	(B); To execute, to do, to satisfie (BsCH).
119.837	(B); Thy letter will, thy det, and legacie (BsCH).
120.838	carit (B); he passit (BsCH).
120.841	Lines 841 and 842 are transposed in BsCH.
121.848	Oyas! Oyas! (B); on this wyis (BsCH).
122.852	his (CBHt); ane (BsHS).
	buste (BCHt); bus (BsH).
	bill (BCHt); bull (BsHS).
125.873	Thre (B); The (BsCHHt).
	a (B); with (BsCH).
125.877	pollis (B); towis (BsH).
130.908	gay (BHt); gray (BsCH).
	the (B); with (BsCH).
143.993	My Lord (B); now see (BsCH).
148.105	This (B); This writchit (BsCH).
	on his wayis (B); thus on he (BsCH).
150.1052	This new-maid (B); Speir at your (BsCH).
152.1067	garray (B); merines (BsCH).
156.1095	Basare (B); Bowcher (BsCH).
159.1111	contemplatioun (B); gude contitioun (BsCH).
159.1112	Off pennance (B); As Pilgymes (BsCH).
159.1113	(B); Approvand that for richt Religioun (BsCH).
159.1114	That presis God (B); Thair God onlie (BsCH).
159.1116	In . . . pomp (B); Fechtand with lust, presumptioun (BsCH).

162.1134   That . . . of (B); Assaultand men with sweit (BsCH).
            religiounis [religioun] (B); preswasionis (BsCH).
162.1135   (B); Ay reddy for to trap thame in ane trayne (BsCH).
162.1139   Mary . . . mercy (cancelled in B); Mediatour! mercifull and
            (BsCH).
162.1140   Sitt . . . sone (B, with some cancellation); Thow soveraigne
            Lord and King (BsCH).
162.1141   For . . . celsitude (B); Thy celsitude maist humillie we (BsCH).

The Sheep and the Dog

164.1148   unto (B); to (BsCH).
168.1175   up (B); [omitted] (BsCH).
170.1194   as Juge (B); Juge as (BsCH).
174.1216   mony volum (B); Law volumis full mony (BsCH).
174.1218   Contra et pro, strait (Murray, Fox); prowe and contra strait (B);
            Contrait Prostrait (BsCH).
174.1220   nor (B); or (BsCH).
            thay (B); that thay (BsCH).
179.1251   persecutioun (B); the executioun (BsH).
182.1276   be (B); wes (BsCH).
182.1273   porteous (B); portioun (BsCH).
182.1278   swa (CBHt); tak (BsHS).
            skat (B); tat (BsH).
184.1289   frawart (B); hard (BsCH).
184.1292   hair (B); sair (BsCH).
186.1300   syn (B); sone (BsCH).
186.1301   (B); Loist hes baith lawtie and eik Law (BsCH).
186.1304   Jugis (Fox suggestion); Juge (B); Juge it (BsCH).
186.1305   Thay ar (B); he is (BsCH).
186.1306   meid thay thoill (B); micht he lettis (BsCH).

The Lion and the Mouse

189.1321   joly (B); [omitted] (BsCH).
189.1324   lemis (B); bemis (BsCH).
190.1331   gresis (B); gers (BsC).
191.1336   viola (CBHt); violat bla (BsH).
191.1340   the fowlis (Fox emendation); off fowlis (BsCHB).
192.1345   maid a cors (B); cled my heid (BsCH).
193.1350   chymmeris (B); Chemeis (BsCH).
198.1386   dedene (B); not disdane (BsCH).
201.1405   wery (B); war (BsH).
205.1438   prodissioun [Fox, based on promissioun (B)];
            presumptioun (BsCH).
205.1439   Erer (B); The rather (BsCH).

208.1460   Onto (B); Upon (BsCH).
209.1461   A (B); Na (BsCH).
210.1471   spirituall (B); speciall (BsCH).
218.1527   he knet (B); the New (BsCH).
221.1548   thy (B); off thy (BsCH).
            gentilnes (B); gentrace (BsH).
223.1562   abone (B); about (BsCH).
            for (B); of (BsHHt).
228.1599   commoun (B); kinbute (BsHHt).
231.1616   (B); I the beseik and all men for to pray (BsCH).

The Preaching of the Swallow

236.1653   takis (B); tak (BsCH).
240.1678   grene (HBHt); off grene (BsCS).
242.1697   changeis (B); changit (BsCH).
243.1701   ar bethit (B); laifit (BsH).
249.1744   lo se and (B); and gude (BsHHt).
251.1758   befoir and se[e] (B); and foirse (BsCH).
251.1761   ethar (B); the better (BsCH).
266.1863   mocht (CHtS); nocht (BsH).
267.1873   this (CHHtS); thus (Bs).
271.1903   delectatioun (BS); delectioun (BsCH).
275.1938   warldis (B); warld (BsCH).
278.1946   to seis (B); fra (BsCH).

The Fox, the Wolf, and the Cadger

279.1957   breith (C); wraith (BsHHtS).
307.2148   dow not (CHt); he will (BsHS).
310.2168   als wraith as ony (C); wavering as the (BsHHtS).
310.2171   revenge him best he (CHt); revengit on him he (BsHS).
313.2193   fyne (Ht); syne (BsC).
315.2207   men (HHtS); man (BsC).

The Fox, the Wolf, and the Farmer

339.2372   hous (HtS); hors (BsCH).
343.2399   Aa (Fox suggestion); Na (BsCHHTs)
347.2432   Arctand (C); Actand (BsHHt).
350.2454   from (CH); ftom (Bs).

The Wolf and the Wether

352.2468   with [editorial suggestion]; wit (BsCH).
354.2476   wichtlie [T.W.Craik suggestion]; wretchitlie (BsH).

353.2474 that (HtS); [omitted] (BsCH).
359.2516 thay (CH); lhay (Bs).
364.2548 Syne (CH); Tyne (Bs).

The Wolf and the Lamb

375.2628 presomyng (B); belevand (BsCH).
376.2632 this (CB); and (BsH).
377.2638 your (CHB); yuor (Bs).
381.2667 pais (B); prais (BsCH).
381.2668 pyne (B); pane (BsCH).
382.2677 to (CB); [omitted] (BsCH).
          spew (CB); did spew (BsH).
383.2682 audience (audiens) (B); evidence (BsCH).
384.2690 wyis (wys) (B); gyis (BsH).
385.2693 Ha (B); Na (BsCH).
385.2697 Goddis (B); his (BsCH).
386.2701 hedit (B); deid (BsCH).
386.2703 syne (HB); and (BsC).
388.2716 poleit (B); Poete (BcCH).
390.2729 aneuch (CB); full grit (BsC).
391.2738 crufe (Hunterian Club version of (B)); cruse (B); caff (BsCH).
393.2750 Cairt (B); Court (BsCH).
          and (2) (HB); or in (BsCH).
394.2760 be rad (B); dreid (BsCH).
396.2771 extortioneris (HB); exortioneris (BsC).
396.2773 manifest (B); manifestit (BsCH).
396.2776 of (B); out of (BsCH).

The Paddock and the Mouse

398.2789 rauk (CHB); rank (BsHtS).
400.2800 your (B); thy (BsH).
400.2802 withoutin (B); without (BsH).
400.2803 yow (B); the (BsH).
400.2804 your (B); thy (BsH).
401.2806 without (CHB); withont (Bs).
401.2808 droun to wed (drowin to wed) (B); drounit be (BsCH).
402.2815 swyme (B); row (BsCH).
410.2869 How (B); O (BsCH).
413.2893 this (2) (B); [omitted] (BsCH).
          in (B); in to (BsCH).
414.2898 owthir (BsCH) ony (BsCH).
420.2942 wardit (B); wrappit (BsHtS).
420.2946 fische (B); fitche (BsH).

420.2947   wappit (B); wrappit (BsH).
421.2950   twyn (twin) (B); wyn (BsCH).
422.2958   distinyt (B); rycht different (BsH).
423.2967   gud deidis (B); Faith in Christ (BsCH).
424.2972   a sample or (B); exempill and ane (BsCH).

APPENDIX A

Fables prove a natural repository for proverbs[1] because they have so much in common: Both attempt to be morally persuasive by presenting a bit of popular wisdom through a homely but artful form of truth telling; both combine literal and figurative language: both must have the signs of venerability; both appear in different places at different times.[2] The proverb must always sound 'true'; that is, it must be immediately apparent that there are life situations for which the proverb supplies an answer or an analysis. However, most proverbs can be countered by other proverbs, context overcoming text. 'Look before you leap' advises delay before action, while 'a stitch in time saves nine' advises action without delay. Neither invalidates the other, but together they suggest the limitations of proverbs as tools of persuasion.

Henryson plays with this limitation throughout the *Moral Fables*, making several different uses of proverbs. In almost 3,000 lines of poetry, Henryson utilizes 102 proverbs and proverbial phrases. Of these, forty-two are spoken by the narrator, usually for one of two effects: (1) to intone a moral ('Best is bewar in maist prosperite,/ For in this warld thair is na thing lestand' 1939-40); or (2) to supplement a description ('bitter as gall' 609). Nearly all of them are delivered in the tone one would expect from a didactic narrator, especially when they appear in the *Moralitas*. They have a summative and advisory effect; the fable itself has presented the argument, and the poverbs are used as mnemonic devices and shorthand references.

It is with the other sixty proverbs and proverbial phrases, spoken by the animals in the fables, that Henryson plays such interesting tricks, demonstrating how the misuse of rhetoric can cover a world of sins in a sinful world. Of the sixty, fifty-two are misapplied: some are wrenched out of context; others are based on false assumptions; others are intentionally misused to confuse the character being addresed; and yet others are turned ironically on the characters which speak them. The remaining eight all give efficacious advice or present an analysis that is applicable to the situation at hand; significantly, they are all spoken by the innocent, ingenuous, or righteous characters for whom Henryson uses the descriptive adjective '*selie*.' (The word suggests a combination of 'poor,' innocent' and 'holy'; compare the German *selig*.) These characters never misuse proverbs; all the other characters who used proverbs always misuse them.

A few examples should suffice to demonstrate this contrast. The first group below comes from the 52 misused proverbs and demonstrates the variety of possibility for misuse.

> Be blyith in baill, ffor that is best remeid;
> Let quik to quik, and deid ga to the deid. (521-2)

Intentional misuse to convince or free the self to pursue inappropriate action: The hens here confidently rationalize their way to abandoning all grief for Chanticlere. The proverbs have a ring of truth to them, but the first is misinterpreted and the second is summoned inappropriately quickly.

> All ar not halie that heifis thair handis to hevin (2325)

Intentional misuse resulting in ironic application to the character addressed: Hearing this proverb, the Farmer immediately puts his faith in the Fox that uttered it, ignoring the possibility that it might apply to the Fox himself. The Fox, both here and elsewhere, seems to enjoy warning others of precisely the kind of chicanery he is practicing on them at the moment. For a similar example, see the Paddock's advice to the Mouse that 'fair thingis oftymis ar fundin faikin' (2834).

> For everie wrink, forsuith, thow hes ane wyle (1987)
> His dart Oxin I compt thame not ane fle (2402)

Unintentional misuse resulting in ironic application to the speaker: The Wolf does not know at the time of this comment that in the end the worth of a fly will be precisely the value he will realize from those oxen.

> Thow wenis to draw the stra befoir the cat (2010)

Incompetent use resulting in ironic application to the speaker: The Wolf addresses these to the Fox, hubristicly believing himself incapable of being fooled, even by one he explicitly recognizes as a consummate trickster.

> For houngrie men may not weill leve on lukis (104)

Appropriate literal use but inappropriate figurative use resulting in the reader being intentionally misled: A hungry Cock cannot live on looks, it is true; but, as we learn from the Moralitas, a Fool cannot benefit from wisdom even when it appears before him. The reader may have been persuaded by the proverb to approve of the Cock's abandoning the jasper, through which the reader, along with the Cock, becomes the Fool.

> It will not wyn yow worth ane widderit neip (2362)
> Now se ye not the Caboik weill your sell,
> Quhyte as ane Neip   (2394-5)

Linguistic echo resulting in ironic application to the character addressed: This is another example of the Fox's delight in giving clues to his vic-

tims, confident that they will not recognize them in time to take action. In l. 2362 the Fox tells the Wolf to abandon his claim against the
Farmer because it will not win for him 'the worth of a withered turnip.'
Four stanzas later (and many hours later in the narrative) the Fox describes
the supposed Great Cheese to the Wolf as being 'as white as a turnip,'
but the Wolf hears no connection.

> . . . me think it better
> To sleip in haill nor in ane hurt skin (1029-30)
> The greitest Clerkis ar not the wysest men (1064)

Appropriate use but unfeelingly or derisively uttered: The Fox articulates
these 'truths' at the expense of the Wolf, who in the first case has just
been wounded by the Mare and in the second case is embarrassed before
the entire Parliament of Beasts.

The eight proverbs that are appropriately applied and used in timely
fashion make a sharp contrast to the other fifty-two. Three are spoken
by the Country Mouse, who shows her good sense in the one at the beginning
of the tale (236-9) and shows that she has learned her lesson in the other
two at the end of the tale (345a and 345b). The other five are used by
wise characters in attempts to persuade others to provident or just action; two are spoken by the Mouse in the central dream vision (1499-1500
and 1557) and three by the Swallow to the other birds (1754, 1759-60,
and 1789). The three from the Country Mouse are analytical; the two
from the Mouse in the dream vision are persuasive in character and prove
to be effective; the three from the Swallow are persuasive in character
and prove ineffective. Having had the Swallow fail in her use of proverbs, Henryson gives no other sympathetic character proverbs to use.
The Lamb in the twelfth fable tries to persuade with careful logic, not
with homely phrases and sayings; by that time in the work's progression
the tone and weight of proverbs are insufficient to combat evil; even
the more formal rhetoric of the Lamb proves ineffective. The proverbs
are left to the foxes and wolves and paddocks of the world to cover falsehoods.
Proverbs only work when both the speaker and the audience are in earnest,
are guileless, and are in touch with simplicity and righteousness. By the
arrival of the Swallow and the other birds, *haly preching may na thing availl*.

Proverbs and Proverbial Phrases in the Moral Fables

Reference Key:

Whiting	B.J. Whiting. *Proverbs, Sentences, and Proverbial Phrases from English Writings mainly before 1500*. Cambridge: Harvard University Press, 1968.

BJW [AL]   B.J. Whiting. 'Proverbs and Proverbial Sayings from Scot-
                   tish Writings before 1600; Part one A - L.' *Medieval Studies*
                   11 (1949): 123-205.
BJW [MY]   B.J. Whiting. 'Proverbs and Proverbial Sayings from Scot-
                   tish Writings before 1600; Part Two M - Y.' *Medieval Studies*
                   13 (1951): 87-164.
Walther   Hans Walther. *Proverbia Sententiaeque Latinitatis Medii Aevi*,
                   4 vols. Gottingen: 1965.

The Prologue

4.22-31   Whiting B 478
5.31   Whiting M 722

The Cock and the Jasper

15.102   Whiting W 648
15.104   Whiting M 109
21.146-7   Whiting P 89
23.159   BJW [MY] 'Wind (15),' 155

The Two Mice

29.203   Whiting E 184
32.221   Whiting L 457
34.236-9   BJW [AL] 'Good Will (2),' 181
42.290-1   Whiting J 58
45.315   Whiting H 430
47.328   Whiting F 189
50.345a   Whiting G 378
50.345b   Whiting G 11
53.371-2   BJW [AL] 'Climb (1),' 149
54.375-6   Whiting E 126

The Cock and the Fox

74.521   Whiting B 20
74.522   Whiting Q 14
79.552   Whiting F 190
81.568   Whiting F 51
85.595   Whiting S 795
87.609   Whiting G 8

The Confession of the Fox

100.700	Whiting H 430
104.731	Whiting N 51

The Trial of the Fox

115.805	Whiting E 192
118.827	Whiting F 592
120.839-40	Whiting W 668
124.868	Whiting G 310
147.1029-30	Whiting S 361
147.1033	Walther 8952
152.1064	Whiting C 291
152.1065	Whiting H 653

The Sheep and the Dog

181.1270	Whiting S 21

The Lion and the Mouse

193.1349	Whiting M 545
199.1393	Whiting S 763
207.1448	Whiting M 599
214.1499-1500	Whiting M 159
222.1557	Whiting T 533
229.1604-7	Whiting F 523

The Preaching of the Swallow

250.175	Walther 15841c
251.1759-60	Whiting E 84
252.1763	Whiting N 91
252.1764	Whiting B 12
252.1765	BJW [AL] 'Ground (2),' 182
252.1766-7a	Whiting M 157
252.1767b	Whiting D 90
255.1789	BJW [MY] 'Time (10),' 142
266.1862-3	BJW [AL] 'Counsel (2),' 152
266.1864-6	Whiting E 84
277.1939-40	BJW [MY] 'Prosperity,' 114

The Fox, the Wolf, and the Cadger

284.1987	Whiting W 712
285.1996	Whiting B 608
285.1997	Whiting F 51
285.1998	Whiting B 484
286.2001	Whiting C 93
287.2009	Whiting E 320
287.2010	Whiting S 818
291.2036	Whiting S 328
291.2041	Whiting E 217
292.2045	Whiting F 263
292.2046	Whiting B 165
295.2063	Whiting D 202
295.2064	Whiting Y 11
295.2068-9	BJW [AL] 'Fox (8),' 174
301.2108	Whiting M 327
301.2109	Whiting H 275
310.2168	Whiting W 340
313.2189-90	BJW [AL] 'Covet,' 153

The Fox, the Wolf, and the Farmer

320.2242	BJW [AL] 'Hare (1),' 185
321.2251	Whiting K 48
324.2268	Whiting G 86
324.2270-1	Whiting P 250
326.2282	Whiting W 609
326.2285-6	Whiting L 149
326.2286	Whiting F 263
327.2288	Whiting M 128
332.2322	Whiting B 580
332.2323	Whiting G 68
332.2324	Whiting H 344
332.2325	Whiting A 86
333.2335	Whiting H 89
335.2346	Whiting R 41
337.2362	Whiting N 72
340.2383	Whiting B 244
342.2395a	Whiting N 73
342.2395b	Whiting S 118
343.2402	Whiting F 260
345.2418-9	Whiting F 506
346.2421	Whiting B 224

The Wolf and the Wether

372.2608	Whiting H 47
373.2614	Whiting C 296

The Wolf and the Lamb

395.8365-6	Whiting T 195

The Paddock and the Mouse

404.2830	Whiting W 265
405.2843	Whiting T 119
406.2842	Whiting A 18
412.2886	Whiting D 276
417.2922-3	BJW [MY] 'Tongue (3),' 143
419.2939-47	BJW [AL] 'Fortune (7),' 173
420.2941	Whiting B 290
420.2944	Whiting J 46
420.2946a	Whiting F 225
420.2946b	Whiting H 559

1. Throughout this Appendix the term 'proverb' is used to comprise both proverbs and proverbial phrases.

2. For information on the origin and nature of proverbs, see the articles by B.J. Whiting cited below.

APPENDIX B

In 1803 James Hogg wrote Sir Walter Scott the following description of the method of ploughing then in use on the Island of Lewis. It is curiously reminiscent of the Farmer's plight in Henryson's tenth fable.

I could venture a wager that Cain himself had a more favourable method of tilling the ground. The man was walking by the side of the plough, and guiding it with his right hand. With the left he carried a plough-pattle over his shoulder, which he frequently heaved in a threatening manner at such of the horses as lagged behind; but as it had the same effect on them all, and rather caused the most fiery one to rush on, he was obliged sometimes to throw it at the lazy ones. The coulter is very slender, points straight down, and is so placed that if it at all rip the ground it hath no effect in keeping the plough steady. The horses, impatient in their nature, go very fast, and the plough being so ticklish, the man is in a perpetual struggle, using every exertion to keep the plough in the ground, and after all, the furrow is in many places a mere scrape. The four ponies go all abreast, and such a long way before the plough, that at a little distance I could not imagine they had any connection with the man or it. They were all four tied to one pole, and a man, to whom the *puller* is a much more applicable name than the *driver*, keeps hold of it with both hands, and walking backward as fast as he can, pulls them on. Those of them that walk too fast he claps the pole to their nose, which checks them. He finds means also to carry a small goad, with which he strikes the lazy ones in the face, asserting that that makes them spring forward. I had once an old brown mare—if he had struck her on the face he would have got her no farther in that direction. A man can scarcely conceive a more disagreeable employment than that of this 'driver' as he is called. The ploughman's post being such a very troublesome one he is mostly in a bad humour, and if the line of horses angle, the plough in spite of his teeth is pulled out of the land to the side on which the line is advanced. This puts him into a rage, and he immediately throws the pattle, or a stone, at the hindmost. Now, although the man may be a tolerable good archer, yet passion may make him miss, and the driver run a risk of meeting with the fate of Goliath of Gath. But granting this should never happen, and the ploughman's aim should always hold good, yet 'I own 'tis past my comprehension' how a man can walk so fast the whole day in a retrograde direction without falling, when he must that moment be trodden under foot by the horses. In fact

I have seen many people who would often be missing their feet on such land although walking with their faces foremost; and it is a fact that many of these drivers are hurt by accidents of the above nature.

(E.C. Batho, *The Ettrick Shepherd*. Cambridge, 1927. Reprinted in H. Harvey Wood's *The Poems and Fables of Robert Henryson*.)

BIBLIOGRAPHY

I. Modern Editions of Henryson

[For early manuscripts and prints, see Introduction, pp. 32-34.]

Hailes, Sir David Dalrymple, ed. *Ancient Scottish Poems, Published from the Manuscript of George Bannatyne, 1568*. Edinburgh: J. Balfour, 1770; rpt. London: Longmans, 1815.

Maitland Club, rpt. of *Henryson's Fables* (Andro Hart, ed., 1621). Edinburgh: Maitland Club, 1832.

Laing, David, ed. *The Poems and Fables of Robert Henryson*. Edinburgh: William Patterson, 1865.

Diebler, A. R., ed. *Henrisone's Fabeldichtungen*. Diss. Leipzig 1885; rpt. as 'Henrisone's Fablen' *Anglia*, 9 (1886), 337-390.

Smith, G. Gregory, ed. *The Poems of Robert Henryson*. 3 vols. Edinburgh: Scottish Text Society, 1906, 1908, 1914.

Metcalfe, W. M., ed. *The Poems and Fables of Robert Henryson*. Paisley: Alexander Gardner, 1917.

Murray, Hilda M. R., ed. *Selected Fables, The Testament of Cresseid, and Robene and Makyne*. London: Sidgwich & Jackson, 1930.

Wood, H. Harvey, ed. *The Poems and Fables of Robert Henryson*. Edinburgh: Oliver & Boyd, 1933; 2nd edition, New York: Barnes & Noble, 1958.

Murison, David, ed. *Selections from the Poems of Robert Henryson*. Edinburgh: Oliver & Boyd, 1952.

Elliott, Charles, ed. *Robert Henryson: Poems*. Oxford: Oxford University Press, 1963; 2nd edition, 1974.

Fox, Denton, ed. *The Poems of Robert Henryson*. Oxford: Oxford Unversity Press, 1981.

II. Books on Henryson

Gray, Douglas. *Robert Henryson*. Leiden: E.J. Brill, 1979.

Kindrick, Robert L. *Robert Henryson*. Boston: Twayne Publishers, 1979.

MacQueen, John. *Robert Henryson: A Study of the Major Narrative Poems*. Oxford: Oxford University Press, 1967.

McDiarmid, Matthew P. *Robert Henryson*. Edinburgh: Scottish Academic Press, 1981.

Powell, Marianne. *Fabula Docet: Studies in the Background and Interpretation of Henryson's Moral Fables. Odense University Studies in English*, Vol. 6. Odense, Denmark: Odense University Press, 1983.

Rossi, Sergio. *Robert Henryson*. Milan: C. Marzorati, 1955.

Stearns, Marshall. *Robert Henryson*. New York: Columbia University Press, 1949.

III. Dissertations on Henryson's Fables

Carens, Marilyn M. *A Prolegomenon for the Study of Robert Henryson*. Pennsylvania State University, 1974.

Carruthers, Ian Robert. *A Critical Commentary on Robert Henryson's 'Morall Fabillis'*. University of British Columbia, 1977.

Daugherty, Evelyn Newlyn. *The 'Kyrnal' and the 'Nuttis Schell': The Poetry of Robert Henryson*. Syracuse University, 1977.

Fratus, David Joseph. *Robert Henryson's Moral Fables: Tradition, Text, and Translation*. University of Iowa, 1971.

Gabbard, Gregory Norman. *The Animal Human Double Context in the Beast Fables and Beast Tales of Chaucer and Henryson*. University of Texas at Austin, 1968.

Gerke, Robert. *Studies in the Tradition and Morality of Henryson's Fables*. University of Notre Dame, 1968.

Godshalk, Anne M. *Robert Henryson's Moral Fables: Metaphor and Moral View*. University of Cinncinatti, 1973.

Goldstein, Abraham. *Meaning and Structure in Robert Henryson's Moral Fables*. University of Toronto, 1980.

Hildebrand, Joachim. *Robert Henryson's 'Morall Fabillis' im Rahmen der mittelalterlichen und Spatmittelalterichen Tierdichtung*. Hamburg, 1973.

Jamieson, I. W. A. *The Poetry of Robert Henryson: A Study of the Use of Source Material*. University of Edinburgh, 1964.

Jenkins, Anthony W. *The Mind and Art of Robert Henryson*. University of California at Berkeley, 1967.

Kretzschmar, William A., Jr. *The Literary-Historical Context of Henryson's Fabillis*. University of Chicago, 1980.

MacDonald, Donald. *Verse Satire and Humor in Middle Scots*. Northwestern University, 1958.

Proctor, John W. *A Description of the Fifteenth Century Scots Dialect of Robert Henryson Based on a Complete Concordance of His Works*. University of Missouri at Columbia, 1966.

Roerecke, Howard Henry. *The Integrity and Symmetry of Robert Henryson's Moral Fables*. Pennsylvania State University, 1969.

Schrader, Richard. *A Critical and Historical Study of Robert Henryson's Morall Fabillis*. Ohio State University, 1968.

Seiler, Thomas Henry. *Devices of Brevity in the Narrative Poetry of Robert Henryson*. University of Texas at Austin, 1975.

Siegel, Marsha. *Robert Henryson's Quest for a Morality*. University of California at Berkeley, 1977.

Sutton, Robert Francis. *The Moral Fables of Robert Henryson, the Scots Makar*. University of Massachusetts, 1975.

IV. Articles and Reviews

'Account of an Edition of the Fables of Aesop.' *The Scots Magazine*, 75 (1813): 504-10.

Aitken, A.J. Rev. of *Robert Henryson: Poems*, ed. Charles Elliott. *Studia Neophilogica* 36 (1964): 344-6.

_____ and Paul Bratley. 'An Archive of Older Scottish Texts for Scanning by Computer.' *SSL* 4 (1966): 45-7.

Baum, P.F. Rev. of *Robert Henryson* by Marshall Stearns. *The South Atlantic Quarterly* 48 (1949): 623-4.

Bauman, Richard. 'The Folktale and Oral Tradition in the Fables of Robert Henryson.' *Fabula* 6 (1963): 108-24.

Bawcutt, Priscilla. Rev. of *Robert Henryson: Poems*, ed. by Charles Elliott. *N & Q* 11 (1964): 197-8.

Benson, C. David. 'O Moral Henryson.' *Fifteenth-Century Studies: Recent Essays*. Ed. Robert F. Yeager. Hamden, CT: Archon Books, 1984.

Bone, Gavin. 'The Source of Henryson's 'Fox, Wolf, and Cadger.'' *RES* 10 (1934): 319-20.

Burrow, J.A. 'Henryson: The Preaching of the Swallow.' *EIC* 25 (1975): 25-37.

Caird, James B. 'Some Reflections on Scottish Literature.' *Scottish Periodicals* 1 (1937): 6-24.

Carruthers, Ian Robert. 'Henryson's Use of Aristotle and Priscian in the Moral Fables.' *Actes du 2e colloque de langue et de litterature ecossaises (Moyen Age et Renaissance)*, ed. Jean-Jaques Blanchot and Claude Graf. University of Strasbourg (1979): 278-96.

Clark, George. 'Henryson and Aesop: The Fable Transformed.' *ELH* 43 (1976): 1-18.

Conley, John. Rev. of *Robert Henryson* by Marshall Stearns. *JEGP* 68 (1950): 399-400.

Craik, T.W. 'An Emendation in Henryson's *Fables*.' *N & Q* 16 (1969): 88-9.

Crowne, David K. 'A Date for the Composition of Henryson's *Fables*.' *JEGP* 61 (1962): 583-90.

Crutwell, Patrick. 'Two Scots Poets: Dunbar and Henryson.' *The Age of Chaucer*, ed. Boris Ford. Baltimore: Penguin Books, 1963: 175-87.

Dickins, Bruce. 'Contributions to the Interpretation of Middle Scots Texts.' *TLS* 21 (Feb. 1924): 112.

Ebin, Lois. 'Henryson's *Fenyeit Fabils*: A Defense of Poetry,' *Actes du 2e colloque de langue et de litterature ecossaises (Moyen Age et Renaissance)*, ed Jean-Jaques Blanchot and Claude Graf. Strasbourg: University of Strasbourg (1979): 222-38.

Elliott, Charles. 'Sparth, Glebard and Bowranbane.' *N & Q* 9 (1962): 86-7.

Fox, Denton. Rev. of *Robert Henryson: A Study of the Major Narrative Poems* by John MacQueen. *N & Q* 14 (1967): 347-9.

_____. 'A Scoto-Danish Stanza, Wyatt, Henryson, and the Two Mice.' *N & Q* 18 (1971): 203-7.

_____. 'Henryson and Caxton.' *JEGP* 67 (1968): 586-93.

_____. 'Henryson's *Fables*.' *ELH* 29 (1962): 337-56.

_____. 'The Coherence of Henryson's Work.' *Fifteenth-Century Studies: Recent Essays*. Ed. Robert F. Yeager. Hamden, CT: Archon Books, 1984.

_____. 'The Scottish Chaucerians.' *Chaucer and Chaucerians: Critical Studies in Middle English Literature*, ed. D. S. Brewer. London and Edinburgh: Thos. Nelson & Sons, Ltd., 1966: 164-201.

Fradenburg, Louise O. 'Henryson Scholarship: The Recent Decades.' *Fifteenth-Century Studies: Recent Essays*. Ed. Robert F. Yeager. Hamden, CT: Archon Books, 1984.

Friedman, John B. 'Henryson, the Friars, and the Confessio Reynardi.' *JEGP* 66 (1967): 550-61.

Golding, Louis. 'The Scottish Chaucerians.' *The Saturday Review* 134 (1922): 782-3.

Gopen, George D. 'The Essential Seriousness of Robert Henryson's *Moral Fables*: A Study in Structure.' *SP* 82 (1985): 42-59.

Gray, James. 'A Note on Henryson.' *TLS* (13 March 1953): 176.

Grierson, Sir Herbert. 'Robert Henryson.' *The Modern Scot* 4 (1933-34): rpt. *Aberdeen University Review* 21 (1933-34): 203-12.

Hamer, Douglas. Rev. of *The Poems and Fables of Robert Henryson*, ed. H. Harvey Wood. *MLR* 29 (1934): 342-44.

Hammond, H. 'Meat into Fish.' *TLS* 52 (1953): 33.

Harth, Sidney. 'Henryson Reinterpreted.' *EIC* 11 (1961): 471-80.

Heidtmann, Peter. 'A Bibliography of Henryson, Dunbar, and Douglas, 1912-1968.' *Chaucer Review* 5 (1970): 75-82.

Henley, W.E. 'Robert Henryson.' *The English Poets*, ed. T.H. Ward, 5 vols. London, 1880-1918: I, 137-9.

Hyde, Isabel. 'Poetic Imagery: A Point of Comparison between Henryson and Dunbar.' *SSL* 2 (1965): 183-97.

Jack, R.D.S. 'Caxton's *Mirrour of the World* and Henryson's 'Taill of the Cok and the Jasp.'' *Chaucer Review* 13 (1978): 157-65.

Jamieson, I.W.A. 'Henryson's *Fabillis*: An Essay towards a Reevaluation.' *Words: Wai-te Atu Studies in Literature* 2 (1966): 20-31.

_____. 'A Further Source for Henryson's *Fabillis*.' *N & Q* 14 (1967): 403-5.

_____. 'Henryson's "Taill of the Wolf and the Wedder." ' *SSL* 6 (1969): 248-57.

_____. ' "To Preue Thare Preching Be a Poesye': Some Thoughts on Robert Henryson's Poetics.' *Parergon* 8 (1974): 24-36.

Jenkins, Anthony W. 'Henryson's *The Fox, the Wolf, and the Cadger* Again.' *SSL* 4 (1967): 107-12.

Keidell, George C. 'A Manual of Aesopic Literature; A First Book of Reference for the Period Ending A.D. 1500.' *Romance and Other Stories*. Baltimore: The Friedenwald Company, 1896.

Kindrick, Robert L. 'Lion or Cat? Henryson's Characterization of James III. *SSL* 14 (1979): 123-36.

_____. 'Monarchs and Monarchy in the Poetry of Henryson and Dunbar.' *Actes du 2ᵉ colloque de langue et de litterature ecossaises (Moyen Age et Renaissance)*, eds. Jean-Jaques Blanchot and Claude Graf. Strasbourg: University of Strasbourg, 1979: 307-25.

_____. 'Poetry and Politics at the Court of James III.' *SSL* 19 (1984): 40-55.

Kinghorn, A. M. 'The Medieval Makars.' *TSLL* 1 (1959): 73-88.

Kinsley, James. 'The Medieval Makars.' *Scottish Poetry: A Critical Survey*, ed. James Kinsley. London: Cassell and Company, 1955.

_____.'A Note on Henryson.' *TLS* (14 November 1952): 743.

MacDonald, Donald. 'Chaucer's Influence on Henryson's *Fables*: The Use of Proverbs and Sententiae.' *Medium Aevum* 39 (1940): 21-7.

_____. 'Henryson and Chaucer: Cock and Fox.' *TSLL* 8 (1967): 451-61.

_____. 'Narrative Art in Henryson's *Fables*.' *SSL* 3 (1965): 101-13.

MacQueen, John. 'The Literature of Fifteenth-Century Scotland.' *Scottish Society in the Fifteenth Century*, ed. Jennifer Brown. New York: St. Martin's Press, 1977.

_____. Rev. of *Robert Henryson: Poems*, ed. Charles Elliott. *RES* 16 (1965): 224-5.

Manning, Steven. 'The Nun's Priest's Morality and the Medieval Attitude towards Fables.' *JEGP* 59 (1960): 403-16.

Marken, Ronald. 'Chaucer and Henryson: A Comparison.' *Discourse* 7 (1964): 381-7.

McDiarmid, Matthew P. 'Robert Henryson in his Poems.' *Bards and Makars: Scottish Language and Literature, Medieval and Renaissance*, ed. Adam J. Aitken and Matthew P. McDiarmid. Glasgow: University of Glasgow, 1977: 27-40.

McIntosh, Angus. Rev. of *Robert Henryson* by Marshall Stearns. *Speculum* 26 (1949): 456-8.

McKenzie, Kenneth. 'Some Remarks on a Fable Collection.' *PULC* 5 (1943-44): 137-49.

McMillan, Douglas J. 'Classical Tale Plus Folk Tale.' *A N & Q* 1 (1963): 117-8.

Mudge, E. Leigh. 'A Fifteenth Century Critic.' *College English* 5 (1943): 154-5.

Muir, Edwin. 'Robert Henryson.' *Essays on Literature and Society*, rev. ed. London: Hogarth Press, 1965: 10-21.

_____. Rev. of *The Poems and Fables of Robert Henryson*, ed. H. Harvey Wood. *The Spectator* 151 (1933): 290.

Mumford, Marilyn R. "'Merines, Ernistfull Thochtis, and Sad Materis': Kinds of Comedy in Henryson's *Morall Fabillis*.' *Actes du 2ᵉ colloque de langue et de litterature ecossaises (Moyen Age et Renaissance)*, eds. Jean-Jaques Blanchot and Claude Graf. Strasbourg: University of Strasbourg, 1979: 239-49.

Murison, David. 'Studies in Scots Since 1918.' *Anglia* 69 (1950): 387-97.

Murtaugh, Daniel M. 'Henryson's Animals.' *TSLL* 14 (1972): 405-22.

Newlyn, Evelyn S. 'Of Sin and Courtliness: Henryson's Tale of the Cock and the Fox.' *Actes du 2ᵉ colloque de langue et de litterature ecossaises (Moyen Age et Renaissance)*, eds. Jean-Jaques Blanchot and Claude Graf. Strasbourg: University of Strasbourg, 1979: 268-77.

_____. 'Robert Henryson and the Popular Fable Tradition in the Middle Ages.' *Journal of Popular Culture* 14 (1980): 108-18.

Nichols, P.H. 'Lydgate's Influence on the Aureate Terms of the Scottish Chaucerians.' *PMLA* 47 (1932): 516-22.

Olphiant, F.R.R. 'Robert Henryson.' *Blackwood's Magazine* 148 (1890): 497-512; rpt. in *The Living Age* 187 (1890): 537-48.

Perry, Ben. 'Fable.' *Studium Generale* 12 (1959): 17-37.

Plessow, Max. *Geschichte der Fabeldichtung in England bis zu John Gay (1726)*. *Paelestra* 3 (1906).

Pope, Robert. 'A Sly Toad, Physiognomy and the Problem of Deceit: Henryson's *The Paddok and the Mous*.' *Neophilologus* 63 (1979): 461-8.

———. 'Henryson's "The Sheep and the Dog." ' *EIC* 30 (1980): 205-14.

Ramson, W.S. "Lettres of gold written I fand': A Defense of Moral Verse.' *Parergon* 23 (1979): 37-46.

Ridley, Florence. 'Middle Scots Poetry: A Checklist 1956-68.' *SSL* 5 (1970): 32-48.

Ross, Ian. Rev. of *Robert Henryson: Poems*, ed. Charles Elliott. *SSL* 1 (1964): 268-73.

Rowlands, Mary E. 'The Fables of Robert Henryson.' *The Dalhousie Review* 39 (1960): 491-502.

———. 'Robert Henryson and the Scottish Courts of Law.' *Aberdeen University Review* 39 (1962): 219-26.

Roy, J.A. 'Of the Makaris: A Causerie.' *UTQ* 16 (1946): 30-41.

Schrader, Richard. 'Henryson and Nominalism.' *JMRS* 8 (1978): 1-15.

———. 'Some Backgrounds of Henryson.' *SSL* 15 (1980): 124-38.

Smith, M. Ellwood. 'A Classification for Fables, Based on the Collection of Marie de France.' *MP* 15 (1917-18): 477-89.

Smyser, H.M. Rev. of *Robert Henryson* by Marshall Stearns. *MLN* 66 (1951), 409-11.

Spanier, Sandra Whipple. 'Structural Symmetry in Henryson's 'The Preaching of the Swallow." *Comitatus* 10 (1979): 123-7.

Speirs, John. 'Henryson, Chaucer, and the Scottish Language.' *Scrutiny* 2 (1933): 296-8.

Stearns, Marshall. Reply to Francis Utley's rev. of *Robert Henryson*. *MLQ* 12 (1951): 498-9.

Toliver, Harold E. 'Robert Henryson: From *Moralitas* to Irony.' *ES* 46 (1965): 300-9.

Utley, Francis L. Rev. of *Robert Henryson* by Marshall Stearns. *MLQ* 12 (1951): 493-7.

Von Kreisler, Nicolai. 'Henryson's Visionary Fable: Tradition and Craftsmanship in 'The Lion and the Mouse." *TSLL* 15 (1973): 405-22.

Whiting, B.J. 'The Nature of the Proverb.' *Harvard Studies and Notes in Philology and Literature* 14 (1932): 273-308.

———. 'The Origin of the Proverb.' *Harvard Studies and Notes in Philology and Literature* 13 (1931): 47-80.

———. 'Proverbs and Proverbial Sayings from Scottish Writings before 1600.' *MS* 11 (1949): 123-205 [A-L]; and 13 (1951): 87-164 [M-Y].